The Daily Telegraph Electronic Business Manual

"The *Electronic Business Manual's* all-in-one approach is a godsend. Potential online entrepreneurs should seriously consider making this book their Internet bible."
Iain Campbell, business books editor, Amazon.co.uk

"An outstanding book. Not only does it read as if it were written by someone who understands that businesses are meant to make money, it is stuffed with ideas on how the Net can help them."
Mike Flanagan and Liz Leffman, Flanagan and Leffman, London

"An excellent book that dispenses with hype and immediately gets down to business - highly recommended."
The Federation of Small Businesses

"Informative and jargon-free, this is an essential reference book for anyone interested in utilising the commercial possibilities of the Internet."
Robert Eadie, The Map House, London

The Daily Telegraph

electronic business manual

how to make the Internet work for your business

David Bowen

and

Emma Charlton
Ray Hurst
Scott Payton
Ben Schiller
Mark Stevenson
Elliot Wilson

Net Profit Publications Ltd

Net Profit Publications Limited
8 The Leathermarket
Weston Street
London SE1 3ER
Tel: 020 7403 1140
Fax: 020 7403 4160
e-mail: info@netprofit.co.uk
Web site: www.netprofit.co.uk

First published October 1999
Reprinted February 2000

ISBN 0 9529714 3 7

Cover design by Lydia Thornley

Printed and bound in Great Britain by
Biddles Ltd, Guildford, Surrey

Contents

Introduction

Mike Jarman is a bubbly baker in Whitby, North Yorkshire. His wife is a descendant of Elizabeth Botham, who founded the eponymous family business a century ago. In 1995 Mr Jarman decided to investigate the strange new phenomenon called the Internet, to see if he could pick up extra sales. He built a simple Web site, and soon found he was selling his plum bread, tea brack and other Yorkshire specialities around the world. "A man in Kuwait ordered two plum breads, whose cost barely covered the package and posting," he says. "But six months after that he ordered 13 of everything on Mother's Day for his 13 wives – that was worth £500." Elizabeth Botham's Web site does not generate a huge amount of business but it is, he says, "a great marketing tool and it irons out the peaks and troughs of seasonal demand." Mr Jarman is sufficiently enamoured of the Internet to have set up his own Web design company – he built the Web site for Wensleydale Creamery and Alan Ayckbourn's Stephen Joseph Theatre in Scarborough (see case study, page 246 for more).

Scotlens is a Linlithgow-based manufacturer of contact lenses. In 1996 it too decided to use the Internet. Its idea was that opticians would be able to put their requirements (lens strengths etc) into its Web site, rather than faxing or phoning through orders. Apart from the increased speed, the likelihood of errors would be cut right back. Within two years Scotlens had abandoned its experiment. Whatever its logic, Scottish opticians just were not ready to use this new and unfamiliar medium.

Both these stories have been repeated by the score over the past few years. Ever since the Internet first came into the public consciousness, businesses of all sizes have been wondering what to do about it. A handful have had wild success. More (including Botham's) have done well though not spectacularly. More yet have created a Web site and have wondered why they bothered. And the great majority have done nothing – or rather, they have started using e-mail but have yet to be convinced that they should do anything else.

Despite the widespread belief that everything moves at breakneck speed in the electronic world, and that if you haven't done it by next Tuesday you're too late, business adoption of the Internet has been rather gentle. When we started writing about the Internet, six years ago, we were convinced that businesses would quickly see that they could not live without it, and would soon be exploiting it to the full. As time went on, it became clear we were wrong: although e-mail is establishing itself as a standard business tool, there is still almost as much uncertainty – scepticism even – about the business benefits of the World Wide Web as there was several years ago.

The *Daily Telegraph Electronic Business Manual* is designed to reduce this uncertainty. Anybody who says "you must be on the Internet or you will die" is almost certainly trying to sell you a service. On the other hand, there are very few companies that cannot benefit from using the medium – and there are none at all that do not need to know about it.

This book aims to help business managers decide to what extent they should be using the Internet, and how they should go about doing so. It has a slant towards small and medium-sized companies – though it is designed to be valuable to people in companies of any size at all, and in any industry. It should help both non-technical and technical staff, because it is about business not technological issues. And while the contact details are UK-specific, the vast majority of the information is as relevant in Beijing or Bogota as it is in Basingstoke.

It is called a manual because it is designed to be held (figuratively) in one hand while following its instructions with the other – much as an amateur mechanic might follow a workshop manual to change a clutch, or a cook will follow a recipe. The difference is that it also helps readers decide whether the clutch needs to be changed, or whether this is the recipe they really want to cook. But the over-riding aim is to be practical and comprehensive – taking managers from the basics (do I need the Internet at all?) to a reasonable level of sophistication (running a full electronic commerce operation).

The structure is also that of a workshop manual – readers can work through it, following instructions to get straight to the parts they need. It is designed to be read in one general direction (forwards), but there are points where you will have to jump back and forth somewhat to get the information you need for your company, or to read up a case study. There will also be bits you want to skip (much of Chapter One is for people who have never used the Internet, for example). We have tried to make the navigation as simple as possible, and have kept the language straightforward. We have avoided technical jargon where we can – though there is a glossary on page 339.

The manual is divided roughly into sections:

- Chapter One covers the basics – it explains the Internet in theory and gives a practical guide to getting online.
- Chapter Two covers quick returns – how you can use the Internet to help your business as soon as you are up and running.
- Chapter Three carries the signposts for the rest of the book. Its core is a flow diagram that will help you decide your strategy, and also point you to the most relevant sections elsewhere.
- Chapters Four and Five tell you how to set up an excellent Web site, and what to put on it.
- Chapters Six to Nine cover the different ways in which you can use the medium to help your business – marketing, selling, customer service, supply chain management, recruitment, and more.
- The End Note contains some guesses about the future – and also explains why this is the Electronic Business Manual, not the Internet Manual.

The appendices are packed with useful names and addresses, as well as a legal guide and an Opportunities and Threats section – a quick reference listing designed to help you identify the way forward for your business.

The manual has been assembled by the staff of Net Profit Publications, a publishing and research company that has been monitoring and writing about developments in the commercial Internet since 1996. If you would like to know more about us, and our highly-regarded monthly newsletter, please visit our Web site at www.netprofit.co.uk. Additional or updated information will be made available on this site.

The main author is David Bowen, editor-in-chief of Net Profit. The contributors are Emma Charlton, Ray Hurst, Scott Payton, Ben Schiller and Elliot Wilson. We would also like to thank Janet Robson for editing and laying out the book, Lydia Thornley for designing the cover, Charles de Montagnac of deMont Design for help with the Web site building material, Charmian May of Ashurst Morris Crisp for checking the legal section, and Bernice Hurst for proofreading. Thanks too to Susannah Charlton at Telegraph Books (for more information, see the Electronic Telegraph at www.telegraph.co.uk).

Chapter 1 Getting started

All the questions in this book, bar one, have at least two possible answers. The exception is the first, because it has only one correct answer: Do you need to know about the Internet? The answer is "yes". The Internet will become an integral part of so many people's lives that a refusal even to examine its potential is unwise, to put it gently.

That is not to say you should necessarily *use* the Internet. Just as some companies survive without a computer and others have no fax machine, so some businesses will still be trundling along in 10 years' time without ever having had anything to do with the Internet. Almost everything it is used for can be achieved by a combination of printed material, phone, fax, mail and personal meetings.

But there are few companies that cannot benefit from the Internet, because it can save them time or money, or bring in extra revenue. Before diving into the detail, here are some questions. If you answer "yes" to any of these, the Internet can help you:

- Do you have business partners overseas?
- Do you regularly make international phone calls?
- Do you send many faxes?
- Do you spend a lot on postage?
- Do you need to find market information regularly?
- Do you travel by plane or train?
- Do you need to keep in touch with industry news?

A "yes" to any of the first three questions suggests you will benefit from using one part of the Internet, e-mail. The last four will push you in the direction of the World Wide Web. This already raises one complication, because the Internet is not one thing – it is several. And that is the least of its complexities.

The rest of this chapter is aimed at explaining the Internet to people who have little or no experience of the Internet, and telling them how to get going.

- What the Internet is in theory (1.1)
- Where and how to try it out (1.2)
- Getting connected (1.3)
- Getting going (1.4)
- Connecting to a small office network (1.5)

The sections on choosing an Internet Service Provider (1.3.4) and setting up a small office Internet connection (1.5) could well be useful for people who already use the Internet. Otherwise they should go to Chapter 2 (page 27).

1.1 What is the Internet in theory?

One of the reasons many people are worried by the Internet is that it is so difficult to explain, without trying it out. The best way is to look at it in steps. First, what it is in essence. Second, what it is in practical terms. Third, how it has developed. Finally, its consitituent parts.

1.1.1 The essence of the Internet

Forget computers for a moment. Think instead about how communication has developed. First we communicated verbally with people we could see – improvements came from getting them closer together (by horse, ship etc). Setting aside smoke signals, the only remote communication was written, carried by messenger. In the last century the penny post and the telegraph brought the first mass remote communication – again the medium was writing. Then came the phone, bringing voice, and in the last 20 years the fax has added another written carrier.

All these media are "interactive" – communication can go in two directions – but are limited by volume and distance. It is expensive, both in time and money, to bring large numbers of people together. It is expensive too to make a long-distance phone call or fax transmission, and the volume of information that can be exchanged is limited (also, there is usually only one sender and one recipient).

Radio and television arrived too. They can send information (though still not much) to large numbers simultaneously. But they are one-way

– not interactive. What the Internet brings is the theoretical ability to send almost unlimited amounts of material at negligible cost (and independent of distance), between any two points on earth, and to display it on a giant "noticeboard". That material can be in the form of voice, music, text, photographs, graphics, video, or anything else that can be "digitised" (turned into a series of ones and noughts, the language of computers). It is also fully interactive. In other words it brings together the abilities of the post, telephone, television and teletext, vastly increasing capacity and cutting cost at the same time.

The fact that the information is being sent between personal computers is not part of its essence. In 10 years' time, it is as likely we will be sending and receiving data on our TV sets or mobile phones as on a computer (they too will be digital). We may not talk about the Internet any more: it will simply be the carrier for all electronic communication.

1.1.2 The practicalities of the Internet

For now, the Internet is very much to do with computers. If you work in an office with a network, the basic concept should be familiar to you. Several computers are connected together by a cable, and users of each can view material held on the others. They may also be able to send messages across the network. Larger companies usually have a Wide Area Network, by which computers in different offices are connected together. The Internet takes this development to its logical conclusion – connecting millions of computers all over the world, using a mix of private cables and ordinary phone lines.

The Internet is not a "thing" and is not owned by anyone, though it is guided by a number of committees and organisations. It is in essence a set of standards, though it does have certain "things" associated with it:

- services, notably e-mail and the World Wide Web.
- specialised computers to store material (servers) or guide it round the world (routers).

Its ingenuity comes from the way in which it allows computers of all different sorts to talk to each other. Computers, being literal-minded, have to be offered information in exactly the right format. An inexact but useful metaphor is language – a computer that is programmed to speak English will not understand a message in Bulgarian. The Internet uses a universal language, a sort of Esperanto. In the jargon this is a "protocol", and its name is TCP/IP. There is nothing magic about TCP/IP, except that of the many protocols developed to allow computers to talk to each other, it has become dominant (rather like English in the business world).

The system by which messages are sent across the Internet is amazingly robust. This is not surprising because it was designed to resist nuclear attack. The ancestor of the Internet, ARPANet, was developed in the Sixties by the US Department of Defense to move files and information between government computers and defence contractors in such a way that if one computer or telecom line was destroyed they could be sent by another route. The key was to use a "packet" system, which broke messages up into chunks and "wrote" the address on each of them. Just as an envelope that has been dropped by the postman will probably get delivered by someone else, so these packets should find their way one way or another to their destination – where they would be automatically reassembled into the original message.

The Internet is rather like a reliable old tractor: it can get stuck in ruts, and will occasionally stop completely. But it will work in all sorts of hostile conditions, and despite various predictions to the contrary, shows no sign of breaking down for good. So it is that an engineer working in the back country of Papua New Guinea will be able to connect an elderly computer to an erratic phone line and send messages to his head office in Birmingham. The software needed to use the Internet is free, and any computer built after about 1993 should be able to communicate with any other.

How it developed

The original purpose of ARPANet was to transfer computer files (for example scientific documents) between military establishments and academic institutions working with them. It could also be used to send messages – electronic mail (e-mail) is just a way of sending small files between computers. ARPANet gradually became an academic as well as military system, and when the military bit was spun off in the early Eighties, it became the Internet. But it remained little more than a way for people with the right equipment to link up by computer: not only did you have to work somewhere with an Internet connection (probably a US university), you also had to know how to use it, which was not easy. In other words, it stayed in the world of the geek.

That started to change in the early Nineties. The critical driver was the invention in 1990 (by a British scientist, Tim Berners-Lee) of the World Wide Web. He was a scientific researcher, and he was looking for a way of linking huge quantities of documents in a way that made them easy to manage. He used the Internet's protocol, TCP/IP, and added "hyperlinks", so that if you clicked on a highlighted word, you would be automatically transferred to another relevant document. The concept of "browsing" (or clicking from file to file) was born.

Useful as this was, it remained firmly in the hands of academics until 1992, when the first "graphical browser" appeared. This moved the Web beyond plain text to multimedia. The browser was a "window" that appeared on the screen and could display pictures and graphics as well as text. It could even play sounds. By luck, it was about this time that low-cost computers were becoming powerful enough to display such multimedia graphics. (In the last decade, the power of computers per pound spent has doubled every nine months.)

It was the multimedia World Wide Web that triggered the explosion of public interest in the Internet. Americans (and from 1990 Britons) had come to understand that computers could be used to receive data down the phone line through their use of CompuServe – a private service that provided a good range of information, and also allowed members to e-mail each other (the French had had the Minitel information system since the early Eighties, but this was little known outside France). But the World Wide Web quickly came to dwarf CompuServe, because anyone with a little knowledge and a lot of patience could create his own Web page.

Many of the earliest sites were created by students, and could be used to spread information (potholers, mountaineers or pub-goers could publicise their favourite spots), or simply to create an electronic shrine for their favourite bands. It was a formula that intrigued: just as Edwardians would go to watch moving pictures of people walking about, so people would enthusiastically surf sites of whatever quality. The novelty of watching a picture that had been posted by an Australian student appear on a computer screen was appealing to most people who tried it – especially as it cost no more than a few minutes' local phone call to do so.

The novelty has never really worn off, because new people are trying the Internet every hour of every day. But there have been huge developments:

- The number of people using the Internet has exploded – from under 10m in 1994 to around 180m by late 1999. In the UK, the number of regular Internet users has been set at around 8 million for late 1999. For a rundown of online population by country, see page 77.

- The size of the World Wide Web has exploded – it now has over 10m domain addresses, the majority of which identify Web sites (the rest are defunct or unused). These sites range from vast sites from multinational corporations to single pages set up by schoolchildren (building a Web site is part of the US child's normal curriculum).

- E-mail has become a standard communication tool in many countries, and seems likely largely to displace the fax.

- While the student and hobbyist sites remain, commerce has become the great driver of Internet growth. Companies use it for all the reasons you will read about in the rest of this book, while consumers increasingly use it as a giant shop or source of information (for example, to look up rail timetables).

- As computer power has increased, more and more elaborate Web sites have appeared. It is possible to view video (albeit usually with poor quality) as well as listen to live radio and music tracks at CD quality.

The constituent parts

The Internet has several elements. Some of these, such as Telnet and Gopher, are unlikely to bother the non-technical user. This leaves e-mail, or electronic mail, File Transfer Protocol, Newsgroups and the World Wide Web.

E-mail: The Internet allows anyone with a computer and a phone line to send or receive messages from anyone else with the same equipment. Files (text, graphics or whatever) can be "attached" to an e-mail. E-mail is still used mostly for simple text messages, although modern software allows multimedia to be sent and received: so it can look just like a Web page (see below). See 2.1 for more.

File Transfer Protocol (FTP): FTP allows you to send or receive large computer files or programs. From a business viewpoint, its main advantage is that it can provide large amounts of information to customers or suppliers simply and cheaply. But it needs special software, and its job is increasingly being carried out by e-mail.

Newsgroups: The Internet's discussion areas. Most are related to computer issues or to a range of esoteric hobbies and interests. There are however some 20,000 newsgroups, and it is quite probable that one or more can help with your business, either as a source of information or to ask questions. Taking part in a newsgroup is fairly straightforward once you have mastered the concept of the "thread," which holds each line of discussion together. See 2.4 for newsgroups as information sources, and 8.5.6 for more on how to use them to sell.

The World Wide Web (Web or WWW): The glamorous part of the Internet – a multimedia notice board that can include text, graphics, photographs, sound and even video. The Web appears in a window (the "browser") on the computer screen. The browser has its own set of buttons allowing you to type in the address of a Web site, to move forward and backward, to jump to the home page (the page that automatically appears when you start up), and to adjust the look of the page (eg increase type size).

Most of this book relates to use of the Web – either as a passive instrument (to find information etc) or an active one (eg marketing, selling). See the index for specific references.

Where else can you find out about the Internet?

You will find a wide range of Internet magazines on your newsagent's shelves - most have a heavy consumer bias, and some tap into "youth culture". *Internet* is consumer-focused but runs useful performance tests on ISPs. *.net* has plenty of tutorial information, eg on building Web sites.

Publications specifically aimed at business include:

Net Profit (monthly newsletter, £195 a year, including access to full electronic archive): Produced by the authors this book, *Net Profit* combines reporting with analysis, and is aimed at senior non-technical managers in companies of all sizes. See www.net-profit.co.uk, or call 020 7403 1140 for a sample issue.

Revolution (weekly, £84 a year), published by Haymarket, serves the new media marketing community with easy-to-read features and news.
Tel: 020 8841 3970 or see www.revolution.haynet.com.

Real Business (£3 from large newsagents, £29 a year by mail). Well-produced small business magazine that regularly has electronic business features. See www.realbusiness.co.uk or e-mail subscribe@realbusiness.co.uk

Internet.Works (newstand*: £2.99)*. Features for the business/hobbyist Web user, with a useful directory of hardware, software and designers.

Internet Business (£2.95 from large newsagents). Aimed at small businesses.
Tel: 020 8267 4637

Newspaper supplements on the wired world often carry good features:
Daily Telegraph: *Connected*, published on Thursday
The Times: *Interface*, published on Wednesday
The Independent: *Network*, published on Monday
Guardian: Online, published on Thursday
Sunday Times: Innovation
Express: EX, small business section, published on Monday
Daily Mail: features an Internet page on Tuesday

1.2 Trying it out

By far the best way to understand the Internet's functions is to play with them. Play is the right word: the Internet, or at least the World Wide Web, can be great fun – addictive even (warning: a psychologist reckons that 6 per cent of Net users are addicted). Here are some of the ways you can try out the Internet for yourself before you decide to commit.

- Through friends and colleagues: Many people get their first experience of the Internet by looking over someone else's shoulder. Do not be afraid to ask – most Internet users are more than happy to show off the Web, and demonstrate amusing or interesting sites.

- At a Cybercafé: Here you can hire an Internet computer by the half-hour, and get instruction from trained staff. Cybercafés are now widespread and are a reasonably painless way of becoming acquainted. For a list of Cybercafés see Appendix D, page 325

Here are some things to try to get started.

- Get the e-mail addresses of a couple of friends or colleagues, and try sending them messages (they will not be able to reply to a cybercafé, but should be able to tell you by conventional means whether they have received them).

- Type this address into the Web browser (under File/ Open Location): www.altavista.com. This is one of the main "search engines". In the search box, type anything that you would like to know more about: the village where you went on holiday, the name of your main commercial rival, a prominent friend or relative ... almost anything will generate lists of Web sites. A summary of the content will appear – click on the title, and you will go through to the site itself. Try clicking on any highlighted word (usually a different colour) to see where it takes you – this is a hyperlink. If you get stuck, use the Back arrow at the top of the browser window to return.

- Try this address: www.askjeeves.com. You can ask it any question (What is the capital of Kazakhstan? What is existentialism? What is ICI's share price?), and it is quite likely to come up with answer (it interprets the questions, then pushes you into a Web site it believes contains the answer – a simple form of artificial intelligence).

- Type in www.railtrack.co.uk/travel. Put in a departure and arrival station, a travel time and date, and you will get the best trains to take.

- Type in www.baa.co.uk. Click on Arrivals - you will see the Arrivals board as it appears, live at any BAA airport.

● Look at Chapter 2 – Quick returns – for lists of other interesting of Web sites with a business focus.

1.3 Getting connected to the Internet

If you want your own Internet connection, decide first whether it should be at home or in the office. From a work efficiency point of view, it is probably best to have one at home, because you can get used to the system in the evenings and at weekends. Expect to experience both frustration and a

Technophobia and the Internet

Many people dislike or even fear computers. Even if they use them at work for word-processing, they are unwilling to use them more than they have to. An early 1998 survey showed that 70 per cent of British households without PCs said they had no intention of ever buying a computer. And 30 per cent of Britons declared they had no intention of ever using the Internet. If you are a technophobe, but want to get to grips with computers, here are some thoughts and tips.

● Although computers are complex (over-complex often), the Web and e-mail are two of the easier functions to use. The Web, in particular, is possibly the only computer software that is genuinely intuitive – when you see a word highlighted, it makes sense to click on it, and so go to some sort of linked area. And that is what happens. If you want to go back a page, click on the back button. Etcetera.

● Setting up on the Internet used to be horrendously complex. No more: put a CD-Rom into your drive, and it should be easy (see 1.4)

● Things do go wrong on computers, and particularly on the Internet. Sometimes you will lose your connection, or be unable to log on, for no apparent reason. Computers are so sophisticated they can appear to have moods. Do not give up – disconnect, dial up again, try later then, if necessary, get help.

degree of addiction. The other advantage of starting at home is that you can choose your own equipment – it may well be that computers at work are getting long in the tooth, and it is worth having a reasonably powerful machine. On the other hand, unless you have suitable offspring or neighbours, it may be easier to find people who can help you out in the office than at home.

To get connected to the Internet, you will need

- a computer (1.3.1)
- a modem (1.3.2)
- a phone line (1.3.3)
- an Internet Service Provider (1.3.4)

- Similarly, the Internet will sometimes run very slowly – it can get jammed up at certain times of day (the mornings are usually best because the Americans are not surfing). It is natural to expect everything to happen instantly on computers. On the Internet, it does not. Go and put the kettle on or do something else while you are waiting for a page to load.

- Find someone who will help you if you do get stuck. Almost everyone's son is an expert on the Internet – you almost certainly know someone who has some level of expertise, and is prepared to help out. Because it is still "new", many people are more than happy to muck in and see what they can do.

- Computers can be very frustrating, but they cannot bite. You will find you quickly discover how to solve common problems: it is remarkable how often a non-technical person is fiddling around to fix something, calls in an expert, and then finds the expert is fiddling in exactly the same way.

- Ultimately, the Internet is not about computers any more than a book is about paper. Many of the functions we now carry out by computer will in the future be delivered on interactive television or even via mobile phone – and anyone who can use a TV remote control will be able to order books, look up information and so on.

1.3.1 Choosing a suitable computer

You run the risk of frustration if you try connecting with a computer built before 1995 – the Internet may work on it, but slowly. On the other hand you do not need the very latest machine. Any PC or Apple Macintosh that runs at 166 MHz (Megahertz) or above should be powerful enough. If you have a suitable computer, go to 1.3.2.

If you are buying new, choose an "Internet-ready" computer, which will have a modem built-in and the connection software loaded. It should also have

- a 17-inch screen, or larger, because small screens can limit the display of Web pages.
- at least 32 MB of RAM (internal memory) – 64 MB is better.
- good telephone back-up – it is essential to have a helpdesk that you can ring with any queries. A "big name" computer should have reasonable support. If you are buying from a low cost store (or mail order), check carefully what level of back-up you will receive.

Where to buy?

If you buy from the high street, you will probably not get the lowest price, but you can try a machine out before you use it (though it is difficult to tell much difference between them). Mail order from the mainstream press can offer good prices (but check carefully on the helpdesk). News stand computer magazines offer a bewildering number of mail order options, which can provide both good prices and good back-up. But the choice is daunting.

Mac or PC?

It is difficult to give categorical advice on whether to choose an Apple Mac or a PC (that is, a computer that runs Windows software). Both will run the Internet equally well. Here are some points to consider:

- Much Internet-specific software (especially plug-ins – see page 132) is released first in PC format, and sometimes will not appear in Mac format at all. Some online services, such as banking, may not run on Macs. That is because PCs have 90 per cent of the market.

- PCs (at least desktop, as opposed to portable ones) tend to be cheaper than Macs - though the iMac and iBook are good value.

- Mac users claim they are easier to use and more reliable than PCs: there are technical reasons to believe them, though no computer is completely reliable.

- If you intend to have an ISDN connection (see 1.3.3), it is much more expensive to connect a Mac than a PC.

- If you intend to use the computer to transmit material for printing, choose a Mac: most printers are Mac-based.

- Macs are more “fun” than PCs – they tend to have more frivolous software (to customise the look of the screen, for example), because they are the favoured machine of the graphical community.

- Many offices run both PCs and Macs – there is no reason why they cannot be connected together on an office network.

1.3.2 Choosing a modem

You can buy a modem by mail order (look in a PC magazine), or from a computer retailer. Go for the fastest one you can, likely to be 56 kbps (unless you choose an ISDN option – see 1.3.3). There are two sorts: internal, which slots into the computer, and external, which sits separately and is plugged in to the computer at the back.

- Internal modems are slightly cheaper and take up less space. They can be fitted quite easily, though you will probably need help from someone with a little computer knowledge.

- External modems simply plug in. Their main advantage is you can sometimes solve a problem by switching them off and on again, which you cannot do with an internal modem.

- The magazine *Internet.Works* runs a monthly-updated “product buyers’ guide” to available modems, providing ratings, prices and contact details.

1.3.3 Will you need an extra phone line?

You will need an available phone line. Although it is possible to share an Internet line with a phone or fax machine, by fitting a double socket, you are blocking the phone line – and Internet sessions tend to be lengthy.

If you are fitting another phone line, try to find a suitable package – if possible talk to both BT and cable companies. If you are likely to use the Internet mostly during the day, try to get a phone package that trades lower peak rates for higher evening rates. Best of all, have one set of phones that operate like this, with the other on a conventional expensive day/cheap evening schedule – and swap the phone lines round when you are going online in the evening or at weekends.

Should you consider ISDN?

If you plan to make heavy use of the Internet, or if you want to send large files (eg photographs), consider an ISDN line. Integrated Services Digital Network (ISDN) uses ordinary phone lines, but clever electronics installed at the telephone exchange and in your own premises increases the speed. BT has two packages, Business Highway and Home Highway, which convert an existing line to ISDN – you will end up with one ISDN line and two ordinary lines from the same connection (see the BT Web site at www.bt.com/business/index.html). This means you can use the Internet, make phone calls and send and receive faxes simultaneously – through the same phone line. Although ISDN can run at 128kbps, access to the Internet is not necessarily much faster than on a 56kbps line, because much of the delay is caused by the computer at the other end.

If you are on cable, ask your cable provider what services it can provide. Although BT has moved faster on ISDN, cable companies are expected to offer "cable modems", which will at least in theory provide very fast Internet access. This is an area where there is likely to be much competition and much movement, so shop around. Heavy Internet users should ask about permanently-connected "leased lines".

See also: Getting connected on a small office network (1.5)

1.3.4 Choosing an Internet Service Provider (ISP)

You will need to sign up with an Internet Service Provider. ISPs act as a bridge between individuals and companies and the "permanent Internet". They have large computers (servers) that are constantly connected by high-capacity cable to the Internet's main backbone. They also have banks of modems, each of which can be connected to an individual subscriber. Most will also provide corporate services, including ISDN links.

It is not easy to decide which ISP to use. More than 200 companies in the UK offer connection services to the Internet (for an up to date list, see the newstand magazine, *Internet).* Some have tens of thousands of subscribers, others a few hundred. Some offer basic dial-up connections through a modem, others a whole raft of services. Some offer their own "content" as well as an Internet connection (AOL/CompuServe and VirginNet are among them). There are ISPs specialising in connecting businesses to the Internet and others with a more populist portfolio. Since the launch of Freeserve by Dixons in 1998, there has been a great surge towards free Internet provision, though some still charge and claim to provide a better service as a result.

To add further to the confusion, many ISPs are "rebranded" – they are marketed under a household name (for example Nationwide, Tesco, Virgin, WH Smith), but are actually provided by an ISP (WH Smith's service is provided by BT). So there are fewer ISPs than there are ISP brands.

This is, in other words, a minefield. Here are some questions and answers to consider when making your choice:

Is one ISP as good as the next one?

Like most things, they are when they are working well. They are all likely to provide 56 kbps access, and will provide you with a CD-Rom with all the software you need to get started. The theoretical differentiation, apart from price, comes from the inclusion of "proprietary material" (CompuServe prides itself on serving small business particularly well), and a handful of bells and whistles such as a roaming service. If you travel abroad with a portable computer, you want to be able to dial into your Internet account at a local rate, rather than paying the phone charge to the UK (see next section).

The practical differentiation comes in the quality of service offered. This includes the helpfulness of the support desk and the reliability of the connection. It is however rarely possible to say "This ISP is reliable" or "This one is unreliable", because reliability fluctuates. As traffic grows an ISP will become clogged up and will start to offer a poor service. It will then install a new set of modems, and the service will improve dramatically. Meanwhile other ISPs will be running into problems. And so on.

So how should I choose an ISP?

There are two ways: carry out careful research before choosing, or suck a few ISPs and see.

The research route: A good starting point is the newstand magazine *Internet* (see 1.1.2), which not only lists ISPs (including business specialists), but also rates them in terms of reliability. Note that because reliability goes up and down like a yo-yo, a one month snapshot is not much use - use the six month ratings. The other source of research material – as so often with the Internet – is friends and colleagues. Ask around to see what experience they have had with their ISPs.

Other questions to ask:

- Does the ISP offer you a local rate dial-up service? If you live or work away from a major population centre, you may find you have to pay a national phone rate to connect. The answer is to choose an ISP that offers national coverage at local rates (most of the large ones do now).

- Are you intending to build a Web site? Most ISPs offer a limited amount of "free space" (enough to build a small company site) but there are different levels of service. A specialist business ISP should give a better service, although it is easy to build a Web site with one company (for example a specialist host service - see 4.6) and gain Internet access via another.

- Do you want ISDN (see 1.3.3)? Not all ISPs support it.

- Do you want to use the Internet when travelling abroad (for example to check your e-mail from a laptop)? AOL and CompuServe have local numbers all round the world, while others belong to international twinning arrangements. So do some of the bigger US-owned ISPs such as UUNet. Or use an iPASS member. iPASS is a "roaming" alliance that allows you to dial in locally wherever a member is operating.

The UK ISPs that offer the iPASS service are:

Bta	www.bta.com
Cerbernet	www.cerbernet.net
Direct Connection	www.dircon.net
Enterprise	www.enterprise.net
ICL.net	www.icl.net
Internet Central	home.netcentral.co.uk
I-Way	www.i-way.net.uk
Mistral	home.mistral.co.uk
Netcom	www.netcom.net.uk
PLR	www.plr.co.uk
PSINet	www.psi.com
SAQ Net	www.saqnet.co.uk
Worldwide Web Serv	www.webs.co.uk
Zoo Internet	www.zoo.net.uk

To check the list, look on the Web at www.ipass.com/partners/isp-partners/europe

- Does the Help Desk offer 24-hour service (few do)? Is it available at weekends and in the evenings? What are its call charges (free ISPs tend to have very high call charges: 50p or £1 a minute)?

- Are you attracted by the additional content provided by for example CompuServe or AOL? You will only be able to judge this by trying them out (see "Suck-it-and-see", below).

- If you are setting up a link for your business, reliability will be ultra-important. Look at the sort of guarantees ISPs offer business customers (see "What should business class ISPs provide?", below).

Suck-it-and-see: It is easy to get hold of start-up disks for the big ISPs, because that is the way they get new business. If you bought a new computer, you probably have the software already loaded for a number of providers. PC and Internet magazines have "cover disks" offering trial periods or free access. And the free ISPs will do everything they can to spread their disks. You can pick up a Freeserve disk at any Dixons, a WH Smith Online disk at Smith's, while the other companies offering free access are handing out disks wherever they can.

There is a temptation to load more than one ISP's disk on at the same time. This can produce "conflicts" that are difficult to unwind. The best bet is to "uninstall" one set of software before loading another. Some software will have an "uninstall" icon that appears when it is first loaded. Simply click on this. An alternative, with a Windows-based computer, is to double click with your mouse on My Computer, double click on Control Panel, double click on Add/Remove Program, select the software you want to remove, and click on Remove. With a Mac, search for the different elements of the program by using File/Find, then drag them to the rubbish bin.

Can it make sense to pay for an ISP?

Perhaps, especially if the Internet is likely to become an essential communication channel for your company. Free ISPs are by their nature mass market. Those that continue to charge are either resisting the trend (and will eventually go free) or are selling themselves on their ability to provide a more reliable service, especially to businesses. As we have said, they should also provide better (and less expensive) customer support.

The problem is that there may be a gap between claim and reality. Some companies may claim to provide a "premium business service," but in reality are no different from others. Ask around, and also ask the company how its service is differentiated (see next section).

What should "business class" ISPs provide?

The answer is "better service" – but this should be underpinned by a specific contract called a Service Level Agreement. An SLA might include:

- a refund if down-time (when the service is not running) is above a certain level.

- “escalation procedures” detailing what alternative support is offered outside help desk hours, or if a problem occurs that is outside the ISP’s control.
- specified response times for support and maintenance.
- systems for backing up and restoring data, because even the most reliable computer can “crash”.

1.4 Getting going on your ISP

You will normally get going on the Internet by installing the software from a CD-Rom. Installation should be straightforward (if it is not, be suspicious of the ISP). The software will include:

An e-mail reader. Well-known ones are Microsoft’s Outlook Express (supplied as standard on most PCs), the Messenger facility within the Netscape Communicator package, and Eudora, a more powerful “standalone” e-mail reader.

When you sign up initially, you will be asked to provide a screen name and a password. The name will have to be unique for your service provider, so “John” will not normally be accepted. This is the name the outside world will know you by (it makes up the first part of your e-mail address), so if you are a company chairman, it is probably best not to call yourself “Bunnykins”. Some companies tell their staff to use a set formula - initial and surname, or both names run together, for example.

If you have signed up with more than one ISP, you can run into problems with a proliferation of e-mail addresses, which will confuse both other people and yourself. It is possible to configure the software so that it recognises the same e-mail address, even if it “belongs” to a rival ISP. You will have to ring the help desk to find out how.

You could also consider having a (free) e-mail account that is “ISP-neutral”. The advantage is that it can be accessed from a Web site – handy if you are away from home and want to check your e-mail from a cybercafé. Sign up from a Web site, for example from Hotmail (www.hotmail.com), Yahoomail (www.yahoomail.com) or Alta Vista Mail (altavista.iname.com).

E-mail readers are broadly similar. When you log onto your Internet service, you will be given a list of incoming messages. You click on each to display it. You will be able to reply by pressing the Reply button – this means you do not even have to know the e-mail address of your correspondent, although you can also build up a personal e-mail "phone book". You can also store incoming text as a document in your computer using the "save as" function. As you become more familiar with e-mail, you can use it to subscribe to newsletters (see 2.2.2).

Files can be "attached" to e-mails, so that your correspondents can open them up in their original program (Word, Excel, etc). Attachments are however a source of many headaches: see 2.1.2. Anyone using e-mail should have virus-checking software installed. The most common way of spreading a computer virus (which can cause havoc) is through attachments on e-mails. Most modern computers have virus-checking software included.

A Newsgroup reader. You may have a separate program, or you may have to use the system built into your browser or e-mail reader. Netscape Communicator includes a news program, as does Outlook Express. When you first try to activate the news session (make sure you are connected to the Internet), you will be asked if you want to download a complete list of newsgroups. The titles of all 26,000 groups will then be downloaded. You can go through them and "subscribe" to those you want to look at. On the Internet the word "subscribe" rarely implies any payment – it simply means you want to see or receive something. Two ways of making the choosing process easier are to use the search facility built into the newsgroup software – so you could look for all groups with "insurance", "Scotland" or "export" in their titles. Or you can go to the Web site www.deja.com, and search for any words used in newsgroups in the last 12 months. This lets you browse the groups in detail before choosing the ones that interest you.

Every time you connect to the Internet, the newsgroups to which you have subscribed will be updated so that you can read and if necessary contribute to them. (See 2.4 and 8.5.6 for newsgroups that can help your business.)

A Web browser. This will probably be Netscape Navigator or Communicator or Microsoft's Internet Explorer. The browser is a "window" on the computer screen that fills with whatever Web page has been requested. When you first connect, you will be presented with a set "home page" – perhaps of Netscape or your ISP. You can switch across to any site on the Web simply by typing its address in the "open location" box (Click File, then Open location; alternatively hold the Control or Apple button and click on L or O). All addresses begin with http:// and can be very long (note that with modern browsers, you do not need to type in the "http://", which is why this book does not include it in addresses). To access a Web site, you must enter the address exactly – the computer will not make allowances for missed dots or typing mistakes.

If a Web page is taking a long time to appear, you can switch off the graphics, which means you get nothing but text. In Netscape, click "Options", then turn "Autoload Images" off; in Explorer, go to Web Content in Preferences. You can store pages you want to use regularly in "Bookmarks" (Netscape) or "Favorites" (Explorer) – just click "Add" when you are in that page. Bookmarks can get crowded, so it is worthwhile categorising them into electronic folders. Web pages can be stored in your computer by clicking "File", then "Save As". They can also be printed out, though the result may not be satisfactory.

Some sites include features that require extra software called "plug-ins", which you download by clicking on links and following the instructions carefully. Be aware that some software takes a very long time to download, so decide if you really need it first. Unrestrained downloading of software will soon clutter up the computer (see 5.2.7).

Browsers have built-in security systems (see 8.3). When you are buying something from a "secure" site – that is one where your credit card and other details are scrambled before transmission – the padlock or key icon at the bottom of the browser will close up.

Note that you do not have to use Netscape or Internet Explorer. Here are some simpler ones you can download (see page 29):

***Windows*:**
AtomNet: very small program, $79, from change7.com/atomnet.
Netcaptor: free, from www.netcaptor.com.

Opera: small program, good for older computers and people with visual handicaps. $35, from operasoftware.com.

Mac
Cyberdog: Apple's own browser. Free, from www.cyberdog.org.
MacLynx: text only, so very fast. Good for information-finding and for the visually handicapped. Free from www.lirmm.fr/~gutkneco/maclynx.

1.5 Getting connected on a small office network

If you want to connect more than one computer to the Internet, you do not need a separate phone line for each. Because information is going down the line for only a proportion of the time you are online (eg when a Web page is actually loading), the line can be shared between a number of people. The benefits to your phone bill are obvious. One way to provide this is to have your own "router", a box that distributes connectivity around the office. The biggest maker of routers is Cisco (www.cisco.com). Look in the PC magazines for advertisements – you will probably pay between £200 and £400, depending on the number of users. The alternative is to use software:

- Windows 98 Second Edition (£59 to upgrade to this) includes an Internet-sharing system.
- Wingate (www.wingate.com) offers software that can be downloaded from the Internet (see page 29) – you can use it free for a month, then pay according to the number of users ($80 for three business users, $700 for unlimited users).
- WinProxy (www.ositis.com) is similar, starting at $60 for three users.
- Macintosh users can pay $89 for unlimited use of IPNetRouter (www.sustworks.com).
- VicomSoft (01202-293233; www.vicomsoft.com) offers both Windows and Mac versions of its SoftRouter Plus.

For other modem software, go to www.tucows.com (see page 29), and look under "modem sharing".

Chapter 2 Quick returns

Whether or not you decided to use the Internet as an active part of your company's strategy, it is worth seeing what it can offer you passively – that is, with hardly any effort on your part.

The answer is, quite a lot. E-mail use is spreading like wildfire (2.1), many businesses use the Web for finding information (2.2), and some are starting to use it to make their purchasing easier and cheaper (2.3).

2.1 E-mail

E-mail (electronic mail) is the standard tool of the Internet. Despite its lack of glamour, many more people start using the Internet because of e-mail than the World Wide Web, because its uses are so much more obvious. A 1998 survey by AFP Technology, a UK-based electronic document delivery company, found that IT managers expect e-mail to make up 65 per cent of all business document traffic within five years. Even today, according to a recent report, 30 per cent of large companies specify e-mail as a pre-requisite for companies that want to do business with them.

2.1.1 Strengths and weaknesses

E-mail is particularly well suited to business:

- It encourages brevity – there is no preliminary chatter, as on a phone, or elaborate beginnings and endings, as in a letter. It is no way to conduct a love affair, but it is excellent for exchanging information or ideas – the basis of most business communications.

- It is easy to use. There is much less fiddling about than with a fax or a letter. If you receive an e-mail, you do not even have to know the address of the person who has sent it. Simply press "reply", type in a message, and press "send".

- It is much faster than a letter, it can be as quick as a fax (depending on how clear the networks are), and it does not depend, as a telephone does, on the recipient being at his desk. It is possible to have "conversations" by e-mail, as long as you are prepared to wait a few minutes for a reply.

- E-mail messages come directly into a desktop computer. The "fax lost somewhere in the office" syndrome is thus eliminated.

- It is cheap, especially for international communication. Unlimited e-mail is included in an Internet service provider's subscription, no matter where the messages are going. Microsoft's Hotmail, Yahoo! Mail and similar services offer completely free e-mail accounts to anyone who can reach an Internet connection (see 1.4).

- You can send any file that is readable by a computer program as an "attachment" to an e-mail. Pictures, word processor documents, photographs, animated presentations, even videos can be sent on the back of an e-mail.

- As encryption becomes more secure, it will be possible to send important documents by e-mail. Lawyers or merchant bankers, who at the moment rely on a stream of motor-cycle couriers, could find they can finalise documents much more quickly by e-mail.

These are the disadvantages:

- It is not yet as secure as a fax or courier, and it is less easy to be certain that your message has arrived. (See 2.1.5 – e-mail security.)

- It is less personal than a phone call.

- If you have a dial-up connection, you have to make the effort to check regularly for e-mail.

- It can be technically infuriating, especially when sending or receiving attachments (2.1.2).

- It can get clogged up with "junk mail" (2.1.3)

- It is the main carrier of computer viruses (2.1.3).

- Libellous e-mails are too easy to send, and potentially ruinous (2.1.4).

Downloading software

Most people, after a short while on the Internet, will find themselves downloading software (except big company staff who are not allowed to – see 5.2.7). It is plentiful, mostly cheap, and can make e-mail or Web more effective or fun. Be careful not to overdo it – it is easy to jam so many goodies into your computer that it starts slowing down or feeling sick.

Software is divided into three broad categories: commercial, where you pay a full price; shareware, where you will probably pay $50 or less; and freeware. Freeware tends to have been written by someone for fun, while shareware usually relies on your honesty to pay up. Shareware and some commercial software allow you a 15 or 30-day evaluation period. You can buy commercial software from the appropriate company site; shareware and freeware are available from software libraries (see below).

Downloading is usually straightforward. On a PC you will be asked if you want the program opened or stored. Click store, select a suitable folder (or create a new one called Downloads), and click download. If the file is less than 1MB, it should appear quite quickly; otherwise go and have a cup of tea. When the download is complete, locate it (it should have a name ending in .exe), and click to start the installation process. You will be asked where to put the program – choose an area where there is plenty of space (maybe not the C drive). The program will install. If the file that downloads ends with .zip, it has been compressed. You will need an unzipping program such as Winzip or PKUnzip – if you do not already have one, download these from www.winzip.com or www.pkware.com or take them from a PC magazine cover disk.

Mac downloads are simpler. They normally expand themselves if necessary and sit on the desktop. Just click on them to start the program.

There are several huge software libraries. They include:
www.tucows.com
www.softwarenow.com
www.shareware.com
www.download.com
www.hotfiles.com

2.1.2 Technical hiccups

Pachamama is a clothing manufacturer based in south London. It commissions and distributes products manufactured on three different continents. In the past, it used courier and fax to send design information between London, Bali, Nepal and Ecuador. The company is now saving time and money by liaising with its manufacturers in Ecuador via e-mail, sending photos and mock-ups of designs back and forth for approval. But Pachamama still exchanges patterns and designs with its partners in Bali and Nepal via the more expensive courier and fax – because of incompatibilities between its own e-mail software and that of its suppliers.

Pachamama's problems are common. Messages sent with one type of e-mail software can be impossible to read for another. Here are some tips on how to avoid the most common compatibility problems with e-mail:

1 Sending and receiving attachments (computer files attached to an e-mail message). Attachments can only be opened using computers that have the following:

- The correct type of software application (eg Excel software is needed to open Excel attachments).

- The correct version of this software application. So, recipients need a copy of Excel 97 (or a later version) installed on their computer to open an Excel 97 attachment. If a sender does not know which version of a software application the recipient has, it is safer to send the file in an early version of the application (for example, send an Excel document as an Excel 95 file, not an Excel 98 file). When sending text-based attachments, it is best to send files in Rich Text Format (RTF) or (even safer) Text (.txt). You will lose any formatting in Text, but the message should get through.

Because Macs do not add three letter "extensions" to file names, as PCs do, it may help if the Mac-using sender changes the file name by adding an extension manually: .doc for a Word document, .xls for an Excel spreadsheet etc.

If you click on an attachment and your computer does not know what created it, ask your correspondent what the application is, and try opening the file in that application. On a Mac, it may be worth dragging the offending file on to Stuffit Expander (commonly installed on Macs).

2 If you open a message and it is full of garbled nonsense:

- Try scrolling down to see if the text starts lower down – this often happens when the applications are not quite compatible. You will have lost the formatting (fonts etc), but you have the text.

- You may have been sent an HTML (Web) page, but your e-mail software cannot handle it. Ask your correspondent to send a text version (the giveaway is lots of sharp brackets like this < >). He can do this by switching to text-only message in his e-mail software's preferences.

- The attachment is not text, and your e-mail reader cannot understand the "protocol" with which it has been encoded (pictures etc have to be turned into a string of letters and numbers, because that is what computers understand). There are several protocols (eg Base 64, BINHex and UUencode), and not all e-mail software can understand them all. There are particular problems sending attachments between PCs and Macs.

One answer is to ask your correspondent to resend using a different protocol – UUEncode is probably safest. He should be able to change the preferences in his software to do this.

Alternatively download a "decoder" from the Web (see page 29 for more on downloading). Here are three that may help:

DropStuff/Stuffit Expander (www.aladdinsys.com) – Windows and Mac. $20, with 15 days free evaluation.
Decode Shell Extension (www.funduc.com) – Windows. Free.
UUD Win (execpc.com/~mspankus) – Windows. Free.

3 If the message arrives in several e-mails, each full of junk, your correspondent has used a system that chops large messages up – but yours cannot reassemble them. It is possible to string them all together and decode them using a decoder. But it is probably easier to ask your correspondent to send the attachment again. If he cannot disable the "breaking up" function in preferences, suggest he compresses the attachment first, using Winzip (PC) or Stuffit (Mac).

4 Other possibilities if you cannot open an attachment:

- If it is a forwarded message, ask the person who forwarded it to open it on his computer, save it as a different file, and send it again as an attachment. Alternatively, if it is text, get him to copy and paste it into the main message window. Then send it again.

- The attachment may be hopelessly corrupted. Ask your correspondent to try again.

If you want to give yourself a technical tutorial on all this, have a look at pages.prodigy.net/michael_santovec/decode.htm.

2.1.3 Unwanted messages

Junk e-mails: Marketing pitches, get-rich-quick schemes, chain letters or other unsolicited material (often called spam) can waste time, increase connection costs and clog up computers' hard disks. There is no single way to prevent all junk e-mail, but some e-mail applications offer "filters" that enable users to limit the size of incoming mails, and automatically file different kinds of mails (such as those from particular people) into different folders.

So, for example, you could arrange for all e-mail from your accountant and suppliers to go into a separate mailbox. This makes it quicker and easier to separate the electronic wheat from the chaff.

Anti-spam software is available. For example CYBERsitter, $19.95 from www.solidoak.com and DL Mailfilter, $12.90 from web.singnet.com.sg/~leemhc/mailfilter.html. Plenty of others from the software download sites (see page 29).

Viruses: E-mail is a major channel for viruses (computer files that can play havoc with your computer). It is important to use a virus checker software package to scan files for viruses. Most modern computers will come with anti-virus program loaded. Otherwise you can download virus protection software packages such as Norton Antivirus (shop.symantec.com/region/uk/) and McAfee VirusScan (www.mcafee.com).

Making a fax into an e-mail – and vice-versa

You have long been able to send and receive faxes from computers, given the right software. Now you can handle e-mail, fax and even telephone messages from a single program. This means you can easily send messages to people who have a fax but no e-mail, and can also pick up messages of all three sorts from any Internet-connected machine.

Freeserve, the Internet Service Provider, offers a fax/e-mail service from Telserve. Users are given one phone number and e-mail address for their unified mailbox. As well as creating a single source for all faxes, calls and e-mails, Telserve allows users to:

- read incoming faxes on any computer screen connected to the Internet.
- listen to incoming e-mails via a telephone (the e-mail text is automatically converted into synthesised speech).
- arrange for phone calls, faxes and e-mails from other numbers and e-mail addresses to be automatically forwarded to the unified mailbox.
- forward e-mail and faxes to any fax machine, using any telephone or Internet connection.
- store faxes and voice phone calls as digital files on a computer.

Telserve costs £9.95 per month, plus 10p per minute for fax forwarding. As well as offering all the above features, Telserve and other unified messaging services enable businesses to create an additional "virtual" phone line for their offices, without any physical installation. Similarly, home workers can create a business number with voicemail and fax services, without adding a physical line.

Telserve is available at www.freeserve.net.
Other unified messaging services:
Contact Box: www.contactbox.co.uk
Digital Mail: www.digitalmail.com

2.1.4 Legal issues

When an employee sends an e-mail from within a company, the firm faces legal liability for its content. For example, in 1997 a British Gas area manager sent an e-mail about a colleague's departure to establish a rival gas company. The message instructed staff to avoid contact with the employee or the rival company. The former employee sued British Gas for defamation – it had to pay him more than £100,000 in damages. Norwich Union made an out-of-court settlement of £450,000 in an incident involving alleged e-mail defamation of a competitor. These examples highlight the likelihood that it will be the publisher – that is the company – that will be found liable, rather than the author.

Another potential legal problem with e-mail is the ease with which the sender's identity can be forged (see next section). In a survey by Content Technologies, 73 per cent of business e-mail users said that if a company director requested confidential information via e-mail, they would supply it without checking whether the e-mail was genuine.

The best way to avoid these problems is to develop a set of guidelines for e-mail use. This may not make sense for smaller companies, but managers should make sure employees know what the dangers are.

For more information on the legal issues of the Internet, see page 311.

2.1.5 How secure is e-mail?

The answer is: hardly at all, unless you make an effort. The most common security breach comes from other people reading your e-mail. This may not be on purpose (if a number of people share the same e-mail box, it can be difficult to avoid). But it may be: anyone who knows your user name and password can configure their e-mail reader to pick up your messages. Real hackers can also tap into the Internet as messages are sent and read them – in August 1999 Microsoft had to suspend its Hotmail service for two hours because hackers worked out how to get into the 40m account holders' e-mail boxes without their passwords. Most e-mail users will not mind if anyone sees their e-mail: the most that will be revealed is that their friends send them embarrassing messages (and irritatingly large attachments – see 2.1.2).

But if you do want to make e-mail more secure, what can you do?

● Protect your own computer, perhaps with password protection to make it more difficult for other people to log into it. Keep your own password secure, and change it if you think other people may have obtained it.

● When you send e-mails, ask for a receipt. The recipient will be asked to click a button, which sends back to you an acknowledgment that he or she has seen it. This has a security aspect, because it gives some comfort that the right person has seen your message. If you have regular correspondents, suggest that they all use the receipt system. Only certain e-mail software (including Eudora) allows receipts, so look in the help guide to set them up.

● If you have Microsoft Outlook, you will be able to apply a security system called S/MIME and also obtain a digital certificate (see 8.3 to see how these work). Between them they are designed:

- to assure the recipient that the message is coming from you
- to verify the identity of someone who sends you a message
- to guarantee it was not tampered with in transit
- to encrypt the message so it can be read only by the intended recipient
- to read encrypted messages meant for you (note you can only do this if your correspondent is using compatible software).

Follow the steps on the next page if you would like to set yourself up with a digital certificate on Outlook Express – you can download a copy of Outlook free from www.microsoft.com/windows/ie/download/windows.htm.

What's the point? Well, digital certificates are likely to become increasingly standard on the Internet because they provide an approximation to a real signature. Electronic signatures, usually involving digital certificates, are likely to be given legal standing, in some cases with the same weight as handwritten signatures (See Legal issues, page 311). Be aware that the digital ID you can set up on Outlook does not in itself provide much extra assurance - it guarantees merely that the sender of the message is using a particular e-mail address and computer. It does not stop someone else getting a certificate in your name (this would require validation of the sort a merchant has to obtain - see page 245).

Trying out a digital certificate on Outlook

The easiest way to get a digital certificate with Outlook (this is for Version 4.72 of Outlook Express – yours may differ) is to click on Tools/Options/ Security. Select Get Digital ID. This will take you to a Microsoft Web page where you can choose a certificate supplier. If you are in the UK, it may make sense to choose BT. Its Trustwise system is a rebranded version of leading US system Verisign (though we can expect many other well-known names, including banks and retailers, to start offering digital certificates).

You will be directed to the Trustwise Web site (www.trustwise.com) where you will fill in details including a "challenge phrase" (which you may be asked if you are trying to prove who you are). You send these off by e-mail, and get an e-mail back with a 32-digit PIN. Follow the instructions, cutting and pasting the number, then installing it onto your computer's hard drive. This means your e-mail address is bound to your computer, with Trustwise (ie BT) guaranteeing that binding. You will now have to install the certificate into Outlook: the instructions under Help are clear.

You can set up Outlook's options always to add a digital certificate and/or encrypt the message. Alternatively you can click on buttons when you are composing to switch these options on. You can send a digital certificate to anyone: they can click on the icon, which unless they too have S/MIME appears as an attachment, and will be able to see that the certificate belongs to you and has been guaranteed by BT. You must not however encrypt unless the recipient has the appropriate software – if he does, the message will be garbled on all computers but his.

It is very early days for digital certificates. The fact that they are bound to particular machines means they are useless if you switch between computers. This should be overcome, in 2000 or 2001, by the introduction of smart cards, plastic cards with inbuilt computer chips: they will carry your digital certificate, so that you can use it on any computer.

Digital certificate providers:
Trustwise: www.trustwise.com
Verisign: www.verisign.com
Globalsign: www.globalsign.com

2.2 The Web as the world's biggest library – and shop

The Internet is an excellent information resource. It is a gateway to a constantly updating pool of data on everything from stock prices to basket weaving. Increasingly it is a library that also acts as a shop – so as well as telling you stock prices, it lets you buy and sell shares. Many of the travel sites also allow you to buy: some Web sites are in effect travel agencies. American business people do not think twice about looking up a flight and buying a ticket on the Internet – and Europeans are following the same path.

The problem is that the Web is so vast, it is difficult to know where to start looking. It does not help that there is no single entry-point, cataloguing system, index or filtering process. And the dominance of the US on the Web can make looking for information relevant to European businesses particularly tricky. Yet there are ways to filter the Net to find what you are looking for. It is easy if you know where to start...

2.2.1 Search engines and Web directories

Two essential tools for finding information on the Internet are search engines and Web directories. Simply type a key word or phrase into an on-screen box, and a list of related sites will appear. Search engines do this using special software, while Web directories match your keywords against a database of sites compiled by a team of real humans.

The major search engines are:

Alta Vista	www.altavista.com
Infoseek	www.infoseek.co.uk
Lycos	www.lycos.co.uk
Excite	www.excite.co.uk
HotBot	www.hotbot.com
WebCrawler	www.webcrawler.com
All the Web	www.alltheweb.com

The problem with these gigantic search engines is that they can come up with hundreds of matches to the keywords you enter – many of which will probably be of no use to you at all. They can however be made more useful by following these guidelines:

- When typing in your key words or phrases, use the most obscure words possible. In particular, avoid very common terms such as "the" and "Internet", which some search engines ignore altogether.
- If you know the exact phrase you are looking for, enclose it in quotation marks (eg “Daily Telegraph Electronic Business Manual”).
- Search engines have various advanced search features (also known as "Boolean Searching"). For example, typing "AND", "OR", "NOT" between keywords narrows a search accordingly. Alta Vista’s "Refine Search" facility is particularly easy to use, allowing you to repeatedly tweak your search until you find what you need.
- Use software that runs multiple search engines simultaneously. Try www.dogpile.com, www.monstercrawler.com, www.allonesearch.com.

Get to know the difference between search engines. They ignore different words, and look for different elements within sites. That means a search on Lycos is unlikely to throw up the same sites as one on AltaVista.

For details on how the engines work, see the Web site searchenginewatch.com.

If you are looking for information in a broad area (eg “Which are the companies that do this?” “What Mexican newspapers are online?”), it is best to use a directory such as Yahoo!, which allows you to drill down through increasingly specific categories until you reach the information you want. For example, in order to find currency exchange rates, you can click on “business and economy”, then “finance and investment”, then “currency”, then “quotes”, and finally “exchange rates” to reach a site giving the information you require. Yahoo! has a UK and Ireland version at www.yahoo.co.uk.

Two points to note about Yahoo!

- It is not comprehensive – if a site has not been submitted to Yahoo’s indexers, it will not be included.

- In Yahoo! UK and Ireland, a search will by default look in “All Yahoo”. Select instead “UK only”, “Ireland only” or “This category only”.

A number of other local and specialist directories are available.

They include:

Yell	www.yell.co.uk
Search UK	www.searchuk.com
EMAP's UK Internet Directory	www.emap.com/id/uk
Global Directory Online	www.god.co.uk
EuroBusiness Centre	www.euromktg.com/gbc/en.htm
UK Index	www.ukindex.co.uk/
Scotland.com	www.scotland.com/ (Scottish sites)
Interview	www.interview.co.uk/ (UK sites).
Seniorsearch UK	www.seniorssearch.com/ssuk/homedirectory.htm
UK Web directory	www.scit.wlv.ac.uk/wwlib/newclass.html
FinanceWise	www.financewise.com (financial sites)

All of the major search engines and Web directories have sections dedicated to business sites. Infoseek's UK Plus directory (www.ukplus.com) allows users to search the Web for sites by business category (advertising, law, etc).

Finally, try Ask Jeeves (www.askjeeves.com) - see 1.2, page 13. Its ability to interpret and answer questions is more than a gimmick. Because its administrators spend so much time categorising Web sites, it can save time. Alta Vista offers a similar system, but it is not as well developed.

While getting to grips with search engines and Web directories is vital for finding your way around the Web, it is also helpful to be familiar with the limited number of sites that are either valuable in their own right, or which act as gateways to the best information. A pick of the best ones follows. Remember that although there is plenty of free information on the Web, you may be able to save time (and therefore money) by paying on occasion.

But even if you have to pay for information, the Internet does have huge advantages over the private dial-up systems that have dominated the last two decades. First, it is an access point to vastly more data than was ever available before. Second, it can be used by anyone with a computer, rather than just librarians. As a result, all employees – from directors to secretaries – can become researchers. The advantages (lower costs and better-informed employees) are obvious. And smaller companies now have access to information that only wealthy corporations could previously obtain.

2.2.2 News

News sources abound on the Web. The main problem, apart from the volume, is the domination by US providers. Some sites offer "push" services - they will e-mail subscribers updates every day.

General news

All the big media organisations have their own sites.

BBC News (news.bbc.co.uk) is one of the most heavily-used UK sites.
ITN (www.itn.co.uk)
Reuters (www.reuters.com/news)
Press Association News Centre (www.pa.press.net)
Electronic Telegraph (www.telegraph.co.uk) is the longest-established major UK newspaper site, with a searchable archive.
The Times (www.the-times.co.uk) has an archive.
The Independent (www.independent.co.uk)
The Guardian (www.guardian.co.uk) also has a series of specialist sites, mostly sports-related.

Business news

- Financial Times (www.ft.com) includes a big archive of FT and other material, some of which has to be paid for.

- CNN's Financial Network (www.cnnfn.com) provides US-slanted free business news in a number of categories including small business, markets and industry. The site is exceptionally well laid-out and easy to navigate. If you enter some personal details and an e-mail address, CNNFN will send you automatic updates of key business developments.

- News Page (www.newspage.com) is a good place to find technological information. It allows registered users to receive technology-related news updates (from more than 700 mainly US trade magazines) on subjects they are interested in – on the Web or by e-mail. Some articles must be paid for, at $3 each (you set up an account, and are billed at intervals).

- Newsnow (www.newsnow.co.uk) is an excellent UK-based source of information, including business and Internet-related topics.

2.2.3 General business information

- The Business Bureau (UK) (www.u-net.com/bureau) is an excellent gateway to information for small businesses. It has pages of links to subjects including human resources, self-assessment, sales and marketing, and business travel.

- Business Researcher's Interests (www.brint.com/interest) provides links and special search engines to help you find information on subjects including accounting, electronic commerce and knowledge management. It manages to be comprehensive without overwhelming you with data.

- Michigan State University's International Business Resources on the Web (ciber.bus.msu.edu/busres) is designed to distil the ocean of good, bad and ugly sites into a select pool of valuable if esoteric ones. It allows visitors to search sites by name, region or category. The results are not exhaustive, but they are of a high quality. Its links to European business information sites are particularly good, with a refreshingly cosmopolitan range of sources - including south and east European business sites.

- Strathclyde University's Business Information Sources on the Internet (www.dis.strath.ac.uk/business/index.html) describes and provides links to 600 British sites. It reaches only the tip of a very big iceberg, but quality again makes up for quantity.

- Doing Business in Ireland (www.dcd.net/payroll/dbi.html) is a useful guide. Coverage ranges from the tax system to local small business associations.

- Lexis-Nexis (www.lexis-nexis.com) is a subscription-based legal, news and business data bank with more than a billion documents. It is now available via the Web. Services include Lexis-Nexis Tracker, which offers subscribers personalised industry information from 5,800 sources delivered via e-mail. Lexis-Nexis reQUESTer offers access to a range of international business sources (including newspapers and journals) for $169 per month. The main problem is that it is so big (and US-biased) that it can seem as overwhelming as the Web itself.

- Dialog (www.dialog.com) boasts a database "over 50 times the size of the World Wide Web". Its database is an amalgam of Knight-Ridder's (a US firm rather like Lexis-Nexis), and the London-based company formerly known as MAID, which bought Knight-Ridder in 1997 (and is now called Dialog). MAID's traditional strength is market research information, and its most powerful product is Profound (www.profound.com), which carries 100m pages of research data. Access is not cheap, at £6,000 a year plus a per-user fee. A low-cost option is to tap into Dialog's 10 industry-specific information sites, all accessible from www.dialogselect.com. Users are charged per article, with a monthly usage fee of $75.

- An intriguing site, Company Sleuth (www.companysleuth.com) offers users a daily personalised e-mail report giving news on up to 10 chosen public US companies: the clever bit is that it finds this information by scouring the Web. It is free (and rather fun), but does not yet cover European companies.

2.2.4 Government information

The quality and quantity of online government information varies greatly. The UK is quite strong. The main British government site, with a mass of links, is at www.open.gov.uk. A section of the site is dedicated to business, with links to government information from electricity regulation to Companies House. You can also connect to sites dedicated to public services, government agencies and organisations, the G7 countries, and more.

The government wants businesses to be able to conduct government business online. A handful of sites show the way the rest might go:

- Inland Revenue (www.inlandrevenue.gov.uk) publishes tax regulations, consultation documents, and policy updates on a clearly laid-out site. There is also an electronic version of the self-assessment tax return.

- The Patent Office (www.patent.gov.uk) lets you track your patent and trademark applications online.

Other useful sites:

- The Department of Trade and Industry (www.dti.gov.uk) has plenty of useful information on business support, regulation and especially exporting. (See 8.5 for more sites for exporters.)

- Companies House (www.companieshouse.gov.uk) has a searchable database of every UK company director currently disqualified by the courts. Presumably the entire database of company accounts and filings will soon be available online.

- Foreign & Commonwealth Office (www.fco.gov.uk) includes travel advice on unstable destinations.

- Business Link (www.businesslink.co.uk) includes a clickable map of the UK to help locate a local Business Link, as well as a useful information directory.

- Enterprise Zone (www.enterprisezone.org.uk) is an information site designed specifically for SMEs.

International

- The European Union's main site (www.europa.eu.int) is a surprisingly usable multi-language monster containing a huge number of official documents, regulations and announcements.

- Cordis (www.cordis.lu) is the EU research programme, where you can search for projects your company could get involved in, and possibly find new sources of funding.

- The Organisation for Economic Cooperation and Development (www.oecd.org) publishes reports, forthcoming events and recommendations.

- The International Monetary Fund (www.imf.org) is a vast repository of economic information.

- The World Bank (www.worldbank.org) has a huge amount of data on developing countries, including the subscription-based Africa Live Database, which allows you to download figures onto an Excel spreadsheet, and manipulate them as you want.

2.2.5 Company directories

Search tools for UK company information are multiplying on the Web:

- The Yahoo! UK Business Directory (scoot.yahoo.co.uk) is very easy to use. Visitors can search for businesses by name, category and location. There is even an online map showing where the business is located, along with telephone, fax and Vodafone short messaging service numbers.

- Thomson Directories (www.thomweb.co.uk) has a similar service, with more than 2.2m businesses on its database.

2.2.6 Credit checking and debt collection

The Internet is greatly increasing the number of companies doing business together that do not know each other. Not surprisingly, credit checking companies have decided they should provide their services online – some have added a debt collection service too.

- Dun and Bradstreet (www.uk.dnb.com) offers two online credit checking services. Globalseek provides one-off information on companies – detailed data on US companies costs between $20 and $89, while $5 snapshots are available for non-US companies. Pay by credit card. D&B Access for the Internet is a subscription service for regular users, and provides greater detail. You can place debt on the site, which D&B will use its clout to collect: minimum debt £400, with a fee to D&B of between 9 and 30 per cent.

- Business Credit Management UK (www.creditman.co.uk) provides ICC information on 5m UK businesses, live and defunct. Cost ranges from £6 for a basic report to £24 for a full report, which includes the ICC/Juniper Risk score: this uses a predictive scoring model designed to detect which companies are likely to fail in the next 12 months. Pay by credit card.

- UK Data (www.ukdata.com) provides reports on every company in the UK. Costs range from 80p for a single registered address to £24 for a full company report, including principal activities, full company accounts for the past three years and a list of any county court judgment summaries. You can get a scanned image of the latest report and accounts displayed on the Web.

- Euler Trade Indemnity (www.tradeindemnity.com). This credit insurance company does not provide credit ratings, but it does collect debts online, from the UK and overseas. It does not provide a tariff, but will quote for each enquiry.

2.2.7 Financial information

Investors are well-served by the Web – many large company sites will provide live, or slightly delayed, stock market prices, as well as plenty of historical financial data. In addition, there are many sites that gather together financial information, providing useful research tools for other companies, as well as investors.

- Carol (www.carol.co.uk) gathers together reports or other financial information from UK and other companies. The quality depends on what the company has put on its Web site and ranges from annual reports and analyst presentations to a few lines of figures.

- Hemmington Scott (www.hemscott.com) provides data on all quoted UK companies. Detailed information can be bought online at £10 a company.

- Interactive Investor (www.iii.co.uk) provides a wealth of free information on UK stocks, shares and other investments.

- Reuters (www.reuters.com) provides near-live market indices from around the world.

- Investext Group (www.investext.com) has more than 1.8m analysts and other reports, with a price each of about $20.

- GEE Publishing (www.gee.co.uk) offers a subscription-based online reference service for company secretaries. Registered users of the service, called Factfinder, can access information on subjects including company law, health and safety, and buying and selling a business. It also enables users to set up a personalised page of topics of particular interest. Subscriptions cost £575 per year.

- Electronic Share Information (www.esi.co.uk) has information on quoted companies, and links that let you buy and sell shares.

2.2.8 Legal

- Lawlinks (libservb.ukc.ac.uk/library/netinfo/intnsubg/lawlinks), from the University of Kent, gives access to primary material and legal journals.

- Collyer-Bristow (www.collyer-bristow.co.uk) offers a table of links to national and international legal information, from UK cases to New Zealand legislation.

- Multilaw (www.multilaw.com), an international association of independent law firms, has a "business tool kit" on its site, with links to an eclectic range of law-related information.

- The International Centre for Commercial Law (www.icclaw.com) is a good place to look for recommended law firms and solicitors around the world. The site is searchable by continent and/or country.

- LawNet (www.lawnet.co.uk), backed by a national network of UK law firms, offers introductory law advice for businesses. Users can also search for a lawyer by name, town, county or region.

See page 310 for more on Internet-related law, and a list of lawyers who specialise in e-commerce issues.

2.2.9 Industry-specific sites

Some of the most useful sites are those that have been set up to serve particular sectors. They act as information sources, discussion forums, and business meeting points. They include:

www.archinet.co.uk	architects
www.bioindustry.org	bioindustry
www.breworld.com	brewing
www.cateringnet.co.uk	catering
www.egi.com	commercial property
www.fmb.org.uk	building industry
www.teacouncil.co.uk	tea
www.timberweb.co.uk	timber

Case study: industry-specific information sites

Farming On-Line, a subscription service costing £4 a month, offers a wide and growing range of information for farmers. Daily prices provided by Dow Jones and the Meat & Livestock Commission keep them aware of changes that happen too fast for print publications.

Farmers who are reluctant to pay a subscription can still look at a big choice of agricultural sites on the Internet, including Farmers Weekly Interactive, Dot Farming, the Internet home of Miller Freeman farming journals and Galaxy PrecisionAg. This site, set up by agricultural supplier JH Bunn, gives farmers satellite pictures of their land - showing how well it is draining.

Jason Rankin has set up a Web site for his dairy farm in Northern Ireland. It contains information he has compiled himself and from contact through e-mail discussion groups with other farmers. His favourites are Graze-l and the US-based Dairy-l. "We exchange ideas on subjects like quotas, climate and building," says Mr Rankin. "I get a lot of very positive feedback which I often apply to the management of my farm."

FOL has been overwhelmed with enquiries from farmers who want to know more about the Internet, and has held a series of roadshows about the medium.

Farming On-Line	www.farmline.com
Farmers Weekly Interactive	www.fwi.co.uk
Galaxy PrecisionAg	www.jhbunn.co.uk/galaxy
Dot Farming	www.dotfarming.com
Jason Rankin	www.loughries.demon.co.uk

2.2.10 Travel

The Web is an important source of travel information, and increasingly a booking office too. As travel operators try to persuade customers to use the Web (because it saves the operator money), some are even offering slightly lower rates for people who book online.

One-stop shops

- *A2b Travel* (www.a2btravel.co.uk) is a "portal" site aimed at the UK traveller. It links seamlessly to other sites to allow you to check prices and book flights, look up coach times, book a holiday, reserve a hotel room, buy a tourist guide, compare car hire prices, get road directions to any destination in Europe, look up global weather forecasts, view detailed maps of any British post code, search for ferry times, and view live flight arrivals at eight UK airports. The site includes information, products and services from 200 different hotel chains, 19 ferry companies, and 420 airlines.

- *P&O Trave*l (www.potravel.co.uk) is another one-stop shop for UK business travellers. Flight, car hire and hotel booking facilities are all offered online as well as access to hotel directories, timetables, security advice, maps and related travel information. The site gives direct access to Sabre, the world's biggest online booking system, and has a variety of different search options including best fare deals.

- *Bradmans* (www.bradmans.com) is a business travel site with well-organised information ranging from economic conditions, via hotels, to the weather in 100 cities. It is kept up to date by journalists on location, although users are invited to contribute their comments.

Online travel agents

A number of online travel agents are linked into giant airline reservation systems and claim to be able to find the best deals:

Seaforths (www.seaforths.com) is an Aberdeen-based business travel specialist. For now you have to download special sofware to use the system, though direct Internet access is planned.
Travelocity (www.travelocity.co.uk) is the UK end of a giant US operation.
Expedia (www.expedia.co.uk) is the UK version of Microsoft's travel service.
Flightbookers (www.flightbooker.co.uk)
Cheapflights (www.cheapflights.co.uk)
Travel agents with more of a leisure bias, but possible sources of rock-bottom flight prices:
Bargainholidays.com (www.bargainholidays.com) offers flight-only bookings.

Bridge the World (www.b-t-w.co.uk) is an online agent offering hotel and flight bookings.

Air

British Airports Authority (www.baa.co.uk) provides real-time flight arrival information for all its airports, including Heathrow and Gatwick.

Many major airlines offer online customers flight schedules, arrival and departure updates and even direct ticket booking on their sites:

British Airways (www.british-airways.com) offers booking.
Virgin Atlantic (www.ezbook.virgin.com) offers booking
British Midland (www.iflybritishmidland.com) offers booking.
Go (www.go-fly.com), BA's budget airline, offers special discounts for tickets booked on its site.
Easyjet (www.easyjet.com) does the same.

Aer Lingus	www.aerlingus.ie
Air France	www.airfrance.com
Lufthansa	www.lufthansa.com
SAS	www.flysas.com
Alitalia	www.alitalia.com
Iberia	www.iberia.com
United	www.ual.com
American	www.aa.com
Delta	www.delta-air.com
Qantas	www.qantas.com
Singapore	www.singaporeair.com
Cathay Pacific	www.cathaypacific.com

Rail

UK rail information tends to be dispersed between the rail companies, who are moving online at different speeds. There are however sites that cover the network:

- *Railtrack* (www.railtrack.co.uk/travel) has an excellent interactive timetable. It is updated twice a week (to take account of engineering works),

Tips on how to get the cheapest flights

The golden rule is shop around: there is no single outlet – either online or offline – that can guarantee the cheapest seat on any given flight.

- Like their physical counterparts, online agents are intermediaries, so airlines' Web sites quite often offer the biggest discounts. They can also offer "Cyber Specials", selling flights off at bottom dollar rates. But sometimes traditional travel agents offer the best deals because of the byzantine way in which seat allocation works.
- Look for the best price online, then ring up a flight specialist: you may or may not get a better deal.
- If your travel dates are flexible, try keying in different dates and times on the same Web site to find the lowest price.

and can be better at finding the best route than a telephone-based operator. Railtrack is currently working on the development of an online booking system.

- *UK Railways on the Net* (www.rail.co.uk) includes travel news, timetables and links to rail operators and other travel-related firms.

- *TheTrainLine* (www.thetrainline.com) is linked to Virgin but provides online booking, as well as travel information, for all mainland services.

- Deutsche Bundesbahn's timetable (bahn.hafas.de) covers the UK – as well as a dozen other European countries. It will tell you how to get from Peckham Rye to Odense in 18 hours, and offers booking for German journeys. Its disadvantage against Railtrack is that it is not adjusted for engineering works.

Other UK rail sites

Rail Travel (www.cpoint.co.uk/tw/uk/rail.html) provides a simple map of all British Rail Express routes. Links are provided to maps of Network South East and London Underground services.
London Transport (www.londontransport.co.uk). Visitors can download a variety of printable underground maps, and find the latest information on

line closures and engineering work.
Heathrow Express (www.heathrowexpress.com) gives information on the Heathrow-London link.
Eurostar (www.eurostar.com) has no online booking, but offers timetables, fares and contact numbers.
FirstNorthWestern (www.firstnorthwestern.co.uk) has real-time running information.
Midland Mainline (mml.rail.co.uk) has real-time running information.
GNER (www.gner.co.uk) has real-time running information.
Virgin Trains (www.virgintrains.co.uk) is linked to TheTrainLine for booking.
Great Western Trains (www.great-western-trains.co.uk) has a guide to times, fares and pricing information.
Wales and West (www.walesandwest.co.uk) includes times, fares and a journey planner supplied by Railtrack.
Great Eastern (www.ger.co.uk) is a functional guide to all routes, tariffs and times.
ScotRail (www.scotrail.co.uk) is a basic but useful information site from Scotland's rail operator.
Central Trains (www.centraltrains.co.uk) has an interactive map.

Road

- The *RAC* (www.rac.co.uk) calculates the quickest route between specified destinations, and gives travellers detailed directions, complete with a map. Users can then say when they will be travelling, and will be sent an e-mail before they leave detailing traffic conditions and hold-ups on the route.

- *Vauxhall* also offers visitors traffic updates on its site at www.vauxhall.co.uk.

- *Michelin* (www.michelin-travel.com) offers a formidable continental travel planning system, linked to recommended hotels and restaurants. You have to pay for each route, and it takes a little work to understand the intricacies of the site.

- *National Express* (www.nationalexpress.co.uk) offers online timetables and booking.

Hotels

As with airlines, the Web can be used to give direct access to reservation databases.

Gateway sites

- UK Hotel and Guest House directory (www.s-h-systems.co.uk/shs.html) is a crude-looking but huge database of UK accommodation, searchable by airport, county, town or city. Every hotel and guest house is depicted on an online map, and online booking is available for the majority of destinations.

- HotelWorld (www.hotelworld.com) lets you find and book rooms in nearly 9,000 hotels in 204 countries. It provides background on facilities and nearby amenities and has special offers for business travellers.

- AA Hotel Guide (www.theaa.co.uk/hotels) combines reviews, information and online booking.

- Expotel (www.expotel.co.uk) is an agent offering online booking.

Chains

Marriott (www.marriott.com) lets you see a photo of a room, check availability and make a reservation. If you are in the US, it even gives you driving instructions from anywhere within 1,000 miles.
Inter-Continental Hotels and Resorts (www.interconti.com) has similar facilities, with special booking rates exclusively for online customers.
Thistle Hotels (www.thistlehotels.com) has a comprehensive online booking service.
Bass Hotels (www.basshotels.com) is a gateway to online booking for Holiday Inns, Inter-Continental hotels and other Bass hotel brands.
London Hotels (www.london.hotels.co.uk) is an online booking service for Forte hotels in London.
Forte (www.forte-hotels.com), which includes Travelodge and Le Meridien, offers online booking (though this is not clear from the home page).
Stakis Hotels (www.stakis.co.uk). Rooms and conference facilities can be booked online.

2.2.11 Couriers

Air couriers pioneered the use of the Web as a customer service tool (see 9.1.2). If you use one of the companies, you can go on to their sites, punch in the airway bill number of your package, and see where it is and when it is likely to arrive.

FedEx	www.fedex.com
DHL	www.dhl.co.uk
TNT	www.tnt.co.uk
UPS	www.ups.com
Parcelforce	www.parcelforce.co.uk

2.3 Buying online

Businesses can save money by buying online – it means they can cast the net wider, buying from abroad if necessary. The most popular business product is the air ticket (see Travel, above). But that is just a start – it seems likely that most standard company requirements will soon be available online.

Will it save you time and money? Probably, though you have to balance lower prices against the possible extra hassle of dealing with someone you do not know. It may even be worth running a credit check (see 2.2.6) on your supplier.

Business-to-business e-commerce is one of the fastest growing areas. Supplies of non-production equipment – from paper clips to furniture – are moving online so fast that the Web may quickly become the standard purchase channel. Many suppliers are already geared up for direct delivery – it is not difficult to add a Web "front end" to take orders (see Chapter 8 if you are one of these suppliers). From the customers' point of view, the Web is an efficient way of choosing from a large catalogue – it combines the visual advantage of a print catalogue (easy to choose, unlikely to make a mistake) with the speed of the phone or fax.

Should you buy from an Internet-only company, or from the e-commerce wing of an established name? Brand should not play too much of a role here.

The secret is to try out the different suppliers with a fairly small purchase, and use them if their prices and service are good. Internet-only companies should have set up efficient distribution arrangements, are not cluttered by traditional ways of doing things – but they do lack the experience of the established players. Be prepared to change supplier if service drops off (most such companies are growing fast, and have dips in performance). As a customer, you have the luxury of being able to abandon brand loyalty.

Here are some of the things you may be able to save time and money on:

Business equipment, stationery and supplies:

Viking Direct	www.viking-direct.co.uk
Office Shopper	www.officeshopper.com
The Office Shop	www.owa.co.uk
Office Supplies On-Line	www.office-supplies.co.uk
Ashfields	www.ashfields.com
Office Furniture	www.byweb.com

Rank Xerox (www.rankxerox.com) offers a limited range of its products for online ordering.
Signs & Labels (www.safetyshop.co.uk) stocks products ranging from safety notices to speed bumps.

Furniture

Standard office furniture can be ordered safely online, because it is ordered mainly on the basis of dimensions and specifications. We can expect to see more suppliers emerging in the UK soon: one that is already running is Space2.com (www.space2.com), which sold 130 desks, worth £250,000, in the three months after its launch in May 1999.

Printing

The Card Corporation (www.cardcorp.com), a small printer based in London, provides a cut-price, small volume, business-card service with fast turnaround. You can design your cards directly on the site (choosing colours, fonts and layouts) and order cards either via the Web site or by phone.

Case study: Cutting purchasing costs

Non-production equipment – stationery, office supplies etc – is regarded as one of the most intriguing areas of the Internet. Because these products are standard but come in complex ranges, they are ideal for buying online (see 7.2 for why). They have an additional advantage – which puts them even above books – in that they are business-to-business products. Most businesses have computers, and many have Internet access.

The big office suppliers have already put their catalogues online, and are using the Web as just another communication channel – they already have the delivery end set up. But in 1999 a company that works from the buyer's end established a Web-based system aimed at helping small and medium-sized businesses get the best deal.

The Cost Reduction Partnership, a London-based purchasing consultancy, uses its skills to find the best deals, and to aggregate buying power. Large companies can already take advantage of this (usually through an intranet-based system), but CRP also has a Web site (www.buy.co.uk) designed to help organisations of any size.

Companies can take advantage of specially negotiated price deals, purchase products online, create regular item order lists, and receive quotes online for printing and printed stationery. CRP says the system will eventually be available for products and services ranging from office cleaning to cars. It claims that administration costs can be halved, while purchasers can save themselves as much as 10 per cent on the item itself.

CRP collects and organises the information "manually". We can however expect to see the arrival of automatic systems that scour the Web looking for the best deal. These already exist for consumer products: Bottom Dollar (www.bottomdollar.com), Jango (www.jango.com) and in Europe Taxi (www.mygroup.co.uk) allow visitors to type in what they are looking for (book, CD etc): semi-intelligent software ("bots") will then go to the sites of potential suppliers and list the results. The visitor can click across to his chosen store, and buy online.

Because designs are held on the company Web site, you can change layouts and details as you need, so there is no need for the endless exchange of proofs.

Computers, electronic equipment

Dell (www.dell.co.uk). PC manufacturer.
Gateway 2000 UK (www.gw2k.co.uk). PC manufacturer.
Computer Warehouse (www.cwonline.co.uk). Macintosh hardware and software seller.
Software Warehouse (www.software-warehouse.co.uk). Computer software seller.
Net Shop UK (www.net-shop.co.uk) sells computer peripherals.
Morgan Computers (www.morgansco.com). Surplus computer stocks seller.
Mac Warehouse UK (www.macwarehouse.co.uk). Macintosh hardware and software seller.
Ace Quote (www.ace-quote.com) enables you to find the best quote for a computer supplies request (see case study opposite).
IBM UK (www.ibm.com/uk). Computer equipment manufacturer.
Dabs Direct Online (www.dabs.com). Computer hardware and software seller.
Online PCs (209.8.183.235/onlinepcs/web_store.cgi). Computer hardware seller.
Simply Computers (www.simply.co.uk). Computer equipment seller.
Tiny (www.uk.tiny.com). Computer seller.
Insight UK (www.insight.com). Computer equipment seller.

Some of the best deals have come from the online auction company, QXL (www.qxl.com - see case study, page 266). As it has become popular, it has become more difficult to find bargains – but they do still exist. There are also plenty of "person-to-person" auctions – though here you are usually buying second-hand and are taking a risk on the seller. They include www.ebay.com/uk and www.ebid.co.uk.

The secret with online auctions is to look for products where no-one else is bidding: check that this is not because the starting price is too high (you should be able to find an approximate retail price by searching on the Web), and bid as late as you can. If you believe you have a bargain but someone

Case study: Giving power to the buyers

Ace-quote is an online service allowing businesses to post requests for computer equipment and services, compare prices offered by sellers and choose the best deal.

Buyers can use Ace-Quote free of charge to post requests for computer-related products and services. Sellers pay the company £695 a year to receive the requests and place quotes. "A buyer can post the request in 20 seconds, and receive 10 different quotes within an hour," says Gary Munz, managing director of Ace-Quote. He says the service, which is in effect a reverse auction, is particularly useful for buyers with specific computer needs. "For example if you are looking for 40 computers with a specialised network connection and bespoke software, you can use Ace-Quote to instantly field suppliers for the best deal – without spending any time finding out which have your requirements in stock."

The service, launched in June 1999, has "many thousands" of registered buyers and sellers. Around 150 businesses are joining per day. Ace-Quote is currently available to UK businesses but hopes to expand to the US, France, Germany and other parts of Europe. "There is no reason why German sellers cannot offer deals to UK buyers, and vice-versa," says Mr Munz. Although large firms already look abroad for computer suppliers, small and medium sized firms, along with consumers, are largely confined to national suppliers. "This has great potential to open up the computer goods market across Europe," he adds.

Mr Munz says that although both buyers and sellers are enthusiastic about Ace-quote, it can be difficult to persuade them to adopt such a radically different procurement model.

The firm hopes to launch similar procurement communities for other products and services in the future. "The IT sector is the most obvious area to start out with on the Internet, but it holds equal benefits for other goods," says Mr Munz.

www.ace-quote.com

else is fighting you for it, you may have to do some aggressive bidding in the few minutes before the auction closes (sometimes it will overrun, so keep an eye on it). Companies such as QXL are selling end-of-range, returned or refurbished products, so you will not get the same back-up as you would with new equipment. QXL does however have a "return for any reason within two weeks" policy.

Industrial parts and components

Companies that have well set-up delivery systems are starting to put their catalogues on the Web.

Unipart (www.partsdirect.co.uk) offers 20,000 car parts online.
RS Components (www.rswww.com) has 100,000 electronic and electrical

A purchasing community: Marketsite

This virtual marketplace provides companies with a central resource for purchasing indirect goods (products used internally rather than in production) via the Internet. The service gives purchasing managers an international source of suppliers.

It was launched in the US, but has now been licensed by British Telecom for launch in the UK. Buyers can use the service to find and compare new suppliers, and place and track orders. Before they buy, they must make contact offline and agree terms.

As well as running MarketSite in the UK, BT plans to use it for its own internal purchasing. Both Boots and BT expect to do 95 per cent of their indirect procurement via the service by March 2000.

MarketSite gathers all supplier product information into a single electronic catalogue, cutting set-up costs for buyers, as well as providing them with a powerful search tool. It generates revenue by charging clients a monthly or annual maintenance fee, and by taking a commission on transactions made via the service.

www.marketsite.net

components and products. They can be paid for either on account or by credit card.
Farnell (www.farnell.com) has a similar components system.

Higher value business-to-business products are also available through the Web: suppliers of everything from second-hand aircraft via machine tools to riot equipment have realised they can spread their marketing worldwide through the Web. Try typing the name of a product into a search engine, and see what appears. You may find a source you did not know about. See Chapter 7.3.2 for more on specialist sales.

Consumer items

Books

Almost every book under the sun is available from these sites. A fierce discounting war means you should be able to find bargains (the more popular the book, the deeper the discount).

Amazon UK	www.amazon.co.uk
Internet Bookshop	www.bookshop.co.uk
Waterstone's	www.waterstones.co.uk
Blackwell's	www.bookshop.blackwell.co.uk
Bol	www.uk.bol.com
Heffers	www.heffers.co.uk
WH Smith Online	www.whsmith.co.uk
Black Star Books	books.blackstar.co.uk
Book Pl@ce	www.thebookplace.com
Net-MegaStore	www.net-megastore.co.uk
The Book People	www.thebookpeople.co.uk
Alphabet Street	www.alphabetstreet.co.uk

Electrical/household goods

Argos	www.argos.co.uk
Dixons	www.dixons.co.uk
Innovations	www.innovations.co.uk
Shoppers Universe	www.shoppersuniverse.com

Granada	www.granadahome.co.uk
Hutchisons Direct	www.hutchisons.co.uk

Gifts

Worldwide Hampers	www.worldwide-hampers.com
Basket Express	www.baskets.co.uk
Wine Cellar	www.winecellar.co.uk
J Sainsbury	www.sainsburys.co.uk
Thresher Wine Shop	thresher.LineOne.net.
Drinks Direct	www.drinks-direct.co.uk
Interflora	www.interflora.co.uk.
First Flowers	www.firstflowers.com
Flower Net	www.mkn.co.uk
Flowers Direct	www.flowersdirect.co.uk

Second hand items/cars

Adhunter (www.adhunter.co.uk) carries classified ads from dozens of regional newspapers. You can search by product and region.
Loot (www.loot.co.uk) has its entire database online – you have to pay a small amount (£1.35) for the latest issue, but older ads are free.
Exchange and Mart (www.exchangeandmart.co.uk) has a Web-based version of its ads.

2.4 Using newsgroups to find information and products

Although there are 26,000 newsgroups, you will be lucky to find more than a handful that can help your business (unless you are in IT, in which case you will find hundreds). If you get the hang of them, they can be very handy – for carrying our market research, asking for advice, and even buying and selling (for trading, see 8.5.6).

Download a complete list of groups and subscribe to any that look interesting (see 1.4 for instructions). Do not contribute to any until you have got the feel of them – some newsgroups are the equivalent of the old-fashioned pub, where strangers will be stared at and possibly abused. Read the contributions, following "threads" to see if the site is both useful and friendly.

If you use Deja.com (see 1.4), you can sign up to follow particular threads. You will be e-mailed with updates of threads for as long as they are active. You will also be given a special deja.com e-mail address, which is designed to protect you from spam (see 2.1.3 – people who want to spam [send unsolicited e-mail] will collect e-mail addresses from newsgroups).

When you are ready, ask questions. On the next three pages are some real examples, showing how business people have been getting tips, and also how others are using newsgroups to sell their services (most of the names have been changed, though the newsgroups and questions are genuine. We have also put the question in front of the answer, when they appear the other way round in newsgroups).

In the first example, Andy Bigwood is using a signature file, which appears on the end of his e-mail and newsgroup messages, subtly to promote his business.

Note that you do not know if you are getting good advice, and if the question is important you should check elsewhere.

Example 1:

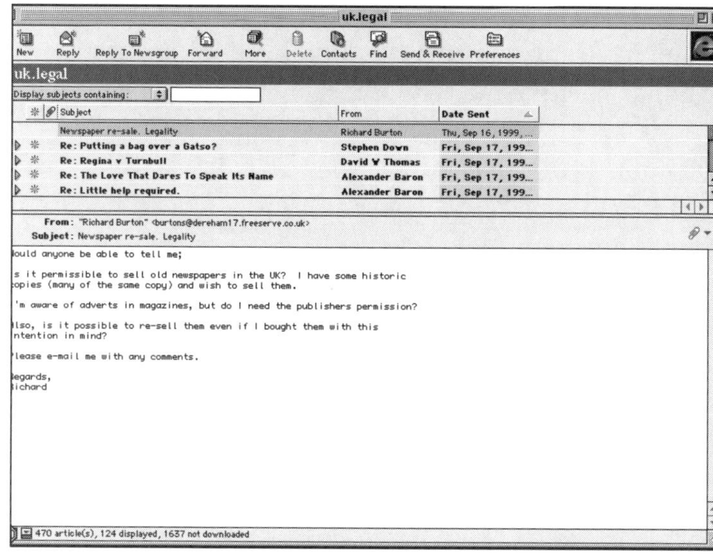

The uk.legal newsgroup

Forum: rec.travel.bed+breakfast
Thread: Advice for new B&B

Subject:
Re: Advice for new B&B

I'm setting up a small B&B in the UK.
Can anyone offer advice or web site address on
- how to set up a GOOD B&B
- what international visitors might want for breakfast?
- how best to cook/serve breakfast
- Ensuite or Shared facilities - should I invest in Ensuite?

Any advice gratefully received>

George Hodges,,
hodges@bandb.co.uk

We operate a new B&B and self catering website covering the UK.
For full details of our free listing service, please see our service descriptions at http://www.country-retreats.com/admin_service.htm

If you have any questions regarding any of our services please do not hesitate in contacting me.

Hope this is of some help to you.
Best Regards,
Andy Bigwood

http://www.country-retreats.com
email:info@country-retreats.com
The Internet Directory for B&B and Self Catering
Accommodation Throughout the United Kingdom

Example 2:

Forum: uk.legal
Thread: Help please! - A limited company

Author: Jim Halifax <tallguy@demon.co.uk>

Could anyone tell me please if a group of people set up a limited company, would that company be obliged to publish finances, expenses, membership etc, at least once a year?

Many thanks in advance.

Cheers,

Jim

Subject:
Re: Help please! - A limited company
Author: Chris Black<blue@netcom.co.uk>

Failure to provide audited accounts to Companies House will get each Director of the Company a fine of up to UKP1,000. Failure to provide audited accounts to your local tax office, in respect of Corporation Tax, can also result in a fine and/or imprisonment (?)

You have to provide accounts whether or not the company is trading.

Chris

Example 3:

Forum: sci.engr.joining.welding
Thread: Magnetized Pipe Re: Magnetized Pipe

A friend of mine asked me a question regarding some 30" dia carbon steel pipe in an off shore oil rig application. The pipe has been sent in and it is magnetized to the point that you can hang a pair of pliers on the side without them falling off. So far it has been next to impossible to weld.

Jim Schwarz

Use a long ground cable and wrap it around the pipe near the side of the weld. It's a pain, but it can negate the magnetism and tame the wiiiiicked arc blow that you get in those situations. If it doesn't seem to work, try wrapping the cable in the other direction (clockwise vs. counterclockwise).

Elliot Turner, Toronto, Canada

This next posting comes from one of the approved commercial newsgroups, which act more or less as for sale and wanted classified columns.

Example 4:

Forum: uk.adverts.computer
Thread: Photocopier Drum Required.

Does anybody know a good source of replacement drums for Photocopiers/Laser Printers please. Thanks.

Richard Carr

If you have not yet had any joy, let me know the make and model number. One of my customers is a photocopier supplier and deals with this type of stuff all the time.

James Burke

The Internet as a time waster

The consultant IDC claims that companies can lose up to £3m a year in wasted time due to personal Internet use at work. In June 1999, a Liverpool-based IT manager became the first UK employee to be sacked for personal Internet use in the workplace. Her employer found that she had conducted more than 150 online searches to book a holiday on the Web. She contested the action, but an industrial tribunal found that she was fairly dismissed.

Time wasting on the Internet can be a big problem. Not only is the Web full of fun (and pornography), a huge number of jokey e-mails make the rounds – fine in themselves, but not when they have large attachments to clog your system.

There is not however a cut-and-dried case against Internet amusement. A moderate amount of playing can encourage familiarity with the medium, enabling workers to use the Web more efficiently in the long term. It also seems reasonable to grant employees the same amount of personal Internet access privileges as they currently enjoy for phone use.

The key is moderation. If employees are using the Internet too much this is probably because:

- they are bored, which is more a management problem than anything else.

- they are addicted. Studies have shown that Internet addiction is a real problem.

How should you control Internet use?

- Draw up a policy, and make it known. Eventually it could become a part of your job contracts.

- Use software to control access. MIMEsweeper (www.mimesweeper.com) and SurfCONTROL (www.surfcontrol.com) allow you to restrict access by individual, time or type of content.

Chapter 3 Planning an Internet strategy

The previous chapter was aimed at any company that has decided to use the Internet in any way. There may be questions about who is given access to the Web and e-mail, but it is difficult to imagine a company deliberately ignoring such a low-cost communication or information-gathering tool.

This chapter moves us into areas of uncertainty. None of the actions described from here on is necessarily suitable for your company. The aim is to give you an overall view of the direction in which you should be heading. Detailed instructions follow in the rest of the book.

Before using the Internet for more than "quick returns", it is essential to ask yourself a simple question: "Why do we want to do this?" Understanding the benefits and pitfalls of using the Internet will make it easier to establish whether your business is suited to the medium. While using the Internet to capture information or for e-mail is relatively cheap, using it as an active part of your strategy will absorb considerable resources – in time mainly, but also in money.

Even a casual look at the electronic business activities of other companies (most visible through their Web sites) is likely to convince you that too many people have been moving too fast with too little thought. Although large company Web sites are improving, the majority of company sites are poor because:

- they have been built by someone for fun. They are unlikely to have any strategic thought put into them and will typically be "brochureware" – an Internet version of the printed brochure (though the design values of the printed version are rarely adequately translated online, because the "Web designer" is unlikely to have as much graphical skill as the brochure's creator). In larger companies this quite often leads to two or more Web sites, neither of any great merit.

- the chief executive suffers from "golf course syndrome". Two chief executives meet on the golf course. One says to the other: "We've got a Web site." The other replies: "Well we'd better have one too." He returns and instructs his IT manager to create one. Once again, "brochureware" is the likely result.

These weaknesses are fed by three potential assets of the Web, which can also be dangers:

- Web design is fun. One of the challenges of management can be to *stop* staff building a Web site.

- The cash cost of building a simple Web site can be nil – especially if the IT enthusiast is prepared to work into the night without overtime (an amazingly common trait).

- There is an industry that lives off building cheap and cheerful Web sites. You may well have received a mailshot from a company offering to build you a site for £100 or so.

In other words it is easy, when confronted with an offer to build a Web site, to say "Why not?" The better response is "Why?" So the first stage of any coherent electronic business strategy is to sit down and think. Think hard, because the whole subject needs extraordinary clarity of vision – as in a game of chess, each move will have an effect on what you can do next, and it is very difficult to see what your position is likely to be after half a dozen moves.

Don't do it unless you know why you're doing it.

3.1 How to establish a strategy

1 Set up a team to consider how the Internet could affect your business. This may initially consist of you and your dog pondering in the park: this is no bad thing, because it helps if you start with some clear thoughts of your own (even if you later discard them).

But the team should quickly develop to include other members of staff. As the Internet can be used for marketing, public relations, research, supplier and customer relations and much else, there will be no shortage of people wanting to provide input. Often Internet activity – especially within small companies – is driven by individual enthusiasm. Self-selecting experts will want to offer advice and to emulate what they have seen elsewhere.

IT experts will tend to want to innovate as much as possible – do not put them in charge, unless they have a broad strategic role within the company. A useful simile is with film making. A studio would not put a couple of cameramen in charge of its latest feature and you should not put "techies" in charge of your Web site. This is not to denigrate the expertise of the cameramen or computer programmers, merely to point out that their skills are "tactical" rather than "strategic" (see IT box, page 70). Listen to them, but make sure overall charge is taken by someone senior – someone who is not driven by the technology itself.

The "director" should be a manager who is instrumental in developing company strategy. He or she should also be someone with the clout to get things done – who will take responsibility for any problems arising and champion the project. This person will make the decisions on how and when functionality will be delivered: which are the most important objectives to fulfil now, given the constraints of time and budget, and which can wait until later phases.

2 ***Research:*** A small team (maybe one person) should be given the task of researching the opportunities and threats. Remember that if you have identified opportunities, your competitors may well have done the same. If you have seen how you can sell to new markets, companies in those markets may well return the compliment:

- The UK is an easy market to sell into (because regulations are light, tariffs generally low and there is no language barrier for US companies).

- US companies are generally ahead of European ones, so if they have decided to target Europe, they will bring their greater experience to bear.

- Competition between sellers of physical products will increase as international fulfilment centres are set up (ie warehouse operations that distribute locally). Much of this activity is likely to take place in the UK.

A word on IT

One of the great mantras is "The Internet is not about technology, it is about business". This is true, in general, but should not be taken too far.

- It is important that people who use the Internet are prepared to get their fingers slightly stained with technicality: otherwise they will not be able to send or open attachments (see 2.1.2) or make plug-ins work (see 5.2.7). Do not allow people to reduce their productivity by hiding behind the excuse that "I don't know anything about technology".

- While it is usually a mistake to give overall charge for a Web site to the IT department (or IT person), it is also important not to irritate them. The Web does after all run on computers, and their expertise should be tapped. Even if you are using an outside agency, you will probably want to use them to keep the site up to date, and to help solve the inevitable glitches that are part and parcel of running a computer.

Use the Web to carry out research both on your markets and on what your competitors are up to (see 2.2). Use it too to find new potential competitors.

3 Brainstorm: If you or one of your colleagues have clear ideas (most of this chapter is designed to help formulate these), give a presentation to stimulate discussion. If you feel there is not enough expertise in the team, bring in an outside expert – a local Web consultancy or other expert will probably be prepared to present their thoughts for free, in the hope of winning work from you later. If the presentation is unsatisfactory, ask another company. Even if you are not impressed by specific ideas, you are likely to be given ideas to stimulate trains of thought. For a list of Web consultancies, see page 320.

Read the Threats and Opportunities section, page 289. This contains a wide range of businesses and industries, one or more of which should be similar to your own.

Also, read section 5.2: it is important to understand the fundamental abilities of the Web. Try absorbing these, then going back to first principles to see how they might be applied.

4 Produce a report for discussion.

5 Implement: one of the big questions is whether you should hold back until you have everything planned in detail, or whether you should move a step at a time. Generally it is fine to move a step at a time as long as you are following a well-conceived outline, and as long as each stage is done well.

On the other hand,

It is better to do nothing than do it badly.

To put it another way,

Don't be rushed.

Why shouldn't I hand the whole thing over to an Internet consultancy?

It may well be that at some stage you will hand the bulk of the work over to outsiders, and it is fine to invite ideas from and bounce ideas off people you trust.

But you are doing neither yourself nor the outsiders any favours by passing responsibility over too early. You know your business better than any consultant, so it is you who must decide the outline of a strategy. Web consultants tend to be busy (worry if they are not …), and you may find yourself "sacked" if you do not have a clear idea of what you want.

See 4.5 for more on choosing an outside agency.

3.2 The thought process

In the broadest terms, you will want to answer these questions:

- Should we create a Web site?
- Should we use e-mail for anything more than simple communication?

In this chapter we have not distinguished between e-mail and the Web, because they should often be used in tandem. Few Web sites fail to offer an e-mail contact, and both media can be used as part of a coordinated marketing effort. For the practicalities of using e-mail, see 2.1. Chapters 4 and 5 are just about Web sites.

One of the characteristics of the Internet is that it blurs distinctions – there is sometimes little difference between selling and marketing. There is no difference at all between above and below-the-line marketing. And the Internet will rarely have one purpose – it can carry out a range of tasks. So when going through these flow diagrams, mix and match – you are likely to end up with a menu of things you believe you can use the Web and e-mail for. Note that the more tasks a Web site is given, the more important its structure and navigation become (see 5.3).

Here are some (if not all) of the things you may want to do online:

1 Sell products or services

2 Market, but not sell, a specific product/service

3 Build your brand

4 Offer customer service

5 Recruit staff

Here are reasons why you would want to do these:
- Increase revenue
- Reduce costs

Note that while the first three activities are related mainly to increasing revenue, all five have a cost-cutting element – you are using the Internet because it is a cheaper way of marketing, recruiting, raising funds etc.

You are more likely to justify an Internet strategy through cost saving than increasing revenue.

That is not to say that the biggest returns cannot come from increased revenue (this is arithmetic: you can only cut costs by 100 per cent, whereas you can increase revenues by any multiple). But to get your Internet activity into profit as quickly as possible, and therefore to generate support for further developments, it is best to look for easy ways to cut costs.

3.2.1 Mapping the demographics

The first question – whether you want to sell, cut costs, recruit or anything else – is "have I got the right demographics? How likely is it that the people I want to communicate with use the Internet?" See pages 74-77 for a breakdown of the "wiredness" of consumers and businesses, in the UK and overseas, remembering always these points:

- The demographic mix is changing all the time as more people start to use the Internet. A year or two ago it was true that the Internet was dominated by young males, and that hardly anyone over 50 used it. Now one of the fastest-growing groups is pensioners. In the US as many women as men use the Internet and Europe is catching up here too. And as "the Internet" moves to interactive television, mobile phone and other devices (see page 287), there is likely to be a fundamental shift in the profile of its users. So do not look just at the market now, imagine how it will be in a few years' time.

- The act of setting up on the Internet will change the demographics of your market. Even if you have never sold anything outside your home town before, you will certainly find you get enquiries from the US, and quite possibly from Russia and Indonesia as well.

Internet and electronic commerce demographics

Estimated number of UK Internet users (Fletcher Research, June 1999)

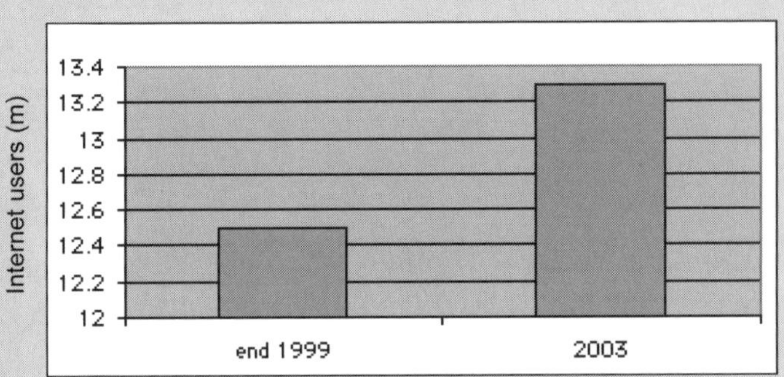

Proportion of UK age groups online (Continental Research, Jan 1999)

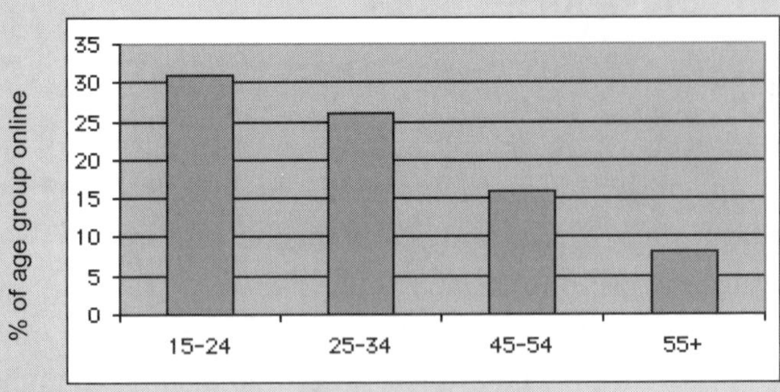

Gender of UK Internet users, by age group (Fletcher Research, August 1999)

%	Female	Male
All Internet users	40	60
Less than18	61	39
18-24	53	47
25-34	45	55
35-44	36	64
45-54	30	70
Older than 55	19	81

UK companies' use of the Internet

Durlacher estimated there were 97,000 small companies and 20,000 medium sized organisations hooked up to the Internet in the UK (Spring 1999)

Internet penetration amongst UK SMEs* (%)

Company size	1998	1999
SME	40	76.6
Small companies	33	61.7
Medium companies	54	88.3

** SME: Small and medium sized enterprise*

Internet equipment amongst SMEs (%)

	Internet-enabled SMEs	Total SMEs
Have online presence	70.8	54
Have an intranet*	33.5	25

** See page 341 for definition*

SMEs offering transaction-based services (%)

	Offer today	Will offer in 12 months
Distributors	15.1	36.8
Manufacturers	5.2	21.9
Retailers	18.4	48.5
SME average	12.6	33.6

Figures on this page are taken from a survey by Durlacher (www.durlacher.com) in Spring 1999

Internet Uptake among UK SMEs

%	Leisure	Retail	Dist/Wsale	Health	Manuf	Telecom
Companies with Web sites	41.1	38.8	50.0	63.6	56.4	78.9
Intranet penetration	8.6	17.4	27.3	36.3	22.8	63.1
Internet penetration	53	64	78	82	85	90

Primary aims of SME Web sites, sector by sector
(% of sector)

All SMEs	
Raise awareness of company products	85.8
Generating direct sales	36.9
Extend geographical reach of company	10.6
Create community/initiate discussion	3.5
Distribution/Wholesale	
Raise awareness of company products	85.0
Generating direct sales	39.1
Extend geographical reach of company	14.3
Create community/initiate discussion	3.0
Manufacturing	
Raise awareness of company products	89.0
Generating direct sales	28.1
Extend geographical reach of company	9.5
Create community/initiate discussion	1.9
Retail	
Raise awareness of company products	80.0
Generating direct sales	57.1
Extend geographical reach of company	7.1
Create community/initiate discussion	1.4

Figures on this page are taken from a survey by Durlacher (www.durlacher.com) in Spring 1999

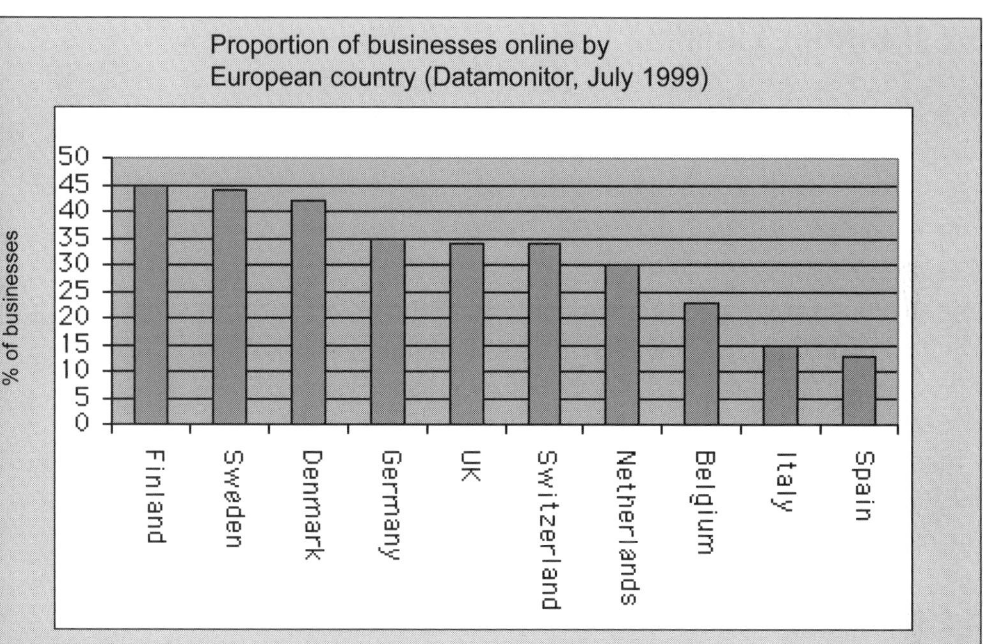

What are the most wired countries in Europe? (Mori 1999)

%population with Internet access	**Home**	**Work**
Denmark	37	33
Sweden	36	27
Finland	21	24
Netherlands	18	18
Switzerland	18	26
UK	15	14
France	7	10
Germany	11	13

Internet penetration worldwide - various sources, gathered by Nua (www.nua.ie)
% of population online (note: these figures are for rough guidance only)

Iceland	45	Switzerland	16	Austria	6
Sweden	41	Netherlands	14	Belgium	5
US	39	Japan	14	South Africa	4
Norway	36	Ireland	13	Czech Rep	3
Finland	32	France	13	Brazil	2
Denmark	30	Israel	11	Greece	1
Australia	30	Germany	10	Egypt	1
Canada	25	Spain	8	China	0.3
UK	16	Italy	8	Saudi Arabia	0.2

3.2.2 Cutting costs

One point to start with:

> *Cost savings will come from saving time at least as much as money.*

Every time someone looks at the Web site rather than phoning/faxing/writing, they are saving you money: not only in the time your staff spends on the phone, but also in the "fulfilment" time – finding the information, sending it off or ringing back.

E-mail can be a more efficient way of handling enquiries, but it must be well handled (poorly handled e-mail is worse than useless, because the nature of the medium leads people to expect a rapid response).

See 9.1 – customer service.

Can you use the Internet to cut costs?

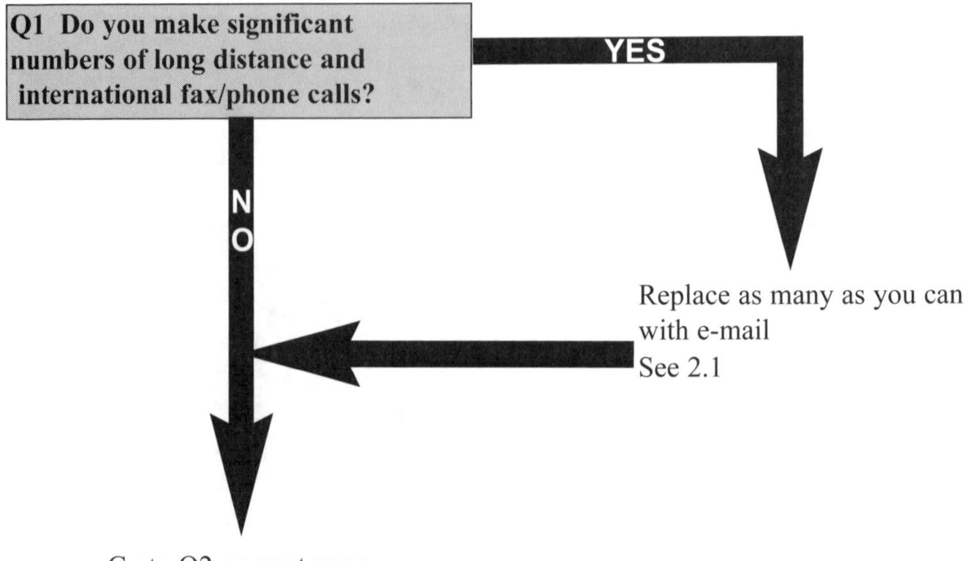
Q1 Do you make significant numbers of long distance and international fax/phone calls?
YES
NO
Replace as many as you can with e-mail
See 2.1
Go to Q2 on next page

Q2 Do you have a printed brochure?

YES

Consider whether a Web site can save you money. (See box.) Then read 3.2.3 to decide whether it can increase revenues. If you decide you need a site, turn to Chapter 4.

Consider the economics of putting a brochure online. A simple home-built Web site can be much cheaper than a printed one, and if well thought out can be highly effective.

Will a Web site save you money?

On the negative side is the cost of the site (see 4.1-4.4). On the positive side is the money you will save on sending brochures out, and a more effective use of your sales staff's time.

If you receive requests for information by e-mail, it is quite reasonable to direct enquirers to your Web site. This will give them the information more quickly, and will save you the cost of postage/packing and, in the long run, printing. Or you can grade your response, directing low-value contacts (eg students) to your Web site, while contacting high-value customers by phone. One of the hidden benefits of the Internet is that you can discriminate much more rigorously between leads – your most skilled sales people can concentrate on the best leads, while the Web offers "self-service" for the less promising enquirer.

Maximum cost benefits come only when you can abandon your print version entirely (unless you are in a high-tech business, this is likely to be years off), but it is never too early to start weaning enquirers towards this low-cost channel.

If you have a constantly changing product range, or want to change prices frequently, this sort of Web site is particularly useful. Many companies produce a printed brochure that they update once or twice a year, along with a separate sheet for prices. Information on a Web site can be changed as often as necessary, so up-to-date price details can always be integrated.

Because a Web site can carry much more information than even a substantial printed brochure, it should reduce the communications (phone/fax/e-mail/letters) being fielded by your staff. A brochure Web site can easily be adapted to provide customer service, and perhaps to sell (an example of "blur").

Go to Q3 on next page

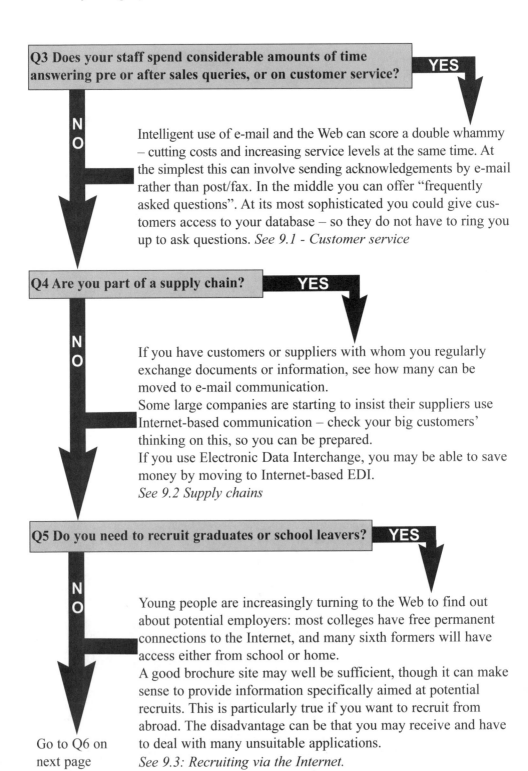

Q3 Does your staff spend considerable amounts of time answering pre or after sales queries, or on customer service?

YES

NO

Intelligent use of e-mail and the Web can score a double whammy – cutting costs and increasing service levels at the same time. At the simplest this can involve sending acknowledgements by e-mail rather than post/fax. In the middle you can offer "frequently asked questions". At its most sophisticated you could give customers access to your database – so they do not have to ring you up to ask questions. *See 9.1 - Customer service*

Q4 Are you part of a supply chain?

YES

NO

If you have customers or suppliers with whom you regularly exchange documents or information, see how many can be moved to e-mail communication.

Some large companies are starting to insist their suppliers use Internet-based communication – check your big customers' thinking on this, so you can be prepared.

If you use Electronic Data Interchange, you may be able to save money by moving to Internet-based EDI.

See 9.2 Supply chains

Q5 Do you need to recruit graduates or school leavers?

YES

NO

Young people are increasingly turning to the Web to find out about potential employers: most colleges have free permanent connections to the Internet, and many sixth formers will have access either from school or home.

A good brochure site may well be sufficient, though it can make sense to provide information specifically aimed at potential recruits. This is particularly true if you want to recruit from abroad. The disadvantage can be that you may receive and have to deal with many unsuitable applications.

See 9.3: Recruiting via the Internet.

Go to Q6 on next page

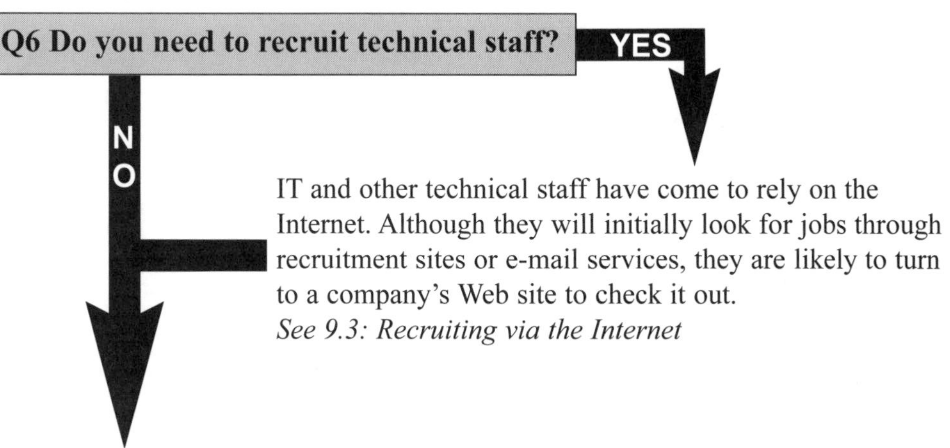
Q6 Do you need to recruit technical staff?
YES
NO

IT and other technical staff have come to rely on the Internet. Although they will initially look for jobs through recruitment sites or e-mail services, they are likely to turn to a company's Web site to check it out.
See 9.3: Recruiting via the Internet

Q7 Are there other ways you can save costs with the Internet?

Analyse your activities to see where a high-cost communication channel can be replaced by a low-cost one:

- Do you spend time or money communicating with people by phone/fax/mail/face-to-face?
Do you, for example, send out a newsletter/information sheet?
Can you put this on the Web and/or e-mail it instead?
See Case study, The Teddington Cheese, page 222.

- Do you have specific communication requirements? For example, are you trying to raise money? A Web site could be a route to potential investors.

3.2.3 Increasing revenues

The highest profile successes on the Internet are "virtual companies" that sell online, bringing in orders from all over the world, processing payments electronically and despatching products by mail (or over the network). They have negligible overheads, but have achieved such high ratings on the stock market that some (such as the retailer Amazon) are – or have been – worth more than established multinational corporations.

Two questions spring to mind for the "conventional" business:

- Can we do that?
- If we can't, what can we do?

The answer to the first – can you set up your own virtual company? – is "perhaps," but only if:

- Your business is well-suited, with the right sort of products selling to the right sort of people. Most of the best ideas have already been taken (or least there is a lot of competition), although there must still be opportunities for European companies to take a US idea and localise it (one previous inhibitor, lack of venture capital, has eased greatly).
- You get the operation just right. Amazon's success comes not only from its business model but also from the astuteness of its management (it was not, by some way, the first Web-based bookseller).

See case studies: QXL (page 266) and House of Tartan (page 232).

The complete selling/payment/delivery operation is only one model for generating Internet revenues. Some companies will be able to sell, but not take payment (eg providers of high-value or bulky products). The majority, including most service companies, do not have anything they can deliver in either electronic or physical form. For them the opportunities lie in marketing online, which – if done well – can be effective. Nonetheless, there is no doubt that the most secure form of revenue generation is by offering trans-actions.

So, the first step is to decide how well suited your company is to selling online. If, having gone through this section, you decide you cannot sell online, go on to the next part, marketing online.

3.2.3.1 Selling online

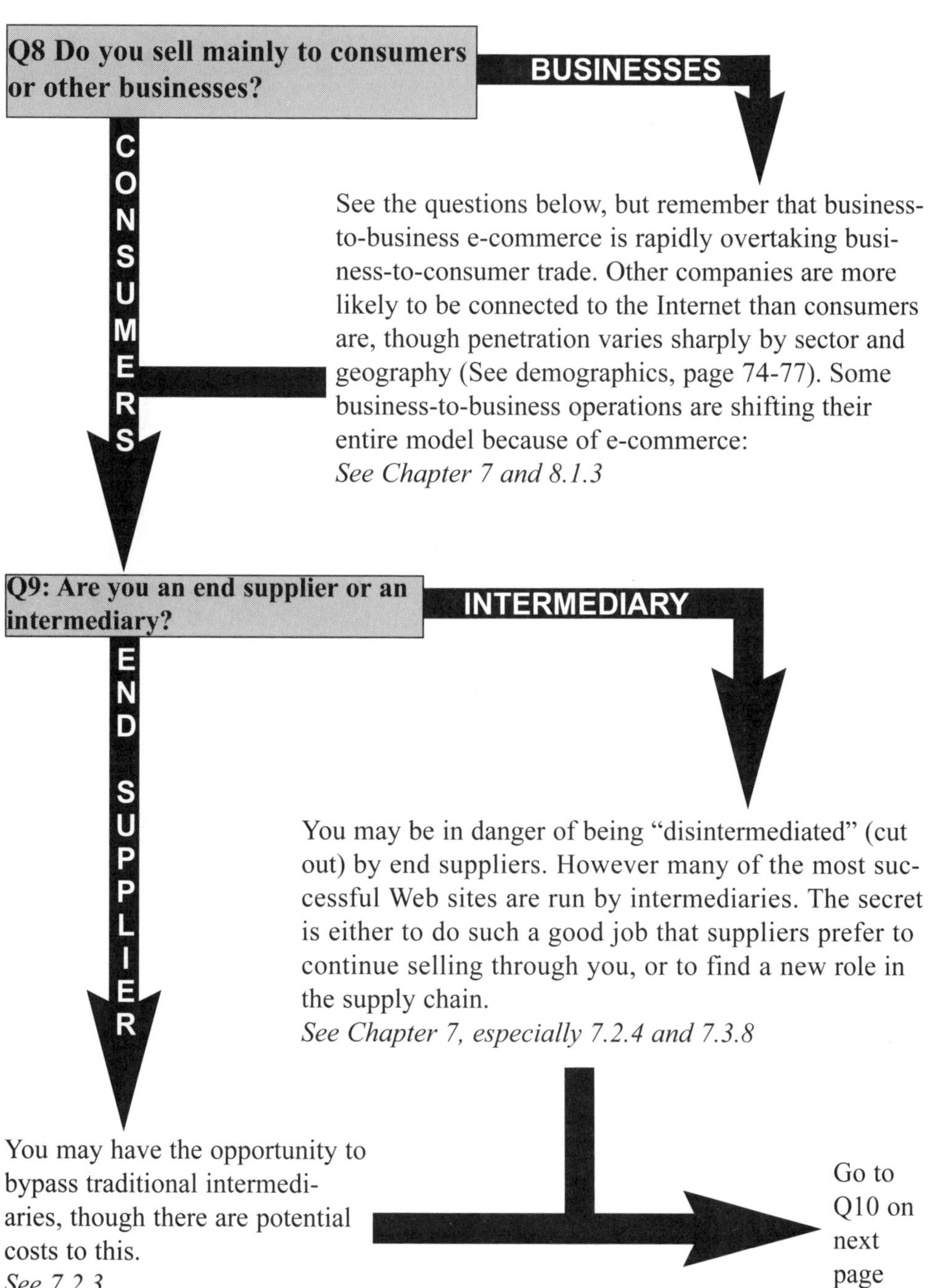

Q8 Do you sell mainly to consumers or other businesses?
BUSINESSES
CONSUMERS
See the questions below, but remember that business-to-business e-commerce is rapidly overtaking business-to-consumer trade. Other companies are more likely to be connected to the Internet than consumers are, though penetration varies sharply by sector and geography (See demographics, page 74-77). Some business-to-business operations are shifting their entire model because of e-commerce:
See Chapter 7 and 8.1.3
Q9: Are you an end supplier or an intermediary?
INTERMEDIARY
END SUPPLIER
You may be in danger of being "disintermediated" (cut out) by end suppliers. However many of the most successful Web sites are run by intermediaries. The secret is either to do such a good job that suppliers prefer to continue selling through you, or to find a new role in the supply chain.
See Chapter 7, especially 7.2.4 and 7.3.8
You may have the opportunity to bypass traditional intermediaries, though there are potential costs to this.
See 7.2.3
Go to Q10 on next page

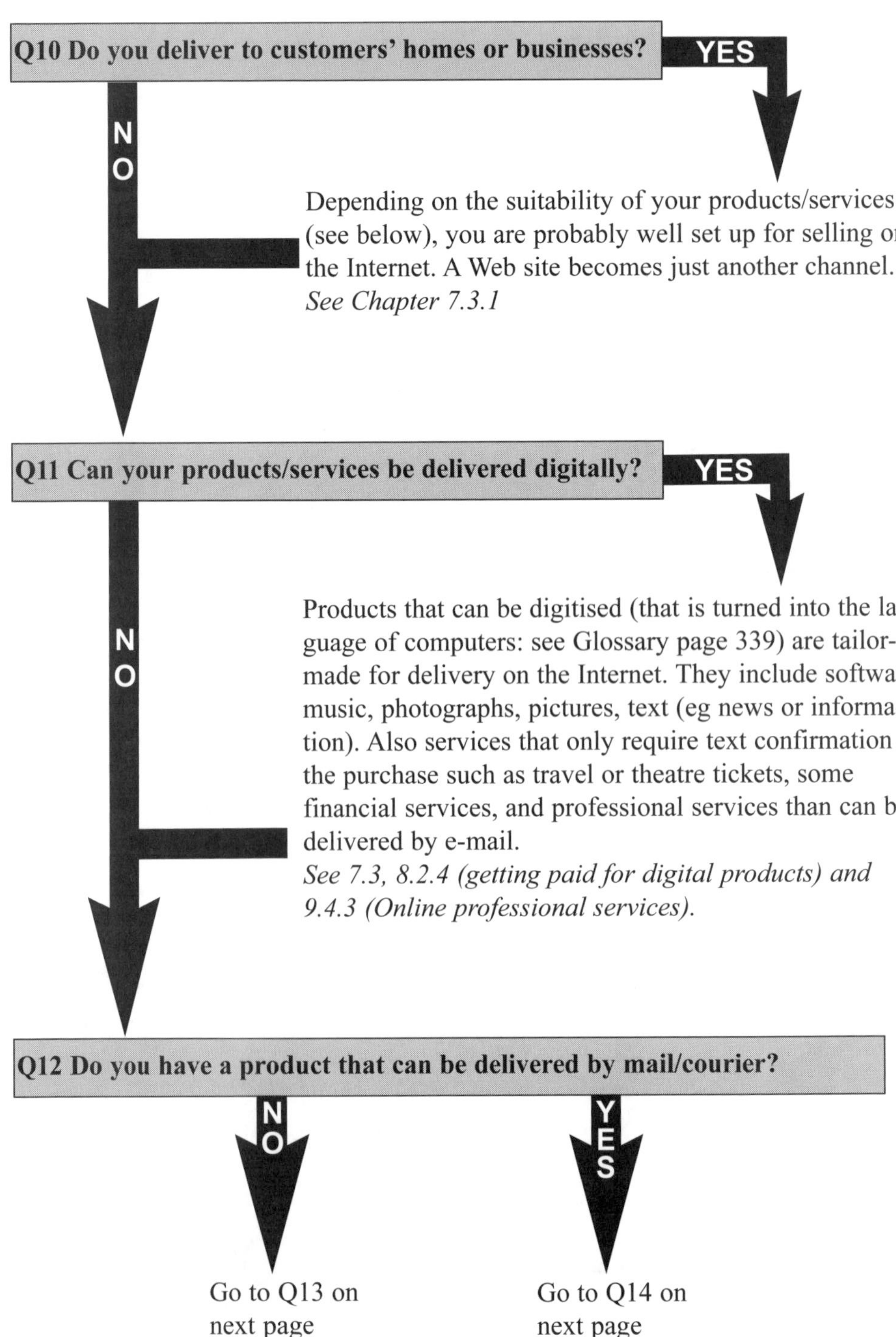
Q10 Do you deliver to customers' homes or businesses?
YES
NO
Depending on the suitability of your products/services (see below), you are probably well set up for selling on the Internet. A Web site becomes just another channel.
See Chapter 7.3.1
Q11 Can your products/services be delivered digitally?
YES
NO
Products that can be digitised (that is turned into the language of computers: see Glossary page 339) are tailor-made for delivery on the Internet. They include software, music, photographs, pictures, text (eg news or information). Also services that only require text confirmation of the purchase such as travel or theatre tickets, some financial services, and professional services than can be delivered by e-mail.
See 7.3, 8.2.4 (getting paid for digital products) and 9.4.3 (Online professional services).
Q12 Do you have a product that can be delivered by mail/courier?
NO
YES
Go to Q13 on next page
Go to Q14 on next page

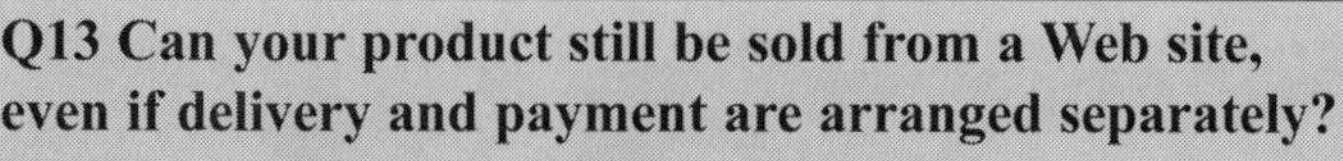

even if delivery and payment are arranged separately?

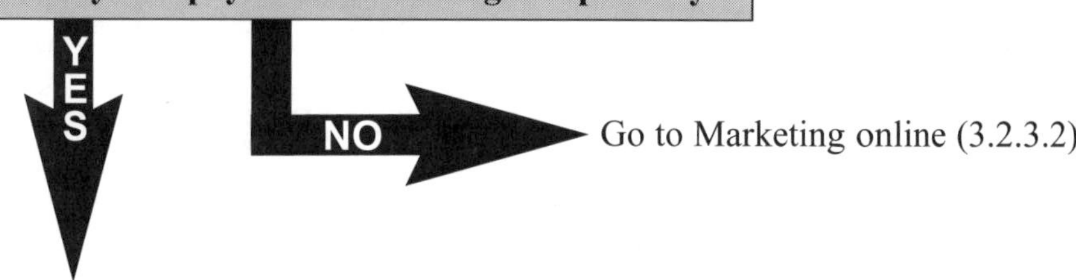

Examples are bulky and expensive items (often business-to-business), where the Internet is just the first point of contact. Products being sold in this way include aircraft, oil rigs, submarines. The Web has proved a fruitful outlet, because the market for such specialist products is so small that it makes sense to put in on a global noticeboard.

See 7.3.2 - Selling big ticket items.

See also Marketing online (3.2.3.2). The distinction between a selling site of this sort and a marketing site is a slim one: the selling site will list specific products, with prices, and will invite offers, whereas the marketing one is more general.

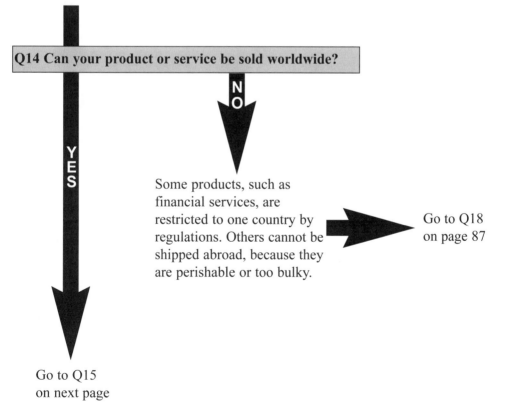

Q14 Can your product or service be sold worldwide?

NO

Some products, such as financial services, are restricted to one country by regulations. Others cannot be shipped abroad, because they are perishable or too bulky.

Go to Q18 on page 87

YES

Go to Q15 on next page

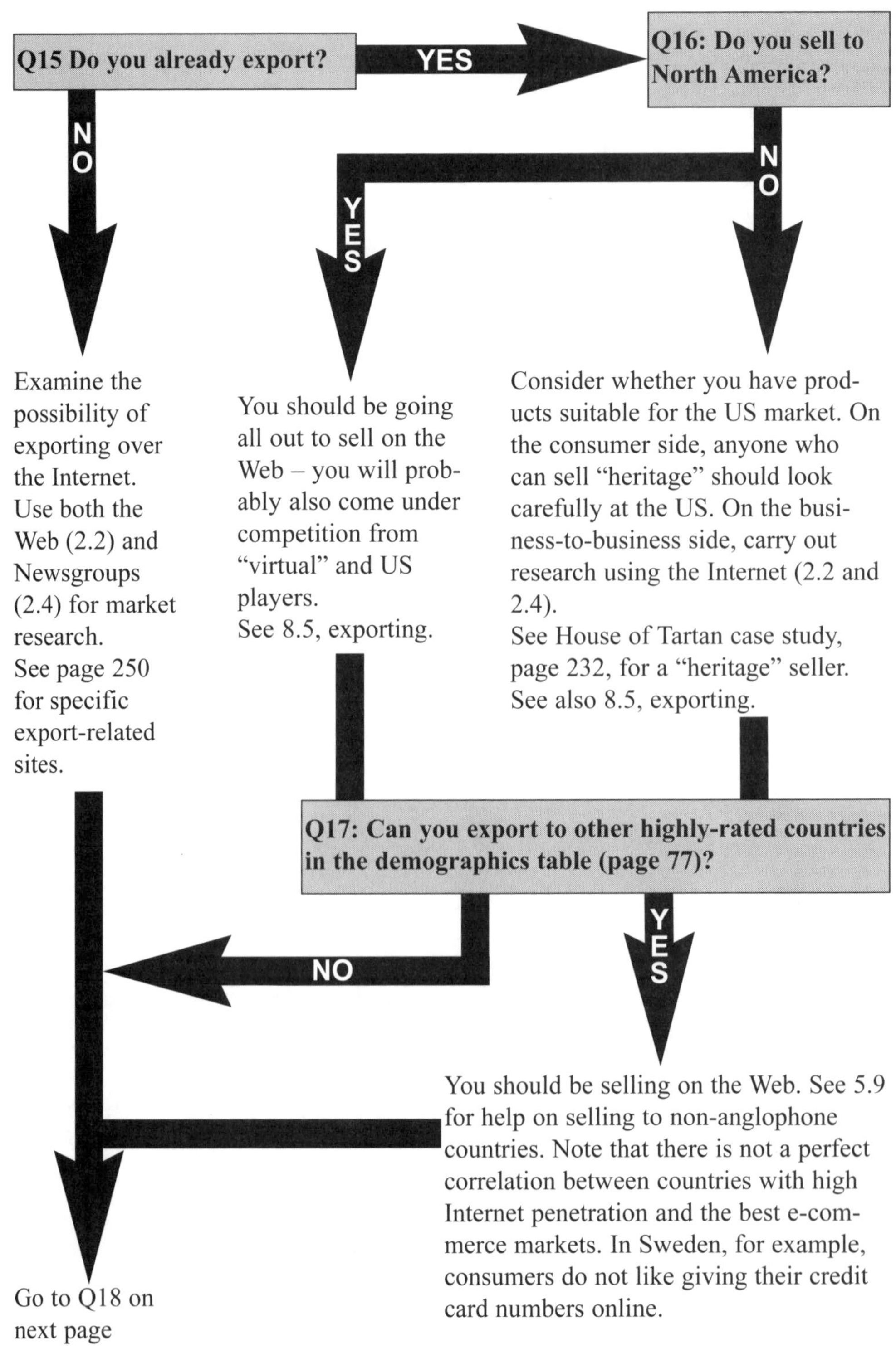
Q15 Do you already export?
YES
NO
Q16: Do you sell to North America?
YES
NO
Examine the possibility of exporting over the Internet. Use both the Web (2.2) and Newsgroups (2.4) for market research. See page 250 for specific export-related sites.
You should be going all out to sell on the Web – you will probably also come under competition from "virtual" and US players. See 8.5, exporting.
Consider whether you have products suitable for the US market. On the consumer side, anyone who can sell "heritage" should look carefully at the US. On the business-to-business side, carry out research using the Internet (2.2 and 2.4). See House of Tartan case study, page 232, for a "heritage" seller. See also 8.5, exporting.
Q17: Can you export to other highly-rated countries in the demographics table (page 77)?
NO
YES
You should be selling on the Web. See 5.9 for help on selling to non-anglophone countries. Note that there is not a perfect correlation between countries with high Internet penetration and the best e-commerce markets. In Sweden, for example, consumers do not like giving their credit card numbers online.
Go to Q18 on next page

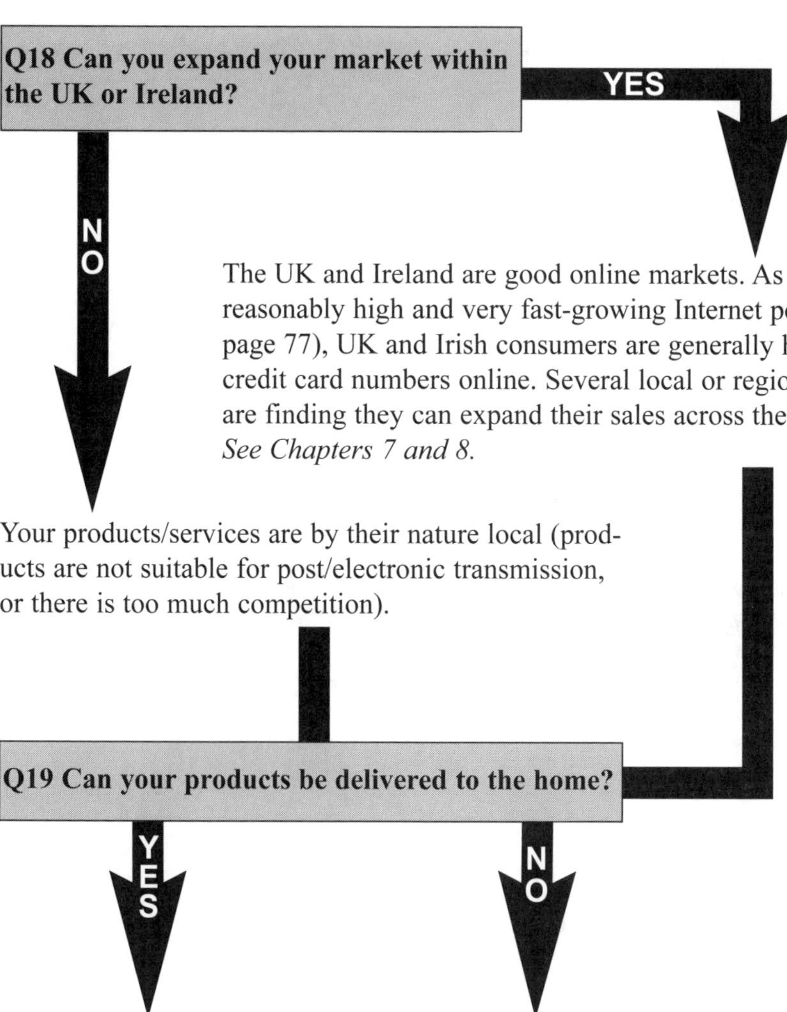

Q18 Can you expand your market within the UK or Ireland?
YES
NO
The UK and Ireland are good online markets. As well as having reasonably high and very fast-growing Internet penetration (see page 77), UK and Irish consumers are generally happy to give credit card numbers online. Several local or regional companies are finding they can expand their sales across the country.
See Chapters 7 and 8.
Your products/services are by their nature local (products are not suitable for post/electronic transmission, or there is too much competition).
Q19 Can your products be delivered to the home?
YES
NO

Consider using the Web to give yourself a competitive advantage.
See also local box on next page, and Chapters 7 and 8.

See local box on next page, for more ideas about how local businesses can use the Internet.

My business is local – is there any point in setting up a site?

There is a tendency to think of the World Wide Web in international, or at least long-distance terms, and it is true that some of the biggest benefits come to those who can capitalise on its indifference to distance.

That does not mean that a purely local business cannot make good use of the Web.

- You may be able to get good traffic to your site. This depends on your own skills in building the site and attracting people to it (see Chapters 4 and 5), but also on the demographics you are aiming at. If yours is a young or professional market, you may well be able to use the Web effectively (estate agents are good examples – see page 216). If your market is less obviously suitable (for example if you are a local retailer or insurance broker), you are likely to find visitor numbers are low (possibly very low).

There may still however be benefits in building a Web site:

- It will allow you to discover the medium, in preparation for the time when visitor numbers become significant (as they are likely to).

- It will give you a public relations advantage, because you will likely be one of the few local businesses to be using the Internet.

Here are some ways a local site can work:

1 You may be able to link your site to a local "community" site. These are widespread, though varying enormously in quality and scope. Many have links to restaurants and estate agents. *See 5.8.3.*

2 You may be able to create your own community site. Do you have a loyal group of customers? Might they like the idea of swapping ideas on the Internet? Is there information you can give that they will find useful – for example if your business is open at varying hours, you could post them online. You could promote special offers: "20 per cent off a Shiatsu massage this week", "Lincolnshire sausages on special". Consider backing it up with an e-mail service, alerting subscribers to these offers.

3 You can use the Web as an online brochure/pricing list. Local search engines such as Yell (www.yell.co.uk), which belongs to Yellow Pages, and Scoot (www.scoot.co.uk) should bring you customers.
See 5.8.1.

4 The first "transactional" Web sites are now appearing. For example pizza eaters in Milton Keynes can order their dinners for home delivery from a Web site (www.mkweb.co.uk). With Internet-based home shopping being established by the supermarkets (www.sainsburys.co.uk, www.tesco.co.uk), it will make sense for smaller retailers and even end suppliers to offer home delivery. The Web is particularly good at displaying a large range of products, such as those offered by an off licence or a takeaway restaurant. Once again, you would be one of the first movers with consequent low traffic, but high PR value.
See Chapter 8 on how to set up a selling Web site.

5 You may be able to offer services locally. Again this is very early days – we know of no examples in the UK although in Stockholm you can order a cab online (www.taxistockholm.se). Again the publicity advantage of being a first mover should not be ignored.

6 To get an idea of how local sites may develop in the future, see www.tref.nl. This site is a "portal" to more than 100 sites, each covering one Dutch town or city. The information is in standard format, and includes community as well as commercial input (see 5.8.3 for more).

3.2.3.2 Marketing online

The vast majority of commercial Web sites are marketing sites – they aim to promote products, companies or brands, but do not attempt to sell. Many also have a vague public relations function.

Marketing online is more difficult than selling because there is no obvious reason why anyone should visit your site, and e-mail marketing takes considerable skill.

It is no coincidence that some of the most engaging sites are pure brand-building ones – they have to be, because they are competing for the audience's attention with the pub, TV, club etc. Most are built by large consumer groups, and have six-figure annual budgets.

The more specific a site's aims, the easier it should be to attract visitors: companies promoting particular products or services will be able to add value with useful details, while general brand-building sites require great skill (though some small companies have succeeded, eg ACDO, page170).

Where transactional (selling) sites can survive with one-off visits (each can lead to revenue) marketing sites need repeat visits. They must therefore be easy to find, and offer compelling reasons to the visitor to return. See Chapter 5 for tips on building a compelling Web site.

The flow diagram here assumes you want to start with the "easiest option" (promoting specific products), and will only attempt brand-building if this is the only option left. You are of course free to ignore this – brand-building sites are the most challenging, and therefore stimulating, to be involved in.

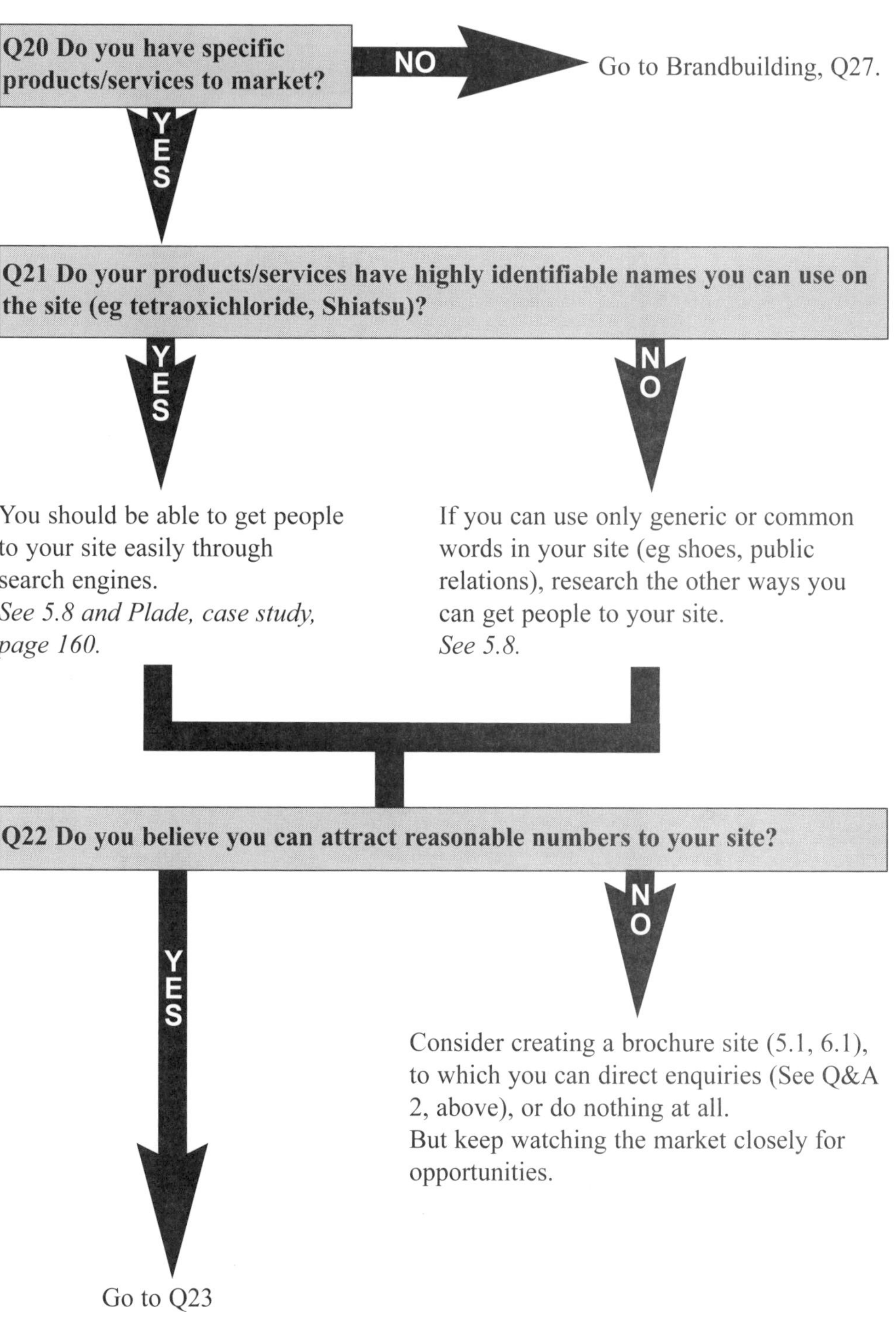

Q20 Do you have specific products/services to market?
NO
Go to Brandbuilding, Q27.
YES
Q21 Do your products/services have highly identifiable names you can use on the site (eg tetraoxichloride, Shiatsu)?
YES
NO
You should be able to get people to your site easily through search engines.
See 5.8 and Plade, case study, page 160.
If you can use only generic or common words in your site (eg shoes, public relations), research the other ways you can get people to your site.
See 5.8.
Q22 Do you believe you can attract reasonable numbers to your site?
YES
NO
Consider creating a brochure site (5.1, 6.1), to which you can direct enquiries (See Q&A 2, above), or do nothing at all.
But keep watching the market closely for opportunities.
Go to Q23
on next page

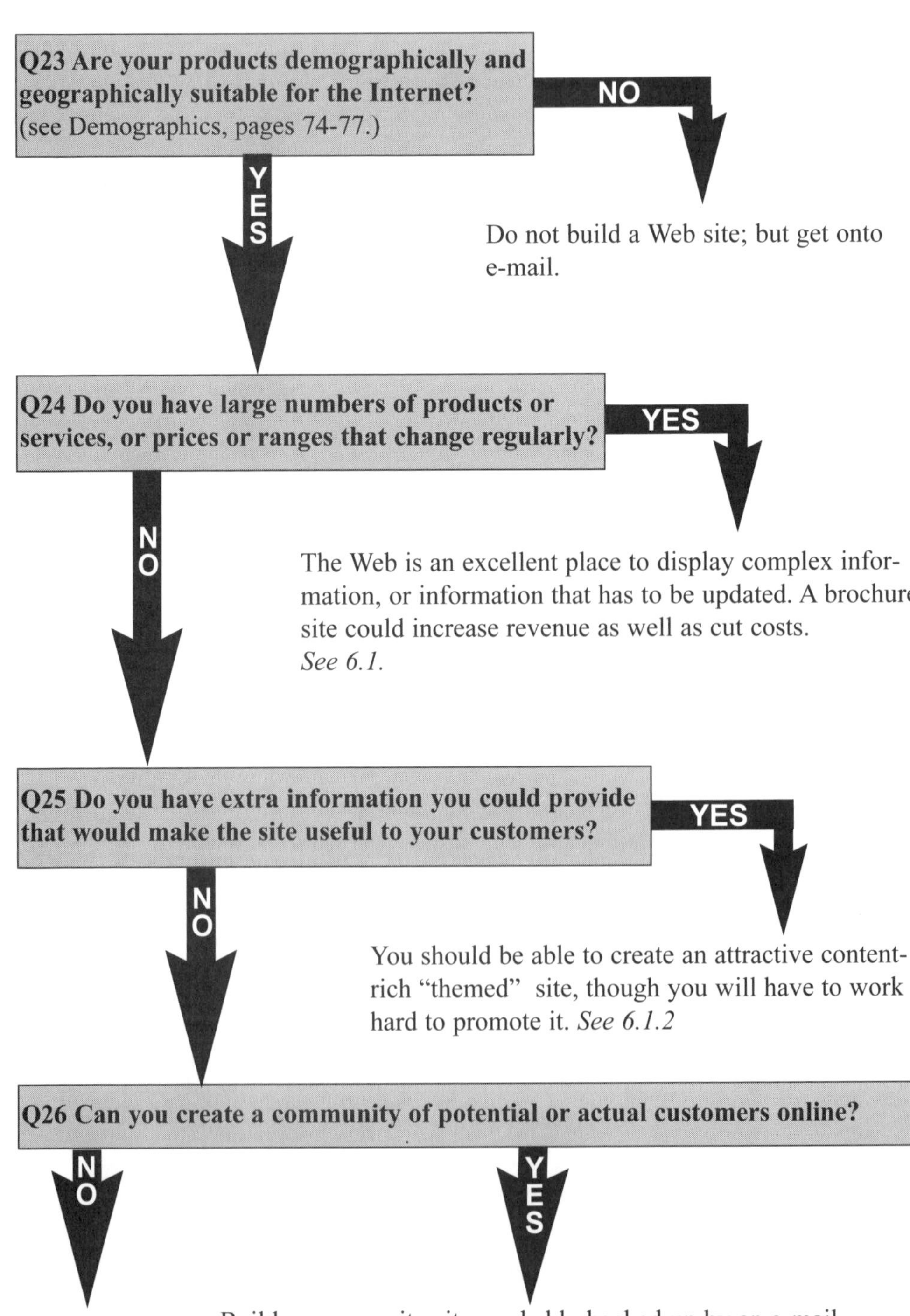
Q23 Are your products demographically and geographically suitable for the Internet?
(see Demographics, pages 74-77.)
NO
Do not build a Web site; but get onto e-mail.
YES
Q24 Do you have large numbers of products or services, or prices or ranges that change regularly?
YES
The Web is an excellent place to display complex information, or information that has to be updated. A brochure site could increase revenue as well as cut costs. *See 6.1.*
NO
Q25 Do you have extra information you could provide that would make the site useful to your customers?
YES
You should be able to create an attractive content-rich "themed" site, though you will have to work hard to promote it. *See 6.1.2*
NO
Q26 Can you create a community of potential or actual customers online?
NO
Do not build a Web site.
YES
Build a community site, probably backed up by an e-mail newsletter. *See 5.2.6, and 6.3 on creating community sites. Also 5.2.3 on e-mail newsletters.*

Brandbuilding

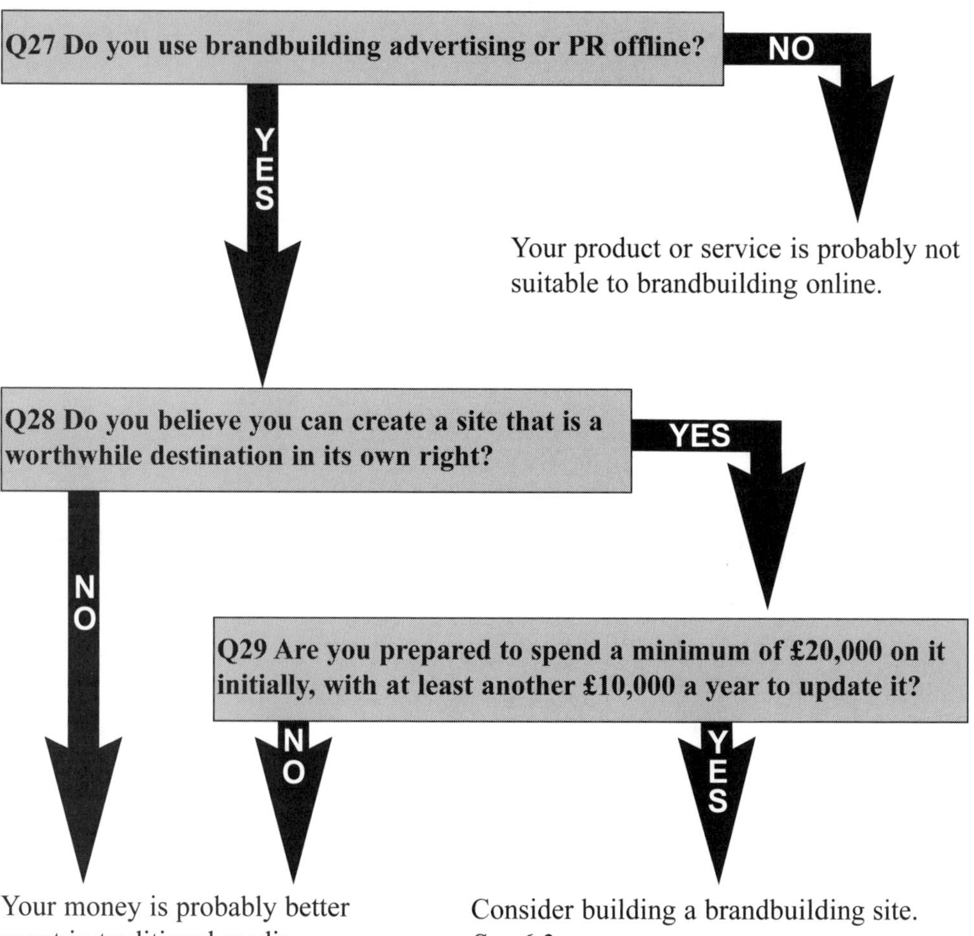

Q27 Do you use brandbuilding advertising or PR offline?
NO
YES
Your product or service is probably not suitable to brandbuilding online.
Q28 Do you believe you can create a site that is a worthwhile destination in its own right?
YES
NO
Q29 Are you prepared to spend a minimum of £20,000 on it initially, with at least another £10,000 a year to update it?
NO
YES

Your money is probably better spent in traditional media.

Consider building a brandbuilding site. *See 6.2*

Should you be bothered about security on the Internet?

This is a difficult question to answer, because there is very little independent research. On the one hand we have the e-commerce and finance industries playing down the risks. On the other are security specialists and police who tend to highlight the problems. Here are two quotes, one from an e-commerce company. "Making a credit card purchase over the Internet is a lot more secure than in a shop." The other from Scotland Yard: "Companies do not appreciate the fact that having an unprotected Internet connection is like having a house without any locks."

First, two apparently contradictory facts. According to CyberSource, a US Internet payment screening company, fraudulent or non-approved credit cards are used in 39 per cent of attempted orders on some Web sites. But only a handful of people have been caught. In fact the first ever conviction for Internet fraud was not made until November 1998, when a Californian court convicted Matthew Bowin of operating an illegal online stock offering that cost investors $190,000. This proves what is obvious when you think about it: that it is near impossible to catch online criminals. Most people entering fraudulent card details would never think of carrying out a "real" crime – but the remoteness and lack of human contact on the Internet encourages the feeling that they will never be fingered.

When we start looking at the issues closely, three points become clear:

- "Internet crime" is almost as vague a term as "real world crime", because there are so many different varieties.
- The concentration on the security of credit-card transactions diverts attention from other issues.
- What is happening now is little guide to what might happen in the future. At the moment, most Internet crime is committed by a collection of old-fashioned scam artists and computer-savvy hackers. But as more valuable information is shared online, and larger transactions are made, organised criminals may start to muscle in.

What, exactly, are the risks involved in doing business over the Web, and what can companies do to minimise them?

As in the real world, Internet crime comes in many forms.

The investment scam: An attractive Web site can be used as a legitimate-looking front for bogus investment schemes. Matthew Bowin recruited investors for his company, Interactive Products and Services, in a public offering conducted entirely over the Internet. Mr Bowin then spent investors' money on himself. Meanwhile, Gene Block and Renate Haag used a Web site to offer fictitious securities, promising to double investors' money in four months. They collected more than $3.5m before the SEC became aware of their activities and froze their assets. And an FBI investigation found 10 fake online banks accepting deposits over the Internet.

These are really just old-fashioned crimes dressed up in new clothing – but there are financial crimes that have grown up specifically to suit the Internet. According to the UK Financial Services Agency, some bogus investment sites have Internet addresses similar to those of well-known companies (see Spoofing, below). There are also online investment newsletters, mass e-mails and bulletin boards that, while purporting to be sources of impartial stock advice, are used to drive up specific stocks illegally for the operators' own profit. Sometimes misleading advice is given (especially in newsgroups and other forums) that may not have criminal intent, but that is plain wrong.
Solution: Be alert, check Web addresses carefully and do not fall for the promise of easy money.

Spoofing: Using special software to falsify the sender identity on an e-mail. This can be used to obtain trade secrets, company research, and other data from a business. One problem here is that companies that fall victim to spoofing are reluctant to talk about it because it makes them look foolish. Spoofing also refers to setting up an illegitimate site that looks similar to a legitimate one (and probably has a similar domain name).
Solution: Watch for telltale signs such as no return e-mail address. Software such as Mimesweeper (www.mimesweeper.com) can run automatic checks.

Cyberwoozles: A piece of computer code hidden in Web sites that enters

your hard disk to siphon data from it. Criminals can use it to steal information from a company's computer network. For example, by clicking on to a Web page, you can unwittingly send your user ID, password and e-mail address to someone who can use them to access your files and online accounts.
Solution: Software such as Mimesweeper will check for woozles.

Hacking: Breaking into a company's computer network. In one incident, the German-based Chaos computer club demonstrated on live TV how money from one bank account can be transferred into another, without anyone knowing. In another case, a German hacker gained unauthorised entry via the Net into the computer system of a Florida-based credit card bureau.
Solution: Avoid putting your most sensitive information on a computer connected to the Internet. For example, put your accounts on a standalone computer. If you have a network, consider putting in a "firewall" – software that should prevent hackers getting into your computer. If you take credit card numbers over the Net, see the next section on e-commerce.

E-commerce fraud: Although many people are offering incorrect credit card numbers online, few companies lose out as a result. That is because the card will be rejected by the card company when it is contacted for authorisation, and the merchants will not ship the goods. Companies can lose money if a) they ship goods before checking the credit card, and b) the customer revokes the deal and the card company "charges the money back" to the merchant. This is a particular problem online, probably because customers feel they can charge back with immunity – orders from some parts of the world, notably Russia, are particularly susceptible to chargebacks.
Solution: Use an encryption system – you are probably breaking the agreement with your bank if you do not. Do not ship goods until you have cleared the card (either immediately, using online clearance or by phone: see 8.2.4). If you are at all suspicious, ask for another form of payment. Digital certificates should soon offer better protection against fraudulent chargebacks. See 8.3 - *How secure is electronic commerce*?

www.yahoo.co.uk/Computers_and_Internet/
MIMEsweeper: www.mimesweeper.com
JCP: www.jcp.co.uk (Internet security specialist)
Internet Fraud Watch: www.fraud.org

Chapter 4 Planning a Web site

You should now have a reasonably clear idea of how you want to use the Internet. This chapter and the next are designed to take you through the process of creating a Web site. You will have to skip back and forth a little between the two chapters, and also drop into Chapters 6, 7 and 8, depending on the site's function or functions.

This chapter covers:

- How much you should spend on a Web site – including whether it should be built in or out of house (4.1 - 4.4).
- How to choose a Web consultancy (4.5)
- Where to put your Web site ("hosting") (4.6)
- Choosing and buying a domain name – your company's address on the Web (4.7)

4.1 What to spend?

This is the question on which all other decisions hang. A Web site can cost anything from nothing to £500,000-plus – with annual maintenance costs going from nothing to £100,000-plus a year. How should you decide what to spend?

1 Decide from the guidelines in Chapter 3 what sort of site you need: a brochure site, a transactional site, a themed site, a branding site, or a combination of two or more of these.

2 Draw up a rough outline of what the site should contain (See 5.1 for help with this). This should give you an idea of the number of pages needed.

3 Work out how much an outside consultancy would charge (4.2).

4 Decide whether you or your team are capable of building all or part of the site in-house (4.4), and cost that work.

After this, you should be able to decide the mix of in-house/out-house you feel will work best, and draw up a budget based on the mix.

A rule of thumb: There is another approach that provides a useful yardstick. It assumes that the Web site comes under the marketing budget (which it usually will, even if the site's role goes beyond marketing):

Calculate the proper level of investment in Web site development by adding up your total annual expenditure on:

- Catalogues and brochures
- Mailshots and leaflets
- Print advertising
- Point-of-sale and posters
- Radio advertising
- TV or cinema advertising

Then divide this sum by the number of media that you are using. So, a company that spends £30,000 on catalogues, plus £20,000 on mailshots and £15,000 on print, but nothing on posters, radio or television, has a total media bill of £65,000. It is using three media – and really it should consider investing about £20,000 in its Web site.

The good news is that costs can if necessary be spread. While it is nice to present an all-singing, all-dancing site in one go, it is often acceptable to launch a modest one that can hum a tune and do a few steps to start with, then build it up slowly.

The keys are:

- To make sure you have an overall strategy to start with (see 3.1, 5.1).
- To work out a plan of delivery. It is likely that if your site is to be even moderately complex it will be delivered in stages. You must decide which bits you want delivered first, and which can wait.
- To impose high standards in all areas from the very beginning (5.4, 5.5, 5.6).
- To be realistic about maintenance and upgrading costs – a small site can be built for a modest amount (say £4,000), but you can easily find yourself paying a consultant more than this annually for upgrading and maintenance.

4.2 What would a Web consultant charge?

A professional organisation asked a number of consultants to quote on an identical Web site: the prices ranged from £2,000 to £40,000. This is not untypical because:

- The industry is so young that no standard prices have emerged
- Many designers are not good business people, and therefore fail to cost their work properly.
- Small companies tend to price low, because they are so keen to get the work and want a portfolio to show off.
- Larger companies tend to have heavy overheads.

This should mean that small companies are cheaper than big ones – but this is not always so, because everyone and his dog is trying to get into the electronic business business. One large consultancy firm reportedly had a policy of refusing work that brought in less than £1m – unless it was related to the Internet, in which case there was no minimum.

What, you may ask, about the company that sent me a flyer offering to build a Web site for £200? Well yes, you can pay to have a single page built for that (or even less). But you could almost certainly build a better one yourself for nothing – and then you would know how to maintain it and expand it (see 4.3). The one occasion when it may make sense to take up an offer like that is if your site will as a result nestle within a well-visited "affinity site" (see 5.8.3).

Coming back to real consultants, it should be possible to work out what they *should* charge – you may be horrified by our suggested figure (£8,500 for a medium-sized slightly-above-average site). In which case:

- Shop around, but recognise when you are getting too much of a bargain. Your relationship with the consultancy is crucial during the building process – if it has given you a very low price, it may be increasingly resentful if you ask it to make more and more changes.
- Try to come to come to a cost-sharing arrangement with an agency. Offer it a cut of your online transaction revenues in exchange for a lower upfront price. Or see if it wants a showcase site (See ACDO case study, page 170).

- Build the site in-house (See 4.3).

This pricing system here is based on figures produced in mid-1998 by Richard King, a talented Web consultant who has since died. They are still valid, though the pressure on wage rates (driven particularly by a shortage of technical skills) is upward.

Workers in the Web business expect, and get, between £25 and £50 an hour gross, and some skills can command even higher rates. Companies will charge them out at at least 50 per cent more than this, to cover overheads.

The Web keeps on advancing, which means some time has to be set aside for research and development. Less than one day a week per person and the company will risk falling behind, so R&D has to be paid for out of work done in the other four days, in effect producing a 20 per cent loading on any "paying" hours.

The basic package: For most sites (those without many bells and whistles), a competent Web author should be able to turn out an average of about one finished page an hour, given a proper brief, layout or storyboard. A fair expectation would be that a Web site of 32 pages with 30 images would take about five person-days to write, decorate with scanned artwork (pictures or photos taken from an existing source), put online, and check that it works.

So paying staff at, say, £33 an hour to do 40 hours of work means the client has to be charged £2,376, just for the company to break even. Add on a moderate profit margin, and the bill for a fairly plain 32-page site is about £3,000.

Adding graphics: This price does not allow for any specially-produced graphics. Graphic origination is much more laborious than simple coding: a good designer rarely works for less than £50 an hour (as a take-home rate) and it can easily take an entire day to produce a single item. So to include two days of graphic design and rather more complex programming would cost £2,000.

Planning costs: If your Web designer is also your site architect (which is likely), you can add another £2,000 to the bill. The ability to produce a scheme that is easy to use, clear, understandable, and comprehensive is a

rare skill, and people who are good at it can command high salaries.
The cost of our Web site is now around the £6,000 mark. The outcome is a well-designed, useful, comprehensive and clear site – but it will be rather dull. To add some excitement and life to it, we will need some JavaScript (a program that allows sophisticated special effects), maybe some animations, sounds or music, perhaps even video or VRML (virtual reality for the Internet). See 5.2.7 for more on such extras. You can spend anything from £2,000 to hundreds of thousands of pounds on such improvements.

Adding animated features: To our theoretical site, we will add an animated menu to the main menu, a site map, a search engine and a single animation to use at various points in the site. A total of two days of coding and a day of animation work, in all costing about £2,500.

Our average Web site is now above average, but only a little, and is costing in the region of £8,500. It is scalable, it does what we want it to, and it has enough bells and whistles to hold up its head in public. But is that a "fair" price? One way of answering that question is to compare the Web site with other media.

What would you get if you spent £8,500 on a catalogue? Or on a mailshot, radio or television advert? The same £8,500 would buy:

- Direct mail: a four-colour four-page leaflet, accompanying letter and reply-form, in an envelope, mailed out to about 3,500 people.
- Print: 30 small advertisements at about £250 a time.
- Radio: 80-odd cheap slots (the graveyard shift) or about eight prime-time slots.
- Television: about 10 seconds of non prime-time, once only. Prime time, about a second, assuming you are very good at getting blood out of stones.

In that context, £8,500 spent on a Web site is very good value for money. The site will last much longer than other types of advertising, it will reach a bigger audience, and it will almost certainly generate more business than any of the other examples. And if you have been following the numbers, you will see that no one has been making unreasonable profits at any stage, and no one has been paid excessively well.

What would it cost to add a selling system – linking a database of your products to an online catalogue and secure credit card payment system? Remarkably little, thanks to the competition in this area. You can buy a catalogue package for as little as £200 (see page 234). Your Web designer will probably take three days to integrate it, costing you perhaps £800. So you can add a full e-commerce facility for £1,000. The chances are you will want to improve the look of your shop, adding photos and specially-created icons – but £2,000 is realistic (unless you have a large database, in which case you will go straight into five figures).

What would you get for another £10,000? Quite a lot – maybe a couple of foreign-language versions of the site, or some really attractive visuals. You could have a non-frame as well a frame version of the site (see 5.3.1). In other words, a £20,000 Web site is a much bigger deal than our slightly-above-average £8,500 one. You will have to cost-justify it, but think always in the context of your other spending.

The truth is that a professionally-designed Web site is cost effective, but not particularly cheap. As a general guide, companies should invest in their Web sites about the same amount of money as they would invest in any other single medium.

4.3 Can you build a site in-house?

Two types of Web sites are typically built in-house – very big ones and very small ones. Large corporations such as Great Universal Stores and Norwich Union have their own well-resourced teams; conversely thousands of small sites are built by owner-managers who cannot, or will not, hire a professional. Most of these small sites, it must be said, are dreadful: ill thought-out, ugly, pointless. The same is true of most sites built by Fred from IT in his spare time. But the main weaknesses here do not relate to technical or even design skill, but to lack of strategic thinking.

Many successful sites are home made. Battersea Pen Home (see case study, page 200) is one. Neil Sherring, whose site sells special telephone numbers (www.future-numbers.co.uk),is another, while Darren Ryan built a site to sell sports equipment (www.a-henkel.com).

The lesson from such people is that it can be difficult and frustrating, and it will be hard work. Mr Sherring warns that at least initially you need someone to hold your hand: “The first month was a nightmare,” he says. Mr Ryan says you have to read everything you can and “just be prepared to burn the candle at both ends”.

It is possible to build a site with no special software, writing all the HTML code yourself (see glossary, page 339). This is not quite as daunting as it sounds, because HTML code is one of the simplest programming languages. Go into a Web page, click View, then Source. You will see the HTML coding of the page. The instructions are written in angled brackets, while the text is unbracketed. A headline for an online *Net Profit* article looks like this:

<TITLE>legal/mar99 - Law firms learn how to offer their wares online</TITLE>.

To edit the source code, you can use a simple text editor:

Simpletext (free): This is part of the basic Macintosh package. It does not contain any shortcuts, but works and has the advantage of being free.
BBEdit 5.0 (£102 inc.VAT) Tel: 01628-660242. Also for the Mac, this is similar to Simpletext but contains many more features, which make it easier to write HTML. A stripped-down version is available for free from the Bare Bones Software Web page (www.barebones.com).
WordPad (free): This is part of the basic Windows package. It does not contain any shortcuts, but works and is free.

To find out more about HTML coding, you can take a look at the Webmonkey site from *Wired* magazine (www.hotwired.com/webmonkey). It offers basic tutorials on Web design and HTML writing. The children's section is good for absolute beginners.

But this is time-consuming, and there are plenty of “authoring” tools that put the code in automatically, and make the creation of a Web page not much more difficult than writing a word-processor document.

Here are a few HTML editors you may want to look at. The list is not exhaustive (check the news stand magazines *Internet.Works* and *.net* for more product reviews). These are among the best-regarded applications for each category of editor.

For the Macintosh
Adobe PageMill 3.0 (£93 inc VAT)
www.adobeshop.com
Tel: 020-8606 4001
This is a WYSIWYG editor – "what you see is what you get". You fill and format pages on your screen, and the program generates the HTML for you.

Dreamweaver 2.0 (£351 inc VAT)
www.macromedia.com/software/dreamweaver
Tel: 020-8358 3837
Another WYSIWYG editor.

For Windows:
Homesite 4.0 (£88/inc.VAT)
www.allaire.com
Tel: 01638-569600
PC magazines rate this as one of the best HTML editors. Not WYSIWYG

Adobe PageMill 3.0 (£79 plus VAT)
See above.

Dreamweaver 2.0 (£351/inc.VAT)
See above

Microsoft Frontpage
www.microsoft.com/frontpage
Tel: 0345-002000
Microsoft new WYSIWYG offering.

Fusion 4.0 (£234/inc.VAT)
www.allaire.com
Tel: 0118-982 9822
A well-regarded WYSIWYG author.

Uploading software

Once you have created a Web site or page (or whenever you want to make changes), you need to "upload" it to the server where the site is kept. The company that hosts your site (see 4.6) will have given you a password that allows to do this. You dial up the Internet, activate your uploading software (see below), and send the pages up the line. If you are making changes, this will over-write the existing page: you can immediately see if the changes have gone through by opening the Web page (sometimes you will get the old version because it has been "cached", or stored on your computer. You can usually force it to upload the new version by holding the Shift key while pressing "refresh").

Here are two efficient and user-friendly uploading packages.

For the Macintosh:
Fetch (free for educators and non-profit making organisations, otherwise $25)
e-mail fetch@dartmouth.edu

For Windows:
CuteFTP (free 30-day trial, then about £22)
www.cuteftp.com.

4.3.1 Building a test site

How do you know whether you can build a site? One way is to try. In less than two hours, you can see whether you feel up to building your own Web pages. The guide on the next few pages will help you build a very simple test site, using one of the standard software tools, Adobe PageMill 3.0. You can download a free evaluation copy of PageMill from www.adobeshop.com. Most WYSIWYG authoring packages work along similar principles, so once you have got the hang of this one, you should find your way around any authoring package fairly easily.
This exercise will help you set up four interconnected Web pages on either a PC or Mac. The aim is to introduce you to the way Web pages are built and linked together. From there you can learn step by step to grow them with your own content, graphics and database information.

Building a simple Web site

You can set these up on your computer, without uploading them – so you do not need a Web site hosting arrangement before you start.

1 Create a new folder on your computer Desktop and give it a relevant name, such as "testsite". This is where you will store your Web pages.

2 Open up your copy of Adobe PageMill.

3 Open a new page by clicking "file" and "new".

4 You will be presented with a blank page, with a grey background. To get started, you will need to open up some toolboxes.
- If you cannot see a window called "inspector", click on "view" and then "show inspector". This is the basic text and background-formatting tool.
- Click on "view" and then "show colour panel". A small window with a dozen colours will pop up. Click on the arrow at the bottom of this box, and the window will expand to display the full array of available colours.
- These two tools are enough to get started.

5 To begin working on your page, you need to make sure it is set up properly.
- Check that the icon in the top right-hand corner displays a scroll and quill. If it displays a globe, click on it once to turn it to a scroll.
- In the left-hand corner of the page, opposite the box called "title", there is an icon representing a small page. If this is grey, click on it to bring it to life.
- Once this is done you are ready to start.

6 Click into the "title" bar, and give your page a name, "index.html". This is the name that would appear in the address box of a Web browser. Then click on "file" and "save page as". Save the page in your "testsite" folder, and call it "index.html". This is not essential for this exercise, but will break in the habit of creating an index page, which is very important once you start broadcasting your pages on the Web.

7 Click back into the main body of the page, and type "Welcome to my homepage". You format text in PageMill much as you would in a wordprocessed document. Highlight the text, and click on the icon marked "0", to change font size. Notch it up to "+4" for example. Then move the text to the centre of the page, move it down a few lines, and change the font, to "Arial" for example.

8 The background at the moment should be dark grey. Change it to a friendlier colour by pointing your mouse at a colour in the "colour panel", and dragging this (by keeping your finger on the mouse button) to the box marked Background. Formatting in PageMill often works by "clicking and dragging" chosen items towards category boxes. With the inspector box, you can customise background and text colour, and build and format tables and boxes (more on this later). Once you get the hang of it, it becomes very easy to make quick changes and to experiment inside your Web pages.

9 Click on "file" and "save". You now have set up a basic Web page. The next step is to make copies, or clones of this basic page, which you can then turn into individual pages. To do this, click on "file" and "save as". Still in the "testsite" folder, save your page as "red.html".

10 Your page should now display "red" at the very top of the page. Click into the "title" box and type "red.html". Change the text inside the page to read "welcome to my red page". And change the background colour to red. Save your page.

11 Then click "save page as" and save it as "yellow.html". You've probably guessed what comes next. Repeat the same steps to name this page, change the text to read "Welcome to my blue page" and change the background colour. Save the page. And then "save as" "green.html". Repeat the same steps again and save.

12 You should now see a green coloured page called "green.html". Behind it, you have three more pages called "red.html", "yellow.html" and "index.html". The next step is to link these pages together by clicking underneath "Welcome to my green page". Type the following page names, one under the other: "red page", "yellow page", "green page" and "home page".

13 Now, you need to turn these names into "links" so you can move between your different pages. Highlight the words "green page" (the order in which you make these links is not important). At the bottom of your page there is a box called "link to". In this box type "green.html". Then press the return key. If all has gone well the words "green page" will now be underlined and coloured in blue (or whichever colour is set as Default for hyperlinks in your Inspector box).

14 Now highlight "red page" and repeat the process, typing "red.html" in the "link to" box and pressing return.

15 Repeat the process twice more, typing "yellow.html" for the yellow page, and "index.html" for your home page. Now save your page.

16 You now have four hyperlinks on your "green page". But you need to build links on the three other pages to move back and forth between all of them. Highlight all four links and click on "edit" and then "copy" (or press Ctrl+C).

17 Toggle the scroll in the top right-hand corner to make it a globe. This removes the formatting buttons from the top of the page and instead displays Web browsing buttons (arrows pointing backwards and forwards).

18 Now move your cursor to one of the hyperlinks, for example "red page". Click on it, and you will move through to the red page. Inside the red page, toggle the globe back to a scroll so you can work on the page again. Click into the page, and move the cursor down a few lines below the "Welcome to my red page". Check that your font size is not too big, and click on "edit" and "paste" (or press Ctrl+V). Lo and behold, you should now have four hyperlinks on your red page.

19 Save your red page, and toggle the scroll back to a globe. Now repeat the process for the yellow and home pages, clicking through to each, pasting the copied hyperlinks in and remembering to save each page before you move on.

20 Once this is done, you can toggle back to a globe and move between your four pages easily. But here is one more thing to do. You have four links on each page – but you only actually need three. For example, you do not need a "yellow page" link on the yellow page. So, on each page, you need to "switch off" one hyperlink.

21 To do this, click into a page, highlight the link you wish to remove, click on "edit", and then "remove link" (or press Ctrl+R). Move between pages, toggling the scroll to a globe and back again, and remembering to save your pages before you move on.

22 The last stage in this exercise is to play around with your four Web pages, now they are up and running. Firstly, you may wish to change the colours of your text and hyperlinks to stand out against your different coloured backgrounds. Do this by dragging colours from the colour panel into boxes in the "inspector".

23 Another simple feature you can play with is the "table" function. Place your cursor at the place where you want to insert a table, or series of boxes. At the top of your page, there is an icon which looks like a small grid. Click on this, and by dragging your mouse you can set the number of rows and columns you want for your table. When you release the mouse, the table will automatically appear inside the page.

24 Once you have a table inside your page, it is up to you what to do with it. Inside the "inspector" window, click on the tab at the top that resembles a small table. You can select the whole table by clicking on its borders. A thin black line will appear, which allows you to set parameters like spacing and padding between cells from inside the "inspector".

25 To select an individual cell, click inside the cell, to obtain a flashing cursor. Then drag your mouse towards the outside of the cell. A thick black line will appear around the edge of the cell. Once this is displayed, you can change the cell colour or size simply by clicking on the option you want in one of the control panels. You can write inside cells, make cells invisible, space them differently, space them around the page. This, you will probably realise, is how a majority of Web pages are designed. It is as simple as that.

26 We are now reaching the end of this exercise. From this point, there is a limitless number of things you can do with your pages – most of which are beyond the scope of this book. Remember that it does not matter if you make mistakes. Simply save your pages regularly. This means that if you do wish to backtrack, you can simply close your page without saving it, to revert to a version you are happy with.

27 Finally, try the exercise again a few days later. You will be amazed at how much easier it becomes with a little bit of practice. The next step is to start hunting for simple and cheap (or sometimes even free) ways of building all sorts of exciting features into your pages. And, of course, actually moving them onto the World Wide Web.

The news stand magazine *.net* offers monthly updated sections on Web site construction. It contains a huge number of links to tutorials on the Web, free downloads, and product reviews.

If you want to build a very simple Web site for free, open Netscape Communicator (downloadable from www.netscape.com, or available on most PC/Internet magazine cover disks).

Click on File/New/Blank Page from Wizard or File/New/Blank Page from Template, and follow the instructions. It is an interesting way of taking the very first steps towards understanding Web site construction, but you would be unwise to use this for your company site. It lacks the flexibility and sophistication you will need.

4.4 Costing an in-house site

Managers of very small companies have a habit of not costing their own time: being paid is a bit of a luxury when you start out. It is possible to build a Web site for nothing: sign up with a free ISP, take advantage of its free Web space offer, build a site using Netscape Communicator, and use a domain name allocated by the ISP (see 4.7). Or for £200-£300, you can buy proper authoring software and buy your own domain name.

If you are prepared to spend rather more than this, but not to pay a consultancy to build the entire site, you will probably need to build a team. These are the main elements you will need in your team:

- Writers
- Web designers
- Technical experts
- (Possibly) reviewers/testers
- A Web master (who looks after larger sites)

You will need one or more of each of the above, and you may well end up "outsourcing" some of the work

Read Chapter 5 for a view of the skills these people will need, before deciding whether your company nurtures them.

When you are building your team, put some thought into how the various skill bases will interact. If the people writing the site are less familiar with Web projects than the technical experts you must make sure that the "techies" do not constrain the writers or that technology comes before content. You must make sure that the site is guided by those influences, or combination of influences, that you see as being most important – whether it be aesthetics, content or technical functionality.

You need to do the sums, because you know how much you will pay people. It is sensible to assume that at first Web pages will take much longer to generate in-house, because the authors will be learning their skills. Fortunately, many people will be thrilled at the idea of creating a Web site – and may well work long into the night for nothing.

4.5 Choosing a Web design agency

A good Web designer can make a small company site as impressive as any giant corporation's. A bad Web designer will leave you with a site that looks like a primary school project (and that's being unfair to primary schools). It is important, to say the least, to get the right one.

You will need a different horse for a different course. Away from the really big (and expensive) agencies, their skills are specialised, even though they may not admit it. Some are strong on the technical side, some on design, some on marketing and brand-building, some on e-commerce and so on. They are all correspondingly weak in some of the other areas.

So how to choose an agency? First, how much do you want it to do? The big agencies call themselves "strategic". That means they will work out your entire electronic business strategy for you, and will tell you how it will affect the rest of your company. These agencies' client lists are dominated by big names – and they charge big bucks for their often formidable skills.

Most medium or smaller companies will go to a medium or smaller agency, probably a local one. It is important to shop around, not just for price but also for skills.

The newstand magazine *InternetWorks* contains a regularly updated list of UK agencies, together with their specialisations and examples of their sites. *Net Profit*'s Web site (www.netprofit.co.uk) also has a listing.

Here are some more hints:

- *Choose a local agency.* Although you can communicate entirely online, a Web site must be built as a partnership between you and the agency. There will be occasions when you want to kill the consultants, and they want to kill you. So regular personal contact is desirable, if not essential.

- *If you need help with your strategy, or a balance of both design and technical skills, go for a medium to large agency* (10 people upwards).

- *Company size is not however a good indicator of eventual quality.* If you know exactly what you want the site to achieve, a small outfit may give you a first-class result at low cost.

- *Make sure a small company has the skills you need.* If you want your site to make use of Java and plug-in technology (see page 130), find a consultancy with a strong IT side. If you do not need such extras, choose a consultancy with graphic skills: it is easier for an artist to learn technology than it is for a technologist to become visually adept.

- You will find small agencies buy in the skills they do not have – *ask to see work done by the freelances/agencies they intend to use.*

- *Look for people with an interest in your business.* Even if you have done the strategic thinking, you want to work with someone who asks smart questions about your fundamental business drivers, and how an online presence will enhance these.

- *Don't accept a single figure quote.* With quoted prices varying so much, it is important to see the components each is made up of – how much time you are getting and from which staff. This will help you weigh up competing quotes against each other more easily.

- *Look for a long-term approach to costs.* Good Web designers should build you a site that does not cost you a fortune to maintain – and train you or your staff to keep it up to date once they leave the project. Any designer that insists on doing all the updating should be avoided. That said, you will probably want an agency to help you with major updates and re-working, so look for someone with whom you can have a continuing relationship.

- *Ask for a portfolio of existing sites.* Get the URLs (Web addresses) of a number of sites they have already built. Under no circumstances take site demonstrations given in an office as the only indication of a company's abilities. Most design houses have high specification machines and fast Internet connections – and of course they can demonstrate their sites "off-line" (rather than over the Internet). Use an averagely powerful computer to visit the sites they have built and see how they perform. If the pages seem slow to load, try again at a time you can be fairly sure the network is not congested (eg 8am, UK time). Check the quality of the site against the guidelines in Chapter 5.

- *Ask for references.* Because the industry is so young, many Web designers have had the opportunity to work with impressively-titled clients. If the list includes Microsoft, it may mean the company produced a banner advertisement for the company two years ago. Cross-examine them, to find out exactly what they did for each client.

For a list of Web designers and consultants, see Appendix C, page 319.

4.6 Where to put your Web site

If you have an account with an Internet Service Provider, chances are that you will be entitled to free Web space – perhaps 5MB. This is enough for a small Web site, perhaps 25 pages, but is not really designed for commercial sites.

You will however have to find a home for your Web site: it will sit on a server – a computer with massive disk space and all sorts of fail safe systems. This server can be:

- at an ISP
- at a specialist Web hosting company
- in your own office
- somewhere else (eg in your Web consultant's office).

If your Web site becomes an important part of your business, you will want to invest in your own server (which will cost a few thousand pounds). It gives you almost limitless space, you have complete control over it, and you do not have to pay a rental. But until you have a big Web presence, it probably makes sense to keep your site somewhere else.

The difference between an ISP and a hosting company is that hosting companies do not have "dial-up" clients. Their sole job is keeping their customers' Web sites safe, and handling their e-mails, so they should be more business-focused. Netlink (www.netlink.co.uk) claims to be the biggest business-only

Web space provider in Europe. Some of the ISPs, especially those that have not "gone free", are putting emphasis on the service they provide to businesses.

As with ISPs, the service level of hosting companies fluctuates, depending on the pressure they are under. Occasionally they might "go down," so that no one can see your Web site or send you an e-mail – this should happen very rarely. It is worth asking them about back-up systems (eg is it possible for them to lose your incoming e-mails?), and to obtain a Service Level Agreement (see 1.3.4).

Typically you will be offered a domain name plus Web space package by an ISP or Web host. Netlink charges £199 plus VAT for a domain name, 20 MB of space (enough for about 100 pages, depending on the number of graphics), and unlimited e-mail addresses.

4.7 Domain names: getting an address in cyberspace

Your domain name (also called a Web address or URL, for Uniform Resource Locator) can be critical to the success of your site. If it is easy to remember (or even better, to guess), you will get a lot more traffic than if it is not. Most really big companies have an "intuitive" domain name – all you have to do is to put www. in front of their name, and .com after it; hence www.microsoft.com, www.ici.com, www.bt.com. British companies that have few international pretensions, or which want to emphasise their Britishness, will have a .co.uk suffix: www.boots.co.uk, www.unipart.co.uk, etc.

If you set up a site on an ISP or host's computer, you will automatically be given an address that reflects this, such as www.bloggs.demon.co.uk. You can change this by registering your own domain name, and asking the ISP to rename your site. This means you will also be able to use your address for e-mails – eg jbloggins@telegraph.co.uk.

Ideally you should try to get a domain name that is identical to your company's name. This is easier if you have a moderately obscure name, because it is less likely that someone else has bagged it. Hence Coastal Cottages of

Pembrokeshire has www.coastalcottages.co.uk, but when Net Profit tried to register www.netprofit.com and www.netprofit.co.uk in 1996, they had already been taken. We had to settle for www.net-profit.co.uk, which is far less intuitive. We have now however obtained the name without the hyphen (see below), which shows that perseverance can pay.

As well as .com and co.uk, you could choose .net (though this is mainly for IT-related network companies) or .ltd.uk. This last is hardly used – you can only obtain it by using the exact name of your company (ie www.johnsmithmetal.ltd.uk), which limits its appeal.

Should you go for .com or .co.uk?

- If you want to be seen to be international, try to get a .com address.
- If you are more interested in saving money, use .co.uk.

The matter may in any case be taken out of your hands by availability. Check whether a domain name has been registered already by going to a name registering company such as Netbenefit (www.netbenefit.co.uk) or Netnames (www.netnames.co.uk), and typing in the name you want. If it has not been taken, you can ask for it on the spot with these organisations.

There are potential complications here. If you already have Web space reserved, it may be simpler to ask your host (or ISP) to register the name. On the other hand there is fierce competition on price, which means name-registering companies can save you money. Netnames, for example, is only charging the administration fee (£99) for .uk domains. It adds £45 for .com names.

For a list of domain registration companies, see: www.yahoo.co.uk/Business_and_Economy/Companies/Internet_Services/Domain_Registration/

What to do if the name you want is already taken: Big names have taken other companies and individuals to court for "stealing" their domain names. Harrods sued the person who had registered www.harrods.com, and won. If the courts decide a name has been registered deliberately to make money (by selling it to the "rightful" owner), they have consistently come down in favour of the established company. If however two companies have an equal "right" to a domain, because they have similar names, the one that bags it first will usually keep it.

A word of warning
If you are employing external consultants and agencies to help you build your Web site, do not let them register the domain name. It is likely that the domain registration will be linked to their company unless specifically stated by them that the name is to be owned by you. It is an easy mistake to make and usually the intent is not malicious, just that the domain is generally registered to whoever makes the payment. Subsequent transference of ownership is troublesome, time consuming and requires the willing participation of all parties.

If the laggard really wants the name, it can offer to buy it. Hence Imperial Chemical Industries paid a substantial sum to the Investment Company Institute of Washington DC for www.ici.com. But www.bbc.com still belongs to Boston Business Computing, and www.apple.co.uk belongs to an Internet company, not the computer giant.

There have also been legal battles. Prince, a British sports company, registered www.prince.com, but when a US company also called Prince objected, the administrator of the .com names, Network Solutions of Virginia, proposed to hand the name over to the Americans. Its reasoning was that they had a US trademark on the name. The case ended up in the High Court in London, with the British company keeping the domain. This is a typical example of the sort of legal skirmish that is gradually bringing some order to the Internet (and making lawyers rich in the process).

Chapter 5 What makes a good Web site?

You know what your aims are (Chapter 3). You know how to go about creating a Web site (in house or out: see Chapter 4) and you have decided your budget. What now? You need to build a Web site that does its job, and is likely to be found.

Whether you are planning to spend £200 or £200,000, the basic rules are the same:

- Give people reasons to come to the site (section 5.1).
- Use the Internet's special strengths (5.2).
- Make sure the site is well-structured (5.3).
- Make sure it can be maintained and improved easily (5.4).
- Make sure it looks right (5.5).
- Make sure it reads well (5.6).
- Make sure it loads rapidly (5.7).
- Make sure it can be found easily (5.8).
- Make sure it caters (if necessary) to a non-anglophone audience (5.9).
- Test it out, over and over again (5.10).

It is amazing how few sites, even expensive ones, obey all these rules. But with a little care, there is no reason why yours should not – immediately making it one of the better sites on the Web. Read this chapter whether or not you are planning to build the site yourself – the knowledgeable client will get much more out of a designer than the ignorant one.

5.1 Why should visitors come to your site?

Not for lack of choice, that's for sure. In the autumn of 1999 there were about 10 million registered domain names – many of them were unused, but there must be more than 5 million real Web sites out there. Why should anyone come to yours?

Here are some reasons:

- They can do something they want
- They can discover something they want
- They can have fun

Your job is to make sure one or more of these is fulfilled – some of the best sites fulfil all three criteria. Don't be afraid to borrow ideas from expensive big company sites – you may be able to use the same principles, even if your implementation is simpler.

"Doing" sites: The main "doing" reason for visiting a site is to buy something. Transactional sites have a big advantage over non-transactional because they have an obvious reason for existing. As long as a retail or other selling site is well-designed, has good navigation and offers desirable products or services at good prices, it should attract plenty of visitors. For more on setting up a selling site – as well as the organisation you need to make it work – see Chapters 7 and 8.

Increasingly companies are using their Web sites as "self-service centres" for their customers. On Barclaycard's site (www.barclaycard.co.uk), customers can pay off their credit card bills, using their debit cards. Other companies allow customers to make appointments online. This is a "win-win" use of the Web, because it is both improving customer service, and saving your company time and money. Can you use your Web site to offer a valuable service to customers? If so, they will make their way there. See Customer service, 9.1.

Information sites: Provide useful or entertaining information on your site, and you vastly increase the chance of visitors both finding it and returning. This is the key to most good non-transactional sites. The information can be

- Strictly related to your products or services, or to the company – a brochure or advanced brochure site. A brochure site is full of facts and figures (though many more than you could fit in printed material). An advanced brochure site sticks to your company's knitting, but uses the Internet's special strengths (see 5.2) to make it more colourful. See 6.1.1 for more on creating brochure sites.

- Loosely related or unrelated, but aimed at the right sort of people – a themed site. See 6.1.2

Fun sites: Pure branding sites are destinations in their own right, competing for the attention of their audience with the pub, television, club etc. Most of them are also fun, because they are aimed at young people: research suggests that older people are unlikely (yet anyway) to use the Internet for pure entertainment. But marketing or selling sites can also have a fun element – if well done they are worthwhile, and can have a useful loyalty-building effect.

It is difficult, if not impossible, to produce a slick branding site cheaply, both because it is going head-to-head with television, and because it must be changed regularly to keep people coming back. Most are the progeny of consumer giants – but some smaller companies have decided to invest heavily enough to make fun sites work. See 6.2.

5.2 Using the Internet's special strengths

"Brochureware" is the dismissive term for a Web site that has been transferred direct from print. Even the simplest site can go a stage beyond print, by using one or more of the Internet's special features:

5.2.1 Space is almost free on the Web

A printed product is limited to a certain number of pages. The more pages you have, the more it costs. Not so on the Web – a Web hosting company or Internet Service Provider charges little extra if you want to increase the size of your site (see 4.6). You are also less constrained by the size and design of a page (though the Web has its own good design practice – see 5.5). The only real limiter is your own company's ability to generate material and, as important, keep it up to date.

In practice, this means that you should not hold back on details – do not include waffle, but do give as much hard or soft information as you think will help. Divide it up into pages and provide links between them – this avoids over-long pages, gives visitors a choice as to whether they want see all the information, and creates the impression of a busy site. As the site becomes more complex, make sure the navigation stays simple though (see 5.3).

5.2.2 Multimedia

Much of the visual appeal of a Web page comes from its ability to carry multimedia: it can display all sorts of pictures (static or animated), text, sound and even video. Many of the most attractive Web sites are built by graphic artists who have conquered the medium, and have produced some stunningly attractive designs.

It is hard for a Web site to match the visual and tactile luxury of a glossy print brochure – but it can be brought alive in a way that print cannot. Good use of pictures, graphics and fonts (see 5.5) will make a site stand out above the mass, while plug-ins (5.2.7) can make it more like a television programme, a cartoon or a juke box.

5.2.3 Interactivity

The Internet is a two-way medium: how can you take advantage of this?

E-mail contact form: The simplest form of interactivity is an e-mail link: make sure visitors can send you a message just by clicking on a link. This will bring up a form with the address ready filled out. Note that these will normally work only if the visitor has suitable e-mail software loaded. It is a good idea to add a message: "If an e-mail box does not appear, please send a message to this address." You may want to offer a number of e-mail forms, going to different departments or relating to a particular product or service. If you really want to divide visitors up (or have very high volumes of e-mail), you can have an e-mail form custom made, so that visitors can use drop-down boxes to choose which product/service they are interested in. Talk to a Web designer about this.

E-mail newsletter: Do you want to create a club or community of customers? The Internet is ideal for this, and an excellent tool for binding the club together is the e-mail newsletter. See The Teddington Cheese case study (page 222) for a good example.

The key to a good e-mail newsletter lies in the content and the writing. Unless you have a fluent writer in-house, it may be worth hiring a journalist, writer or PR company (see also 5.6).

***Interactive features**:* If your budget is big enough (£10,000-plus), you can test the potential of the Web by creating interactive features. You can for example provide an interactive product chooser, or some sort of calculator (see 6.2 for more).

5.2.4 Data-gathering

One of the reasons advertisers believe the Web has such potential (see 6.4) is because it talks back to them, telling them how many people have seen their advertisements, and even who they are. The same is true for every Web site.

Your Web site host will offer some sort of system allowing users to see the log of activity on the site. Part of *Net Profit*'s weekly log is shown below:

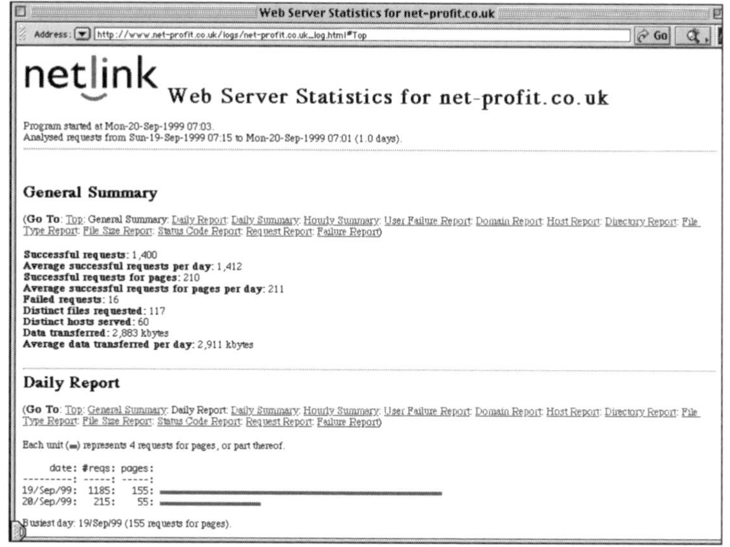

Web Server Statistics for net-profit.co.uk

Address: http://www.net-profit.co.uk/logs/net-profit.co.uk_log.html#Top

netlink Web Server Statistics for net-profit.co.uk

Program started at Mon-20-Sep-1999 07:03.
Analysed requests from Sun-19-Sep-1999 07:15 to Mon-20-Sep-1999 07:01 (1.0 days).

General Summary

(**Go To**: Top: General Summary: Daily Report: Daily Summary: Hourly Summary: User Failure Report: Domain Report: Host Report: Directory Report: File Type Report: File Size Report: Status Code Report: Request Report: Failure Report)

Successful requests: 1,400
Average successful requests per day: 1,412
Successful requests for pages: 210
Average successful requests for pages per day: 211
Failed requests: 16
Distinct files requested: 117
Distinct hosts served: 60
Data transferred: 2,883 kbytes
Average data transferred per day: 2,911 kbytes

Daily Report

(**Go To**: Top: General Summary: Daily Report: Daily Summary: Hourly Summary: User Failure Report: Domain Report: Host Report: Directory Report: File Type Report: File Size Report: Status Code Report: Request Report: Failure Report)

Each unit (▬) represents 4 requests for pages, or part thereof.

```
     date: #reqs: pages:
---------: -----: -----:
19/Sep/99:  1185:   155:
20/Sep/99:   215:    55:
```

Busiest day: 19/Sep/99 (155 requests for pages).

This is the basic form of log, but even it contains a good deal of information:

- the total number of visitors
- visitor numbers for each page
- what days most people were visiting
- what times of day most people were visiting
- the countries they came from (from the last letters of the domain name, eg .uk, .fr (see box)
- some visitors can be identified by their company or organisation (eg domains ending ibm.com, bt.com, gov.uk, etc)

Note that the biggest domain by far, .com, is non-national. It is supposed to refer to internationally-inclined companies, but in reality every US company wants a .com name (the .us domain is little used). Big companies around the world also want .com – so while the probability is that it refers to a US company, it is not certain.

From this, we can see which areas of the site are most popular, and which are hardly visited. That may mean we should be improving the navigation to get people to those hard-to-find spots, or making them more tempting. From visitor times, we can see what factors drive people to the site: this is crucial if you are running an advertising campaign that gives the site's address, or have a mention in a newspaper or magazine. You may discover from a leap in visits from Mexico that your company has been mentioned in a magazine there – leads you can follow up.

There are two follow-up questions:
- How reliable are these figures?
- What can you do if you want more detailed information?

Reliability: There has been much argument (especially in the advertising and publishing worlds) about Web site traffic measurement. Standards for auditing the circulation of newspapers and the numbers watching a television programme are well established. It has been more difficult to do the same with the Web, mainly because it is an international medium. The Audit Bureau of Circulation (www.abc.org.uk/electronic) does now audit many of the big sites, and uses as its key indicator the "page impression" – a request for one page of a Web site. The "hit", which used to be used as a measure, is now discredited because it refers to the download of a single file. The problem is that a page can have dozens of files on it – each individual picture or headline can count as a hit. So distrust anyone who talks in terms of hits – it is not difficult to have huge numbers of them.

The other measure is the "user" or "visitor": this is an individual visiting the site in a single session.

***Getting more detailed information about visitors**:* It is possible to improve on the basic information with tracking software such as Netintellect (available to inspect and download at www.netintellect.com). This will present it in an easier-to-understand format, and may also increase the detail available. But the only way of getting real detail is to persuade visitors to offer it up. This is technically quite simple (though not a DIY job): create a registration form; when visitors fill it in you give them a user name and password. When they want to get into the site, or part of the site, they enter their password, so you know who is visiting. You can then cross-refer usage to details given in the registration form and so build up a profile of your visitors.

Where in the world?

These names are presented in decreasing order of the number of domain names per country. So the biggest national domain is .de, or Germany, followed by .uk, and so on.

.de	(Germany)
.uk	(United Kingdom)
.au	(Australia)
.dk	(Denmark)
.ar	(Argentina)
.nl	(Netherlands)
.ch	(Switzerland)
.jp	(Japan)
.br	(Brazil)
.it	(Italy)
.kr	(Korea)
.ca	(Canada)
.at	(Austria)
.se	(Sweden)
.za	(South Africa)
.nz	(New Zealand)
.fr	(France)
.no	(Norway)
.tw	(Taiwan)
.cn	(China)
.pl	(Poland)
.be	(Belgium)
.mx	(Mexico)
.es	(Spain)
.fi	(Finland)
.ie	(Ireland)
.pt	(Portugal)
.lu	(Luxembourg)
.is	(Iceland)

What is technically possible is not necessarily commercially sensible, though. Do you want to create any barriers to entry, when it so easy for potential visitors to go elsewhere? Do you want to run the risk of irritating them by asking for personal details?

Two questions to ask:

- How valuable is the information you will gather?
- Can you promise enough to the visitor to persuade them to fill in your form?

Visitor information is exceptionally useful if you take advertising on your site (see 6.4), because it provides a profile of your audience. It also provides you with a database of names and addresses for future direct marketing (though be careful to obey the Data Protection Act rules, page 311). But only some sites can reasonably promise enough to persuade visitors to register before they can get beyond the home page: an example is The Electronic Telegraph (www.telegraph.co.uk), which has a database of archived material.

There are however ways of persuading visitors to register:

- Make a small but valuable part of the site password-protected: this is unlikely to annoy visitors, but can yield good information. It could be anything from the advice section to a game.

- Offer extra features to people who register. For example the specialist financial search engine Financewise (www.financewise.com) offers more complete details of sites to registrants.

- Run a competition: visitors will provide their e-mail address and maybe more to take part in it.

- Offer to send a low-value item to visitors who have filled in a form. This could be a mouse mat with your company logo on it, or a full-colour brochure, or some other gimmick.

- Set up a shop online. Every transactional site is by definition data-gathering, and customers will happily hand over their details (see Chapter 7).

What should a registration form include? You will have to compromise between what you want, and what the visitor is prepared to give up. Some US companies ask for details such as incomes and spouses' income. Unless you have a specific reason for wanting to know these (eg if you are selling financial services), do not do this.

But you can ask for basic contact details, and add a couple of bonus questions: "Where did you hear about us?" is a useful one, because it helps you tune your promotional activities. Put an asterisk by questions that are compulsory – some companies do this for the e-mail address, others for every box. Visitors will be told to try again if they fail to fill out compulsory fields. This is annoying, so minimise compulsion.

Other tips

- If a visitor does have to go back to fill in more details, make sure he is returned to the form as he left it. Often it is cleared, which means he has to start again – or give up.

- Be careful with the address and phone sections. Commonly, forms will insist on the "County/state" box being filled in: London is not in a county or state, which makes it a nonsense for Londoners. Some US forms will insist on telephone numbers following the American format, which means foreigners cannot fill them in. Forms often have an alphabetical "dropdown box," from which registrants can choose their nationality. As this includes every country in the world, put your biggest markets at the top.

5.2.5 Personalisation

By combining the Internet's interactivity with its ability to gather data, you can personalise your message – sending greetings on a customer's birthday, offering specially chosen products based on the knowledge you have of him. For some, this is the ultimate special strength of the Internet. Personalisation can be done at a modest level – target different customers with different e-mails; or at an elaborate one, using software that reconfigures your Web site according to who is using it (see RS Components case study, page 226.)

5.2.6 Limited access or community areas

Despite the Web's accessibility, one of its most powerful features is its ability to exclude people – and so to create private areas for a chosen few. Certain pages can be cordoned off, and only people who have the correct user name and password will be allowed in.

Everyone with a password can have access to the same information. For example:

- When used within a supply chain, the private area is the hub of an extranet – that is, it gives access to customers and suppliers to the company's own database (see 9.2, supply chains).

- People who have paid a subscription are given access to extra material. Thus *Net Profit*'s subscribers have access to a password-protected archive of past issues on its Web site, www.netprofit.co.uk.

- Companies can let their customers or suppliers see information they would rather their rivals did not see (eg insurance companies giving controlled access to Independent Financial Advisors).

With more sophisticated technology, different passwords can lead to different information:

- In the Airmiles site (www.airmiles.co.uk), members put in a password to see how many points they have accumulated.

- Bank customers can get access to their own account details.

- Courier customers can type in their airway bill number to see when a particular package is arriving (see 2.2.11).

5.2.7 Special Web technology

The Internet industry offers a bagful of technological goodies to make your site more functional or exciting. As soon as you start using them, you are on the way out of the DIY range – although you may become confident enough to instal simple ones.

These extras come in two broad categories:

- built-in, so they work on any browser
- plug-in based. Visitors to your site will have to use a special plug-in which they may have to download (or get from a cover disk of a PC or Internet magazine). Most regular Internet users will have the most common plug-ins, though they may get irritated at having to download a new version (the software makers regularly update their plug-ins).

In addition, if you are selling online, you will need an e-commerce package. This is a special breed of software that sits alongside your site and is linked to it. See 8.2.

Make especially sure that the technology works on all sorts of browsers. Plug-ins are a major source of glitches.

How to choose what technology to use? Your budget will help you decide (some technology is expensive, mainly in the time it will take a consultant to instal it). See 4.4 for cost guidelines. Otherwise look around the Web to see what sort of functionality you would like to add. See the box overleaf for some of the most popular options in special Web technology.

Big company, low technology

One of the paradoxes of electronic business is that the best technology is available to the smallest companies and to individuals, while employees of some multinationals have to struggle with ancient equipment. If you want people in big companies to use your site, make sure it either avoids plug-ins and power-stretching devices, or offers a simpler alternative.

There are two reasons for this "lumbering giant" syndrome:

- The IT department in a large company wants to run identical software on all its computers – which means it must work on the least powerful machines. Companies are not in the habit of throwing out computers until they are well used, so it is conceivable that Web browsers will be limited to

Popular technologies for Web sites

Built-in:

- ***Cookies:*** When a visitor logs on to a Web site, or a page within a site, the company's server can send a string of numbers and letters – a cookie – to his hard disk. When he returns to the site, it will "read" the cookie. The information can be a tracking aid – the company can see which pages a user has visited, and when. Or it can trigger a further action. If the cookie contains the user's name (gathered from a registration form), it can greet him: "Hello Joe". If it contains his password, it saves him the trouble of typing it in again. In other words, it offers limited personalisation. There are some privacy concerns – although cookies cannot extract information, the fact that they have perched, unasked, on a hard disk is sinister to some. It is probably best to warn visitors if you use cookies (see page 313); they can reject them, or demand a warning, by reconfiguring their browsers.

- Various bells and whistles are available from Matt's Script Archive (www.worldwidemart.com/scripts). They include a visitor counter, a search engine, e-mail forms, time and date display and interactive forms.

- ***A simple animation*** can be created with an "animated GIF". This is a picture file that has certain movement built in – it could be a spiralling logo, or a changing message. Web designers can create them, as can an ambitious DIYer.

- ***A search engine***: Visitors type in a key word, and the engine looks for matches on your site. Basic search engines can be downloaded free from the Internet (eg from www.worldwidemart.com/scripts/). At the other extreme are semi-intelligent engines such as Muscat (www.muscat.com), which cost thousands to instal.

- ***Drop-down boxes***: Visitors click to reveal a list, from which they make a selection. Widely used as a navigation aid (it takes up less space than a series of buttons), and when the visitor is asked to select one from a number of options (eg a country, a recipe ingredient, the model of a car).

- ***Java***: In essence, a plug-in that comes as standard with modern browsers. Java is a programming language that allows you to add all sorts of "intelligence" to a site – examples are mortgage calculators on building society sites (www.abbey-national.co.uk), changing the colour on a pair of shoes (www.kickers.be), bringing up the Wimbledon scoreboards live (www.wimbledon.org, but only in July), and providing "mouseovers". Mouseovers will change the look of a button when a cursor passes over it – they are widely used to add snazziness.

Plug-ins (some of the most popular):

- ***Animation effects:***

■ *Macromedia Flash* is a fashionable plug-in that can provide exciting animation and near-video effects. It is notably fast to download. For examples see Wilson Associates (www.waa.co.uk), ACDO (www.acdo.co.uk, case study, page 170), New Beetle (www.newbeetle.co.uk) and Matinee (www.matinee.co.uk). See www.macromedia.com for more sites.

■ *Macromedia Shockwave* provides even more sophisticated animation, though the plug-in takes longer to download. See for example the horse race game at www.cremeegg.co.uk.

- ***Audio and video:*** Real Audio and Real Video provide "streaming audio" – that is, it does not have to be downloaded onto a hard disk first, but plays almost immediately. The sound quality of Real Audio can be excellent. Real Video plays in a tiny window, and is jerky unless you have a very fast Internet connection. It is adequate for "talking head" video, but not for anything where the visual effect is important. See www.real.com for links to sites.

- ***Virtual reality:*** Three-dimensional Web sites can be used either as a marketing gimmick, or as a useful tool (for example to display the details of a product). Full blown VR plug-ins are Cosmo (vrml.sgi.com), Intervista (www.intervista.com) and Superscape (www.superscape.com). These can be slow to load, so lighter if less complete plug-ins are also available. Quicktime VR (www.apple.com/quicktime/qtvr) and Ipix (www.ipix-eu.com) provide static 3-D effects. The London estate agent Winkworth (www.winkworth.co.uk) uses Ipix to display 360-degree views of interiors – they are created by taking two pictures back-to-back with a fish-eye camera lens.

- ***Formatting***: Unglamorous but widely used, Adobe Acrobat (www.adobe.com) allows you to keep documents in print format. Visitors can download them and view or print them out. RS Components (www.rswww.com) has converted 10,000 technical and other documents into Acrobat format (also known as PDF). This means it does not have to send the printed documents out by mail as part of its customer service operation (see 9.1, customer service, and case study, page 226).

A practical tutorial on Web technologies is at http://snowwhite.it.brighton.ac.uk/~mas/mas/courses/html/html.html

early versions of Netscape Navigator or Internet Explorer. These will not run the latest plug-ins, and may not run Java.

- Computer users are not allowed to download anything onto the company network – including plug-ins – because the IT department fears viruses will be imported. They configure the “firewall” (the protective electronic screen around the network) to stop any downloads. In 1998 Shell International, the oil giant, broadcast two investor relations presentations on its Web site. It hoped that this would be the start of a service that would enable investors, analysts and fund managers to “attend” financial meetings and other corporate events anywhere in the world. But the company found that firewalls limited the audience for the presentations. Ari Miller, a member of the Internet team at Shell International, said: “We have tried to get around the problem by offering a version of the presentations that users can view offline, but this is cumbersome.” According to Paul Reynolds, marketing director of e-TV (www.e-tv.co.uk), the system used by Shell to offer online presentations, corporate users’ inability to access online audio and video is impeding the take-up of services that use plug-ins. “E-TV has not taken off as quickly as we anticipated,” he said. “When our clients use the service to broadcast meetings, they are not reaching a corporate audience.”

5.3 Getting the structure right

The architecture of a Web site is crucial. One that is badly built will be difficult to navigate, and will quickly drive visitors away. It is also important that the site is “scalable” – it can grow without needing a redesign. So the first step is to create a “site map”, the Web equivalent of a storyboard. A good Web site designer should be able to visualise the structure of the entire site in one go, complete with all the linkages. This is a difficult art, which is why you may have to pay more than £1,000 for this element alone if you are going to an agency (see 4.2, Planning costs).

But you should at least understand the structure of the site. Even if you are not involved in building it, this will help inform decisions about what is possible and what is not, how easy it is to make changes and how long those changes are likely to take.

You can examine the overall navigational structure of many sites by looking for the "site map" (it may be grouped with a search engine). This will look like a family tree, starting with the home page and spreading out in different directions.

5.3.1 Frames

The first decision is whether or not to use frames. These are windows into which the screen can be divided, and which can be moved independently from each other. Typically a framed site will have a navigation bar down the side or along the top, with the main page filling the rest of the screen. The navigation bar will have constantly-viewable buttons to take you to other parts of the site – a benefit not only to the visitor, but also to the Web designer, because he does not have to put a new set of links on every page. So companies can save money (in design time) by using this more sophisticated option.

Despite this, frames have been losing ground to non-framed sites:

- They add an extra element of complexity, which means there is more to go wrong.

- Simple design is regarded as "cleaner" (there is a fashion element in this).

- Your site may appear within another company's site (this happens when other companies want to display your information, but do not want to let their visitors go – eg *Net Profit*'s Web Watch database at www.netprofit.co.uk). "Frames within frames" are confusing.

- Blind users of the Web are more likely to be confused by frames (see 5.5.1).

- The original argument against frames – that older browsers and computers will not be able to display them – may still be relevant if you expect your site to be viewed either in the developing world, where computers are made to last longer, or in large corporations (see page 129). But it is no longer as essential to provide a "non-frame version" of a site as it used to be.

Having made the frames/no-frames decision, you need to look at the overall navigation. The most common navigational weaknesses are:

- the home page is confusing (5.3.2)
- it is easy to get lost within the site.(5.3.3)
- broken links (5.3.4)

5.3.2 The home page

By far the most important page on the site – it is where most visitors arrive (though not all: see next section) and it gives an overall impression of the quality of the site, and therefore of your business. It is also the most difficult page, because it has to act as the gateway to a lot of other pages, while remaining easy to use and pleasant to look at.

Here are some tips:

- The home page should be viewable on one computer screen. There is a temptation to make it very long, to fit all the links and puffs in that you want – but the longer it is, the more people it will confuse.

- Though there is an element of fashion in this (a typical '99 home page does not look like a typical '98 home page), you cannot go wrong by keeping the design simple but professional. If you are building the site yourself, it may make sense to hire a graphic designer just to design the home page.

- The home page should reflect the image of your organisation. If you are a robust business-to-business operator, it should be plain but good-looking. If you are a financial services company, you will want it to look solid and trustworthy. If you sell branded goods, inject more artistry. Etcetera.

- Good looks never go amiss: the Royal Society of Chemistry's Chemsoc site (www.chemsoc.org) is little but a sophisticated directory, but its home page, which uses attractive drawings and "handwritten" links, raises the site way above the average.

- The site needs to take visitors where they want to go, but should not be too cluttered. This can be difficult, but is always possible.

For an example of a site that tries to get its message across, look at *Net Profit*'s home page (www.netprofit.co.uk - see page 136). It is designed

- to get the branding across
- to tell people clearly what *Net Profit* is (with a link to "more information")
- to promote particular products
- to provide links to the rest of the site

As the site has grown, we have had to rationalise the link buttons – which means that some pages that used to be directly connected to the home page are now two clicks away. The wording on the links has thus become increasingly important – it must be unambiguous and immediately understandable. Some companies cannot resist using abstract words like "Concepts" and "Focus" – these are far too woolly for the Web visitor in a hurry.

Net Profit's home page is designed for first-time visitors who will want to see what we are offering, and may or may not return. It is therefore essential that they can get where they want without having to think too hard. If a site is designed for repeat visits (eg a themed or branding site), it is possible to be rather softer. For example, the RAC site (www.rac.co.uk) does not attempt to put all the links on the home page at the same time. Instead it uses a "carousel" to rotate its less important links, so they all get a chance to appear, but not simultaneously.

- Buttons on the home page should include a "contact" link, leading to e-mail and phone numbers, an "about the company" link (especially important on a selling site: see 8.1) and, for larger sites, a link to an internal search engine and/or site map.

- Pure branding sites can be more circumspect and imaginative – the Flash plug-in has transformed many into something approaching cinema (see 6.2).

5.3.3 Navigation within the site

A rule of thumb is that visitors should be able to get from any one point in the site to any other in three clicks or less. As some visitors to your site will find themselves set down in the middle of the site, having arrived via a search engine, they must be able to orientate themselves easily.

Navigation should be easier if the site is framed. On a small site, links to every other part of the site should be permanently visible in the frame (these links should not change, because visitors will not expect them to). In bigger sites, the main sections (eg “About the company”, “Contact”, “Buy online”, “Products” and “Home”) should be in the frame. Navigation within each main area can either use another frame (across the top if you already have a side frame), or as unframed links at the top and bottom of the page.
An unframed site should not cause problems if it is quite small: buttons at the top and bottom of each page can lead to the other sections. On larger, multi-layered sites, troubles can begin:

Key points

● Always provide a link back to the home page: that way, visitors can never get completely stuck. The link can be built into the company logo, although a “home” icon is clearer. Ideally the link should be at the top and bottom of each page.

● Keep the navigation consistent. For an example of a huge site that has switched successfully from frames to non-frames, see Dell UK

Net Profit’s home page - www.netprofit.co.uk. See p 135

(www.dell.co.uk). The site looks as though it has frames, but it does not. Instead the same main links are repeated on every page at the top and bottom (Products, Support, Status, Support, Site Guide, Contact), while the sub-sections appear down the side. They change, depending on which main section

Dell UK's site (www.dell.co.uk)

you are in. In addition, Dell uses pop-up browser windows to provide extra information: it is important that only one window can pop up at a time, and that it is smaller than the main screen. Otherwise visitors can get confused about which window they should be using.

5.3.4 Broken links

Make sure all the clickable links work, both those within the site and to external sites. See maintenance and growth, below.

5.4 Maintenance and growth

The biggest giveaway of a site that is not taken seriously by its masters is out-of-date information. We often come across pages that refer to some future event that actually happened months ago. One big company site was still running “a special Christmas offer” in July – why should anyone take it seriously?

Maintaining a site requires discipline. If it has been built by an outside company, you will have to come to an arrangement about maintenance. Most likely it will want you or your staff to carry out minor updates, while it will undertake changes you cannot manage. This means that at least one member of staff will need training in updating a Web site, and will have to be given the responsibility for making changes. Updates can either be entered on an "as required" basis, or every week, fortnight or month. It is simple to make text changes to a site (see page 103).

Check all links regularly. Your site will probably have links to other sites. If they change their address, or disappear, a click will bring up an error message, which makes your site look unprofessional.

Selling sites will almost certainly work on a database system, which should be simple to update in-house (see page 234).

5.5 Making the site look right

Your site's visual clothing should be a) appropriate, and b) professional. Many companies use a) as an excuse for forgetting about b). It is easy to say "We're only small" or "We're in business-to-business" to accept a site that is frankly shoddy: there is no reason at all why even the cheapest DIY site should not look attractive. This is sometimes called the "quality gap": managers are prepared to accept a standard on their Web sites that they would not in other publicly-available material.

Why are so many sites ugly in the first place? Probably, because they have been built by people with little visual skill. Presented with so many easy-to-apply options from a Web authoring program, they add a textured purple background, and put the text in a mixture of yellow, blue and red. As with an amateur cook who throws in ingredients simply because he sees them in the larder, the result is almost invariably disastrous.

Some of the most imaginative Web designers are graphic artists. If you are using a consultancy, it worth finding one that has at least one person with visual flair – and if you are designing in-house, involve the most artistic of your colleagues in the design process. Failing that, ring up a local graphic designer and ask if they can help as consultants – they do not need to create the site, but they can look at your efforts and comment on them. At the least, have a professional help you with the home page (see 5.4).

Here are some tips:

- More is usually less: a simple look is usually more attractive than a cluttered one.

- The cluttered look can work for selling sites – just as a discount store's window will be plastered with posters offering money off this and that. But the clutteredness must still look professional.

- Be economical with photographs – they can seriously slow down the loading of a page. Good designers can reduce the amount of computer data in an image without changing its appearance to any extent. One company found that by reducing the size of an image (in terms of computer data) by 15 per cent, the proportion of people "bailing out" before it loaded dropped from 30 to 8 per cent.

- Think about using thumbnail (less than an inch square) photos that link to a full-size version elsewhere. Only visitors that want a good look at the photo will have to wait for it to load. The Queen makes good use of thumbnails on her site (www.royal.gov.uk).

- A scattering of small pictures or icons can make an otherwise dense page of text light and attractive.

- Most of the text on a site will be in a standard font (which users can alter if they want). If you want to create a striking headline in a different font, it needs to be created as a "picture file" (using graphics software such as Adobe Illustrator).

- Test the site on a range of browsers. Even versions of the same browser (eg Internet Explorer 3 and 4) can produce different effects. You may find that a headline that fits perfectly in one browser is broken in half in another, or that words collide with each other in some versions, but not others.

- A site that looks great on a 17-inch screen may look terrible on a 14-inch one: Web designers usually build sites on big screens. Make sure they are tested on small ones too.

5.5.1 Giving access to the blind and partially-sighted

A building, however beautiful, is no good if people cannot get inside. The same can be said of a Web site. While many companies have given disabled people access to their premises via ramps and improved signage, few have provided (or thought about providing) the blind and partially-sighted with easy access to their Web sites.

According to Julie Howell, Web site editor at the Royal National Institute for the Blind (RNIB), the Internet is "one of the most significant developments in the lives of blind people since the invention of braille," giving people with sight problems access to information and services that were previously denied them in the offline world. The majority of "people with serious sight problems"(the preferred definition of the RNIB) have "some useful vision".

To access the Web, partially-sighted people need to be able to change the size and colour of the text and background of a Web page to suit their individual needs. The RNIB offers a useful facility on its own site that allows users to "freeze" their personal configuration by setting a cookie (see 5.2.7). The RNIB will guide companies wanting to incorporate a similar system.

Blind people, meanwhile, can make use of various types of access technology on their own PCs, including:

- Large print software, which alters the size and colour of the text.

- Speech software that interprets text and reads it out loud.

- "Soft braille" – technology that converts text into "refreshable" braille on a hand-held reader plugged into the user's computer. Some access software is designed to read ordinary Web browsers, while some work on text-based DOS. Lynx, the textual browser that preceded graphical browsers such as Netscape, is still preferred by many people with sight problems, because it does not need a mouse.

The RNIB recommends the following considerations be borne in mind when sites are designed:

- Page backgrounds should be in a single colour, rather than patterned or textured. The colour itself is not important – the contrast between the background and text is.

- Italics, underlined, capitalised or blinking text should be avoided, as partially-sighted people find this more difficult to read.

- Images should have Alternative Text (ALT-TEXT) tags – short descriptions of images that are "read" by access technology.

- Links should have sufficient text to allow the partially-sighted to work out where they lead (they should not just say "Click here"). Also, graphical links should be accompanied by text alternatives.

- Frames (see 5.3.1) are a particular problem, because often access technology cannot read text within them effectively. It tends to read across the screen indiscriminately, taking bits from each frame and so rendering the text meaningless.

- Speech software can have difficulty interpreting information displayed in tables.

- Parallel Web pages should be considered for areas requiring plug-ins, as these are unlikely to be accessible. The RNIB will provide further advice: Mark Prouse, 020 7388 1266. mprouse@rnib.org.uk

5.6 Making the site read well

Stylish writing makes up for many things – but few people are naturally good writers. If your site is functional (eg selling, business-to-business), it is probably not worth hiring a writer or copy editor – just make sure the English is simple, because non-anglophones will be reading it. Avoid jargon too. When Hewlett Packard replaced the word "peripherals" with "printers" on its home page, enquiries improved dramatically.

If you aim to create a site that encourages people to keep reading, and to return, it may well be worth hiring a professional.

Whether you do this, or choose to write the site in-house, it is important to understand the difference between Web text and normal text. As you read a page in a book or magazine, you are guided along a path. Web sites are not linear: each page has different pieces of information, but there is no guarantee that they will be read in a particular order (although you may try to suggest an order, especially on a selling site: see 8.1). That means the writer cannot assume that another page has already been read. Quite probably the visitor will have clicked into the middle of your site from another site, and will click off to another one after absorbing your few pearls. He may even click on a hyperlinked word in the middle of a sentence – so he will never make it to the full stop.

All this must be taken into account by the writer, who has to get used to writing in discrete chunks. He also has to know when to suggest pages, internal or external, to which his words can be linked. Good Web writing skills are hard to find and it is worth either employing somebody who has them or will at least pay attention to how the text will behave in an online environment. Web consultancies should have good writers either in-house or on call. Otherwise you may be able to find a professional writer or sub-editor. A writer will start from scratch, working from your brief. A sub-editor will take your text and smooth it out. Expect to pay £70 to £150 a day for the time of a journalist or sub-editor. A good place to start is with the National Union of Journalists' NUJ Freelance Directory. This is available at £35 from the NUJ, Acorn House, 314-320 Gray's Inn Road, London WC1X 8DP. Tel: 020-7278 7916. A site listing UK freelances is at www.journalism.co.uk.

If you want to train up a Web writer in-house, you may be able to send them on a "writing for the Web" course. You will find advertisements for such courses in the media sections of national and local newspapers. You would do well to run a close check on a course before committing. Try to get feedback from former trainees. There is a large amount of resource and information on the Web which should help you build up a skill base.

Some places worth a look:

- **Contentious** (www.contentious.com) is a Web-based magazine for writers and editors of online material.

- **Inkspot** (www.inkspot.com) is a resource centre for Web writers, with information and debate about the craft, and the Web writing industry.

- **GoodDocuments** (www.gooddocuments.com) has useful information on creating business documents for the Internet.

More tips, plus the results of a survey on how people read Web pages, can be found at www.useit.com/papers/webwriting. If you want to go back to basics, Tim Berners-Lee, the inventor of the World Wide Web, put together a thorough style guide for online hypertext which you can find at www.w3.org/Provider/Style/Overview.html.

When the site is complete, make sure it is proof-read over and over again. It is one of the immutable laws of nature that however many times a piece of writing is read, there will still be mistakes in it. But the more it is read, the fewer they will be. This is an area where the "quality gap" is too often present – if large company managers spotted a spelling mistake in a brochure or advertisement, they would be furious. Yet they seem unperturbed when their Web site is littered with them.

5.7 Making sure the site loads rapidly

Perhaps the most difficult aspect of building a Web site, for the non-technologist anyway, is to make it load fast. There is one obvious point – do not use big photographs. But two apparently identical sites can still load at different speeds because of the way the site has been put together. A good rule is to set a minimum loading speed – say, each page must load within 30 seconds on a 28 kbps modem.
Here are some tips (inevitably a little technical):

1 The total size of a home page should be less than 50 kilobytes.

2 Graphics should use the right format (they can be saved in these formats in the graphics software):

- Graphics containing predominantly solid colours should be GIFs
- Photo type graphics should be JPEGs

3 Use graphics compression tools to remove redundant information.

4 Use a 256-colour Web-safe colour palette.

5 Only use interlaced graphics if it is a large graphic that you want the users to see an outline of before completion of the download.

6 Try to avoid putting information below the "crease" (the lower edge of a browser window, when set to its default size).

7 Use width and size attributes for all tables and images (this allows the page to render the other parts before the table and images have downloaded).

5.8 Attracting visitors

If your site is worth visiting, you will find you get visitors anyway through the Internet grapevine. Visitors will recommend others to take a look at it in newsgroups, in online magazines and in all the traditional ways that people communicate with each other. It is surprising how quickly word about a worthwhile site spreads.

But that is just a start – you should use as many tricks and techniques as you can to get visitors to your site. These are the main ones:

- Getting to the top of search engine lists (5.8.1)
- Using links from other sites (5.8.2)
- Non-Internet promotion (5.8.3)

5.8.1 Managing search engines and directories

Most people, when looking for information on the Web, will turn first to a search engine or directory – see 2.2.1 for a list. When they type in a term, they will be presented with a page listing 10 or 20 possibly relevant sites. There could be several dozen more such pages, but it is unlikely that the visitor will look through more than the first two or three. How, then, can a company improve the odds that its site will appear near the top of the list?

The box on the next two pages provides tips. The first step is to “submit” a page, entering keywords that should lead to your page (eg “oil” or “petroleum” for an oil company). This can be done either to each search engine, or to a multiple submitting system such as Submit-It! (www.submit-it.com). You should also prepare your site to make it as attractive as possible to the search engine robots that run around the Web bringing back news of updated sites. As we explain overleaf, the robots will look for both readable text and invisible “tag words,” which are specifically designed to make indexing more effective.

To increase the chances of an engine finding your site, you should understand the differences between them. For example, AltaVista follows links within a site, so you only need to register the home page; others do not, so you should register every important page. For more information about the popular search engines, how they work and how to promote your site to the top of their lists, see www.searchenginewatch.com.

Directories such as Yahoo! are selective, and usually apply a quality test. So there is no guarantee that your site will be listed. Try to get on regional and specialist directories, which may not be covered by Submit-it! See page 39 for a list.

5.8.2 Links from other sites

Try to get links to your site in as many places as possible. One way is to pay for banner advertising – though as we explain in 6.4, banners only seem to work in particular circumstances. The best bets are specialist sites, where your audience is already likely to be interested in your product – if you make golf clubs, advertise on Golfweb (www.golfweb.com), if you make medical laboratory equipment advertise on Biomednet (www.biomednet.com). If you do not mind putting banner ads on your own site, contact Link Exchange (www.linkexchange.com) to arrange a free banner swap with other sites.

Getting your site up search engine and directory lists

● It is important to re-submit your pages every month or two – to make sure that the search engines have not "dropped" you. If you are using a service such as "submit-it!" (www.submit.com) this can be done automatically, any number of times.

● A directory (eg Yahoo) will not list your address unless you register it. It relies on humans, not automatic indexing software agents, so you have to tell them to have a look. Because directories do not work on the keywords embedded in your site, you need to complete a lengthier registration form for each of them. Your site is not guaranteed inclusion.

● Search engines use automatic software robots to visit sites and collect information:

■ Robots will normally work their way through the site, reading the text and following internal and external links. They will note changes, which is why it is important to change material regularly.

■ Look at the underlying code of a Web page by clicking "view" then "source" on a browser. A page of HTML coding will appear.

■ Look for code that says <TITLE>HEADING</TITLE>. The heading is what appears at the very top of a browser page – this is what a robot reads first. Make it descriptive, rather than just the name of your company.

■ Most search engines are attracted by metatags, words that do not appear on the page but that are detected by the engines. They allow you to provide more detail about your Web pages, and gain greater control over how they are indexed.

■ The description (after META NAME="DESCRIPTION" CONTENT) is what will appear in the summary of the page on the search engine. It should include as many relevant words as possible.

■ The robot will give higher relevance to text at the top of the page. If you have a picture at the top, make sure it has an ALT TAG – text that is hidden under the picture but that will be read by robots. A company logo may be a picture rather than text, so make sure it too has an ALT TAG.

■ The keywords (after META NAME= "KEYWORDS" CONTENT) are not visible but are read by robots. They should contain a string of relevant words – especially ones that do not appear in the title, description or near the top of the text.

■ Give both singular and plural versions of words, as well as different forms of verbs (diet, dieting).

■ Avoid repetition of keywords. Most, if not all, major search engines filter out words and phrases that are repeated excessively.

■ You can tell a search engine robot to revisit you. On the Net Profit home page (www.netprofit.co.uk) there are two lines that do this:
<META NAME= "robots" content= "all">
<META NAME= "revisit-after" content= "21 days">.

■ While you should not "steal" your competitors' tags or keywords, you can reasonably analyse the content of their keywords and look for gaps – keywords they may have missed that you could include in your page to make it stand out.

■ Another useful, if time-consuming, tip is to root out "dead" URLs from the search engine's listings. You may find your site is displaced by a collection of well-tagged but defunct addresses – ones that no longer refer to an active Web page. You can e-mail the search engines pointing this out, and the sites should be struck from their lists.

● For a detailed run-down on the major search engines, and how they work, see the free advice page of the Submit-it Web site, at submitit.linkexchange.com/subopt.htm.

Many sites have "useful links" areas. Look for sites that may be relevant – a trade association, a chamber of commerce, a local site perhaps, and send an e-mail asking if they will put in a link to your site. Offer to return the compliment if they agree. You can only find the sites that suit you by looking around.

5.8.3 Gathering together

The "electronic mall" is a concept that been discredited somewhat. While it may make sense for shops to come together in one physical area, the logic falls to bits on the Web, because location has no meaning. That does not mean that the idea of huddling together on the Web is necessarily a bad one: anything that makes the needle stick out of the haystack a little must help. There are two particular circumstances where grouping together makes most sense – by industry or by location.

By industry

Companies in the same field can set up shop within an "affinity site", in the hope that their customers will get to know it. Good examples are

Under one roof

Property Mall (www.propertymall.com) is a "portal" site for the UK commercial property sector that claims to get 15,000 visitors a month who look at 100,000 pages. It offers free "company profiles" – a single Web page with a link to your proper Web site – but gives emphasis to sites it has hosted itself. It will not host sites of less than 10 pages, which it says do not work, and charges either a set fee (£500 set-up cost plus £35 per page per year), or a fee based on visitor numbers. If your site gets fewer than 200 visitors a month, you do not pay anything. Between 200 and 2,000, you pay 15p per visitor. Above 2,000, you pay £300 a month. The company will also build a site for you.

Property Mall has to be an attractive destination in its own right, so it carries news, a jobs section, and property company financial results. It also has links from Estates Gazette's heavily-visited site, EGProperty Link (www.egi.com).

PropertyMall (www.propertymall.com) which features dozens of companies involved in commercial property (see case study, opposite), Farming Online (www.farmline.com) aimed at farmers, and Highland Trail (www.highland-trail.co.uk), which sells Scottish products and is likely to appeal to Americans with a Caledonian interest. See page 151 for a list of more such sites.

These sites are "portals", aiming to be information sources and meeting points for people in the industry, but they make at least some of their money by hosting Web sites.

Judge whether this is a site you want to act as host to yours by looking at its quality – does it make you want to return over and again? If so, it will probably have the same effect on others. As long as it points visitors clearly towards the companies it hosts, this could be a good place to be.

By location

A number of sites are geographically-focused. Many of these are run by local newspapers, and may provide links to your site but will not host them or promote them. And the only way of getting into the Evening Standard's site www.thisislondon.com is to be reviewed in the paper.

But there are sites that do plug and/or host local businesses. Look up your area up in www.yahoo.co.uk or www.yell.co.uk to see a) if there are any portal sites, b) if they are attractive and c) if they offering a hosting service. B) is particularly important – as with affinity sites, ask yourself if you would ever bother to come back.

Virtual Manchester (www.manchester.com) has a shopping section where retailers can set up electronic commerce sites, while WightOnLine (www.wightonline.co.uk) hosts sites for any Isle of Wight business. Thus the Spyglass Inn, in Ventnor, has its own simple page - a very low cost way of establishing a presence in a well-visited site.

East Midlands Network will list local businesses for free, and will also host their sites. So if someone is looking for a good butcher in the area, they might type "butcher" into the search engine on the home page: the first result is Mike Maloney at Ollerton, whose small but neat Web site (www.emnet.co.uk/mike-maloney) is hosted by East Midlands Net.

Two companies that offer national coverage (with a separate section for different towns and cities) are County Web (www.countyweb.co.uk) and Town Pages (www.townpages.co.uk).

County Web has different levels of business listings, ranging from a "business card" linked to your Web site (starting at £75 a year) to a full scale site. Its visitor-drawing attractions include a Dun and Bradstreet database of UK businesses. Town Pages offers basic information on local businesses free, with rather bigger presences available for £50 or £150 a year. It will also build a full-scale Web site for you.

To be truthful, local sites have yet to have much impact in the UK, both because the Internet is not seen as a local tool and because it is difficult for them to generate revenue. To see the way we might go, look at www.trefpunt.nl, set up by Rabobank. You may struggle with the Dutch, but the idea is clear: from a single Web address (www.tref.nl), people all over Holland can find local shops, services and community information. Rabobank evidently hopes to get business from the business taking place through Trefpunt – for now anyway, it is allowing the system to work without having to scrabble for profits. See also page 89.

5.8.4 Non-Internet promotion

The big advantage of promoting your Web site is that it can increase your bang for the buck: a single line of letters will lead people to a cornucopia of compelling information about your company and products. For example Coastal Cottages of Pembrokeshire has a small ad in the back of the National Trust magazine – it gives a phone number, but also a Web address that leads to an impressively functional site (www.coastalcottages.co.uk). Just above it Wales Cottage Holidays (www.wales-holidays.co.uk) even offers online booking. These companies must have an advantage over those in the small ads column that give only a telephone number.

It is now commonplace to see posters and other advertising specifically promoting Web sites. If both your Web site and its address are memorable

Affinity sites

www.archinet.co.uk – forums, links, news, competitions for architects
www.ace-quote.com – virtual community for the European IT industry
www.bioindustry.org – site for the bioindustry.
www.biomednet.com - virtual community for biomedical researchers.
www.breworld.com – news about the beer industry, trade databases, events listings, bulletin boards and the latest brewing techniques.
www.cateringnet.co.uk – virtual community for the catering industry. Order books, search for job, browse events.
www.classicengland.co.uk – retail mall for "English" products
www.egi.com – commercial property
www.farmline.com – subscription service for farmers (£4 per month). Live commodity prices, market reports, farming advice, weather information.
www.fmb.org.uk – well-presented resource for the building industry.
www.highlandtrail.com – retail mall for Scottish products
www.internetpropertyfinder.co.uk – shop window for UK estate agents
www.pharmiweb.co.uk – news, jobs for the pharmaceutical industry
www.propertymall.com – information for the commercial property industry
www.roadrunner.uk.com – system matching hauliers with spare capacity with those that need to fill it, online shop, news, noticeboards
www.rsx.co.uk - site for the insurance industry
www.teacouncil.co.uk – useful resource for the tea industry.
www.timberweb.co.uk – award-winning site for the timber industry. Trade contacts, noticeboards, jobs and news.

enough, consider bold ads built round the address. In any event all your normal advertising should include your Web address, as should letterhead, brochures, packaging, vans and lorries etc.

You really cannot be too aggressive in pushing the Web address. Easyjet, the UK budget airline, has it painted on the side of half its fleet (the other half has phone numbers). PriceWaterhouseCoopers, the giant professional services firm, has it displayed prominently above the front the door of its main London office block.

Try to get your Web site mentioned in the newspapers. It is almost impossible to persuade someone to write about the site *per se*, except in the specialist Internet press, but if your company is going to be mentioned in an article for any reason, ask if your Web address can be given (instead, if necessary, of your phone number).

You can use conventional direct mail to push people to your site. RS Components (see case study, page 226) sent letters to everyone who had registered on the site, saying that if they bought something online, they would receive a multi-purpose tool as a gift. QXL (see case study, page 266) mailed its members to say they would get a gift if they persuaded other people to sign up – the more sign-ups, the better the gift.

5.9 Handling foreign languages

Whether you intend it or not, your site will be visited by people for whom English is not their first language. If you have no interest in appealing to them, fine. Do nothing. But if you believe they could lead to business, it is worth considering a foreign language element to your Web site.

There are those who will cry "But English is the language of the Internet!" They are right, up to a point, thanks to US domination of the medium. But the non-English speaking user base is growing faster than the English-speaking base, and companies are realising that if they want to sell, they must sell in the customer's own language. Electrolux, the world's biggest home appliance manufacturer, is based in Sweden but has until recently only had a site in English. It is now producing 20 different language versions because it wants to sell accessories around the world, and it does not believe it can do so in English alone.

To take a larger view, it seems quite likely that "location" will become a language issue. Anyone anywhere can access a Web site. The only barriers between a business and a potentially global customer base will be its ability to communicate with its customers in their own languages, and to deliver goods efficiently.
The extent to which you want to localise your site depends on the nature of your business.

Some big companies not only provide different language areas, but also adapt the content towards particular nationalities. Thus on the Durex site (www.durex.com), visitors to the German section can build their own fantasy island complete with date and choice of flavoured condom, while the Saudi area is (almost) a model of decorum.

The next level down is total translation. An example is the Adlon Hotel in Stockholm (www.adlon.se). It has had a Web site since 1995 and has now translated it in full into 18 languages, from Greek and Japanese to Norwegian and Estonian. The result, the hotel says, has been new business from all over the world.

Clifford Chance (www.cliffordchance.com), the London-based law firm, translates a good deal of its site into 17 languages, including Chinese,

Surfers by language (August 1999)

Native speakers of:	*Number with Internet access (m)*	*% of native speakers with with Internet access*
English	129.0	40.1
Non-English	55.7	1.7
Swedish	3.9	39.0
Norwegian	1.5	37.5
Danish	1.7	34.0
Finnish	1.6	32.0
Dutch	4.4	22.0
Japanese	19.7	15.8
German	14.0	14.3
French	9.3	12.9
Italian	5.7	10.0
Spanish	9.6	2.9
Greek	0.26	2.2
Portuguese	3.4	2.0
Chinese	9.9	1.1
Russian	1.4	0.8

Source: Euromarketing
www.euromktg.com/globstats/index.html

Hungarian and Dutch. Users can choose whether they want to view non-Roman scripts, such as Russian or Chinese, in graphics format (which do not need a plug-in) or with a plug-in, which means the script should load faster. Among other things, Clifford Chance is using the site to recruit lawyers to offices around the world. Similarly Civil Defence Supplies (see Case study, page 166) offers five languages including Arabic – much, though not all of the site is translated.

If you are selling from a site, you will probably have a database in English. The best you can do then is to provide navigational help and support in different languages.

The final level is very selective translation – providing an introduction to the company and products, but no more. This is fine for companies that believe their audience reads English well, but that want to show that they have an international outlook.

Admirable though it may be to provide a fully multilingual site, it is an awesome task. Try to cost-justify translation: work out what the likely returns are, then decide which languages are important.

The key to efficient translation is to plan ahead, writing material in a way that is designed for translation and dividing it up into chunks – you can then use software tools such as Translation Memory (which re-uses previously translated text elements) and Machine Translation (which automatically translates) to make a multilingual Web site feasible.

There are already a number of online machine translation services. If the English is correctly constructed and certain rules are followed (see below), these can provide useful, if never elegant, translations.

Rose Lockwood of Equipe Consortium says the key to cost-effectiveness is to treat language just like other data, to be processed in the most efficient way. Consider:

- creating text in reusable, translatable elements which can be managed in a systematic way. Instead of writing chapters, try sentences or paragraphs. You may have a standard description of your company or products. Store these as distinct elements.

- the impact of cultural variants. Do the countries use the 24-hour clock? Do they use commas or full stops as decimal points? Such conventions should be considered at the design stage.

- how your site will handle foreign character sets. Do you have software that can go in two directions, which is necessary for Arabic (an alternative, though an inflexible one, is to create pictures to display the text, as Clifford Chance has).

How to write for machine translation

There is an alternative to translating your Web site into other languages – make sure it (or at least some of it) can be translated by software. If you go into the AltaVista search engine (www.altavista.com) and press "translate", you will be taken to the Systran translation system – the full address is below. This translates text that has been pasted in, or taken from a Web site, in less than two seconds. It offers English to French, German, Italian, Portuguese and Spanish – and vice versa. More powerful, but two-language, versions are available from Systran's own site or from retailers.
Systran can generate complete rubbish – the chances are that if you paste in a piece of text in German or French, the translation will be somewhere between poor and laughable. But if you are careful with the way you construct your text (on the Web site or in e-mails) you can reasonably suggest that visitors can use a machine translation system (provide a link to the Systran page).

Systran has produced guidelines that it sells with the retail version of the software. Here are some of them, aimed at anglophones:

- The use of correct English grammar is essential to getting a good translation.

- Repeat nouns or noun phrases instead of using pronouns; particularly avoid the pronoun "it". Bad: *Wash the car, clean the window and then wax it.* Good: *Wash the car, clean the window and then wax the car.*

- Put phrases as close as possible to the nouns that they modify. Bad: *Engine cover for sale by elderly gentleman with a few bolts missing.* Good: *Engine cover with a few bolts missing for sale by elderly gentleman.*

- Don't leave out prepositions (that, which, who, etc). Bad: *Make sure you select the proper tool.* Good: *Make sure that you select the proper tool.*

- Punctuation is used to divide a sentence into its logical parts. Without clear and correct punctuation, it is often possible to interpret a sentence in several ways.

- Put commas after phrases that begin sentences. Bad: *During the landing personnel should remain seated.* Good: *During the landing, personnel should remain seated.*

- The biggest challenge for machine translation is the resolution of homographs, words that are written the same way, but that have different meanings or act as different parts of speech. In English, the placement of articles often helps to clarify how a word is being used. Use articles to reduce the ambiguity caused by homographs. Bad: *empty file*. Good: *empty the file* or *the empty file*

- Make items in a list into clauses or full sentences whenever possible. Bad: *Rotate the wheels, lubricate, clean head.* Good: *Rotate the wheels, lubricate the joints and clean the head* or *Rotate the wheels. Lubricate the joints. Clean the head.*

- Be consistent in the way you use abbreviations. You will most probably get the same translation for all uses of one abbreviation. Bad: *a 3 min. min.* Good: *a 3 min. minimum.*

- Use punctuation of longer sentences to clarify. Bad: *Press enter*. Good: *Press "ENTER"* or *Press the ENTER key.*

Systran has issued a disclaimer warning that the translator should not be used for important legal, medical or marketing documents.
See these sites: babelfish.altavista.digital.com/cgi-bin/translate and www.systransoft.com

5.10 Testing the site

Although you should have tested and checked the site as it was constructed, it is important to put it through serious pre-delivery trials. There are many barriers to a satisfying Internet experience for visitors that are out of your control – browser failures, Internet congestion and so on. It is therefore vital that everything you *can* control is tested to make sure it does not make the problems worse.

At best a site that "falls over" or fails to work properly will lead to customer dissatisfaction. At worst it could lead to legal disputes with customers claiming, for instance, that they have ordered goods for which you have no record.

There are the key areas to check:

***Robustness**:* Make sure that every link that could possibly be traversed on your site and every action that could possibly be performed works as intended. Broken links (even if they point to other sites) and hit-and-miss implementations of site functionality will do little to improve your image.

Every route through the site and every possible combination of actions should be tested before the site "goes live". On top of this, the site should be tested using a variety of different browsers – check particularly that your special Web technology (Java, Flash etc: see 5.2.7) works on all browsers. You should test on Internet Explorer and Netscape Navigator browsers back to version 2.

***Ease of use**:* Even if your site is robust, it still might be unusable – a link button that may seem clear as day to you could be clear as mud to people who do not know your business. It is a good idea to get somebody who has never seen the site to review it. If they get lost or annoyed so will other visitors.

Another technique is to test it with "dummy surfers". Try to imagine every type of person that might come to your site and see how it treats them. If they have come by mistake does it let them know they're at the wrong place? If the site requires a minimum configuration of "client technology" (eg browser version, plug-in), does it tell visitors this at the earliest opportunity? If you are selling online, but only fulfil domestically, does the site let a foreigner know this straight away? Use your imagination – become a dozen other people and go surfing.

Chapter 6 Marketing

It is relatively easy to attract people to a retail outlet, because there is an obvious reason for them coming. It is far more difficult to get people to come to your site to absorb your marketing message. Hence the need for ingenuity, and maximum exploitation of the Internet's abilities.

From the questions in Chapter 3, you should have come to an idea whether you want to build an information site, and if so what sort (6.1), or a brand-building site (6.2). You may also want to build a community (6.3). Should your strategy go beyond building a Web site to include advertising (6.4), or e-mail marketing (6.5)?

6.1 Information sites

As we pointed out in 5.1, there are three sorts of information sites:

- Brochure sites, which stick to facts, figures and marketing material about a company (6.1.1).
- Advanced brochure sites, which add Internet-only bells and whistles (6.1.2).
- Themed sites, which have information that may or may not be related to the company's products, but that is useful or interesting to the sort of person the company wants to attract (6.1.3).

6.1.1 Brochure sites

A brochure Web site is designed to tell customers and others about your company and/or your products. The vast majority of commercial sites are brochure sites, and of these relatively few do the company any good. The problem, invariably, is that their instigators have gone through a simple but inadequate planning process, with the result that they have a simple but inadequate site.

But there can be good reasons for building a brochure site:

- A brochure site can carry much more information than a printed brochure, and can easily be kept up to date.

- If you do not find it cost-effective to have a well-designed printed brochure, perhaps because your prices or specifications change too frequently, you may find the economics make sense on the Web.

- A brochure site should mean you send out less printed material. If you are e-mailed for information, you can simply send back a link to your site.

Case study: Web site leads to export boom

A Glasgow-based manufacturer of specialised industrial equipment has tripled its exports through its award-winning Web site. Plade, which makes bespoke medical equipment, industrial machines for the medical and semi-conductor markets, launched the site in 1998.

"We thought we should do something on the Internet before someone else did," said managing director Gregor Egan in the summer of 1999. "Now we just can't live without the site. Exports have increased from £200,000 last year to £900,000." Domestic sales stimulated by the site have matched those from overseas.

Plade, which turns over about £2m and employs 30 people, is cutting costs by running its tailored production process entirely electronically. "We are currently producing a set of machines for a Swiss company," says Mr Egan. "Each time they make a change to the product it is sent here electronically, alterations are made and sent back the same way. By doing this we are completing a process that would usually take several weeks within three or four days." He highlights e-mail as an "underestimated marketing tool. People just haven't sussed how powerful it can be. If we sent a letter to Motorola about a product we could offer them, it would probably end up in the bin. An e-mail will go to the head guy's desk and, as all Motorola employees are required to check their e-mails twice a day and respond to every offer or query, you are guaranteed a reply."

Mr Egan says the process has been an enormous learning curve. When the company started its Web site it found that Birmingham University had

- This is particularly effective if the enquirer is abroad, because he will see your information while he is still interested. If he has to wait a week for it to arrive by post, he may have gone off the boil, or found another supplier.

- You will receive interest from buyers or possible partners who would never previously have known about you. They will have found you through search engines, via a link, or through "surfing". It is vital to make the site as attractive as possible to search engines (see 5.8).

written a glowing report on its own site about one of Plade's machines. "We put a hyperlink to the report from our site, but quickly found that people got lost after entering the University's site and never came back. We quickly linked the whole report to our site to prevent people wandering off."

Plade has an advantage in selling products with names such as wet benches, laminar flow hoods and auto disinfectors that will show up well on search engines. But it still works hard to keep its name near the top of search engines. "We have only 30 employees, so compared to our US, Japanese and German competitors we are not large by any means. But our Web site gives us the impression of being a larger company than we actually are."

Because Plade's products are all tailor made, it cannot sell online. But, Mr Egan says, "companies have told us that they would like to see what we've got before they talk to us, to get some idea of how much the service will cost."

"We had a request from Hewlett Packard in Dublin to make them a machine," says Mr Egan, "and asked them if it was supposed to link up with a machine we made for them previously. They didn't know they had a Plade machine – they'd found out about us on the Internet. That's when we realised that people don't take any notice of what's around them every day, but will sit up and take notice when it comes to the Internet."

www.plade.com

Case study: the importance of being seen

A West Bromwich-based heavy machinery manufacturer has pulled itself out of a commercial nosedive by getting itself noticed on the Web – it puts a 70 per cent increase in exports in 12 months down to the strategic placement of its site on search engines.

Eagle Machinery manufactures power generators, machine tools and industrial fridges, which it sends all over the world. But until a year ago the outlook was a lot bleaker, with the company on the edge of disappearing altogether.

"Our Web site has been around for three-and-a-half years, but until a year ago we'd made virtually no orders through it," says managing director Nissr Mijim. "Then a year ago we hired two people to work on the site, and to drive our name and products to the top of search engines. All of a sudden the company took off and hasn't looked back since."

The rocket fuel that supplied this explosion came from an oil company based in Kazakhstan. "They sent us an e-mail last year asking us what sort of generators we produced," says Mr Mijim. "They asked if we could supply them with a couple of generators and we said yes. Then they asked for a couple more. By the end of the year the order had grown to £500,000. That's when we really knew how successful the Web site could be for us."

A few more hefty orders have since come in, pushing the company turnover to £3m, up from around £1m last year. Exports used to make up a fraction of the total output of the firm, but now match the meteoric rise in revenue pound-for-pound: 70 per cent of all manufactured goods get shipped abroad.

- Low priority enquirers, particularly students, can be safely directed to a brochure Web site. It costs you nothing, and should help them.

- Jobseekers, especially graduates and school leavers, will naturally look to the Web for information about potential employees. You may not need a special recruitment section (see 9.3), but they should be able to find out about your company online.

The company's Web site mirrors this new-found cosmopolitanism: it has a currency converter and gives full details of all products in seven languages, including Arabic, German and Portugese. It now finds that half its traffic comes from non-anglophone countries. The company did not have the budget to hire translators, so relied on friends.

But Mr Mijim is remaining guarded about the future of the company. "Hopefully more business will come, but you never can tell," he says. "At the moment we're doing well because of the visibility of our Web site. Hopefully it will give us the chance to make more things."

www.eaglemachinery.co.uk

There are two sub-species – the brochure site and the advanced brochure site. Which you choose will depend on your budget and your market, though in neither case should they be a straight rendering of a printed brochure.

Brochure sites: Business-to-business sites can usually be straightforward brochures - some business-to-consumer sites can be too, though it is usually worth adding the occasional bell and whistle.

What matters is that these sites have lots of information on your products (much more than you could provide on paper), that the information is up to date, and that the site is attractive to search engines. Plade (see case study, page 160) benefits from having products with unusual names, while Eagle Machinery (see case study, page 162) has gone to great lengths to make sure its site is pushed as far up search engine lists as it can be. It certainly helps if the site looks good – at least try to avoid unpleasant backgrounds and clashing colours (see 5.5 for design tips).

Advanced brochure sites: Here you stick to your company's knitting, but you also use the Web-only abilities and gizmos to make the site more colourful or useful. The best way of spotting devices you like is to wander round the Web noting ones that seem to work – their cost ranges from nil to thousands of pounds, with most if not all of the costs going to your consultant for his time.

Here are some examples:

- A detailed street map showing where your office or factory is. Go to www.multimap.com, then to "Maps on your Web site" and follow the instructions (it involves adding a little HTML code to your site). The map will appear on your site, with your premises marked in the centre. It is free, and can be installed by anyone with a little knowledge of HTML editing.

- Bells and whistles such as: a visitor counter, search engine, a forum, e-mail reply forms, a time and date display. Simple ones are free from Matt's Script Archive (www.worldwidemart.com/scripts – see 5.2.7), though each will take a designer a few hours to install. More sophisticated paid-for versions are also available: ask a Web designer.

- An interactive selector. Property sites (eg www.propertyfinder.co.uk) ask house hunters to select from a number of drop down lists (area, price, number of bedrooms etc). The system will interrogate a database and come back with suitable properties (See page 216).

- Tailor-made devices. See 2.2.3, Rail, for examples of the devices rail operating companies are using to attract visitors. They include real time train arrival and departure information, interactive timetables and interactive maps. Marigold, the rubber glove maker, has an "online glove sizer" (www.marigoldindustrial.com). Calculators of all sorts work well on the Web, using the programming language Java (5.2.7); financial service companies have mortgage or pension calculators, builders merchants provide drill bit choosers … they are limited more by imagination (and budget) than by technology.

- Any of the special effects brought by plug-in technologies (see 5.2.7).

Case study: picking up foreign fare

London Taxis International, maker of the famous black cab, created its Web site in 1996 as a link with its parts suppliers. It upgraded it in 1998 to coincide with the launch of its TX1 model. The site has now attracted visitors from more than 70 countries, and has exposed previously undreamt-of demand.

The company says it was taken by surprise by the interest in the site, which almost immediately started generating five or six enquiries from the US alone. The TX1 was not initially available for export, but LTI was able to use response to gauge demand from different parts of the world.

It is also a good example of an "advanced brochure site". Features it uses include:

- a flashing "indicator" on the home page picture.
- a colour picker, so you can see what a taxi looks like in any available colour.
- a downloadable promotional video clip called "Four pounds fifty, luv".
- a clickable map of the UK, which brings up the nearest LTI dealer.
- full specifications downloadable in Adobe Acrobat format (see 5.2.7).

www.london-taxis.com

6.1.2 Themed sites

These need more imagination, and work, but they can be highly effective because they can make the site a destination in its own right. Whereas visitors will go to brochure sites for a specific reason – to find out about that company's products or services – they may well return to a themed site out of interest; your aim should be to get it "bookmarked" as much as possible. Themed sites always have a brochure element, but also build brand awareness.

The link between your company's offerings and the site's theme can be as close or as tenuous as you like. Civil Defence Supplies (see case study,

Case study: essaying a softly softly sell

Civil Defence Supply is a Lincolnshire-based company that was the overall winner of the 1999 ISI/Interforum e-commerce award for small companies. Three years before it was operating in a traditional and declining domestic market – providing riot control and other non-lethal equipment to the police and military. It then launched its Web site which it says has "transformed its performance" by reaching other markets.

The key to the site is its content. Much of the material is available in five languages, including Arabic – visitors choose their language before entering the main site. They are then offered "an introduction to non-lethality and English policing", an essay designed to prove that the English habits of not killing rioters means its control products are more sophisticated than other peoples'.

The "essay" approach is used extensively – making good use of the Web's ability to store large amounts of information. Taken together, the pieces form something of a manual on riot control, which should make it a valuable destination in its own right. Thus the Armadillo riot shield is sold softly via a piece on "early resolution" – it is backed up by photos (including a spectacular one of a shield on fire, showing how its design allows petrol to drain off it). These photos are sensibly provided as "thumbnails", which can be blown up by clicking: a good way of including good illustrations without making the site slow to load.

below) has long articles on riot control, which could be just the sort of primer its potential audience (eg overseas police forces) would find useful – especially as it has translated a lot of the material into other languages. The Teddington Cheese (see case study, page 222) is a selling site, but has some good themed content in the form of the "cheese encyclopaedia." Elizabeth Botham, a Whitby baker and another selling site (see case study, page 246), has a big section teaching children how bread is made – it was built with the help of a teacher, and fits the National Curriculum. Parents will bookmark the site, and may well buy some plum bread too.

To see sites where the link between product and theme has been stretched, you are best looking for big companies (the line between these and "fun"

CDS has made excellent use of the Web's strengths – displaying its products in a way that would be impossible in print, at low cost. It also provides an e-mail list service, so that potential customers can get latest news online – an effective way of gathering names for CDS's marketing database.

www.civil-defence.org

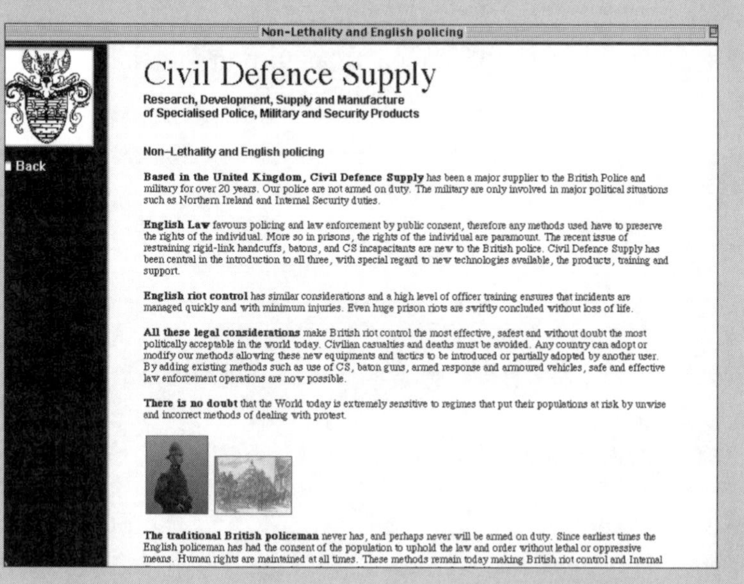

sites – see 6.2 – is a blurred one). Vauxhall (www.vauxhall.co.uk) has Trafficmaster system on its site: you can see in real time where motorway traffic is bunged up. If the link between the Trafficmaster audience and Vauxhall's target is obvious, another link – to snow reports for skiers – is a bit more obscure. The excuse is that it is on thepart of the site that markets the four wheel drive Frontera (rugged, out-of-door image) – but this barely matters. If skiers discover that the easiest way of finding a snow report is to type in www.vauxhall.co.uk, they will (the company hopes) be subliminally picking up its other messages.

Nationwide, which sponsors the First Division, has a big football area on its site (www.nationwide.co.uk). Sport is a favourite source of content, because it generates constantly changing news and is therefore likely to encourage return visits. The Press Association (www.pa.press.net) now has a big division producing "tailored" feeds (mostly news, sport, weather) for companies to use on their Web sites.

Few smaller companies have yet tried to stretch the link between their products or services and the content of their Web sites – but there is no reason why they should not do so (being one of the first to do anything on the Web should generate useful publicity). For example:

- a local builder could offer a guide to the town's pubs.
- an outdoor clothing specialist could offer weather forecasts for walking areas.
- a manufacturer of binoculars could provide a bird recognition guide.
- a retailer could provide local news.

Becoming a bookshop

Anyone with a specialist site can run a bookshop. The big online bookshops run "affiliate programmes" that allow you to offer specialist books on your site. A special pagewill link to the bookshop site, which does the transaction – but you will get a small cut. The TVR Car Club (www.tvrcc.com) uses the Internet Bookshop (www.bookshop.co.uk) to supply manuals about the marque. According to WH Smith, which owns the Internet Bookshop, it has all but cornered the market for these books. See www.bookshop.co.uk (partnership programme), www.amazon.co.uk (associates programme).

- an acupuncture clinic could provide a guide to complementary medicine.

The most effective form of content changes regularly. That could mean it changes by its nature – news, sports results etc. Ask your local newspaper or newswire whether they would be interested in proving a feed (perhaps in exchange for publicity, rather than cash). WightOnLine, the Isle of Wight's local site (www.wightonline.co.uk) takes news from the Isle of Wight News Agency. For a specialist weather forecast (or similar), contact the Press Association – though you can expect to pay at least £10,000 a year.

Feeds of this sort have one big advantage – once they are in place, you do not have to work to change them. But you can create an ever-evolving site simply by hard work and imagination. If for example you have created a guide to local pubs, ask people to e-mail suggestions or reviews. Only take on this sort of task if you have the resources to continue: there are too many sites where we can only say "It started well but …"

6.2 Brandbuilding

Creating a successful brandbuilding site is the highest challenge on the Internet. You have to persuade people to spend time looking at your site, rather than watching television, going to the pub, or visiting any one of thousands of other sites. That is why branding sites tend to be slick and expensive – and thus the province of large companies.

So much for the bad news. The good news is that if you compare your marketing spend on the Web with that on other media, it is trifling. Even though ACDO (see case study, next page) spends £50,000 a year on its Web site, it regards this as excellent value. For the cost of a handful of newspaper advertisements, or a tiny bit of television advertising, it has been able to create a remarkable site. Word has got around the student community it is targeting, and its site has become very popular indeed. A crucial element in its success has been the use of e-mails – you have to remind your audience constantly that you are there, and give them something new to see every time they visit.

Advertising agencies find it difficult to promote anything very particular, so

Case study: consumer midget bites giants

ACDO is a long-established privately held company in Bolton, Lancashire. It employs 60 people and it makes soap powder (ACDO), a range of cleaning aids called Glo White and Doctor Beckmann's range of stain removers. Despite its small size it has a brand-building Web site (www.acdo.co.uk) that stands comparison with the glitziest efforts of its multinational competitors.

The company launched its first Web site in the early years of the Internet, because managing director Brandon Pilling realised it was a good way of providing product information to potential overseas customers (ACDO now exports to 26 countries). The trouble, Mr Pilling says, "was that people didn't really have reason to return. Every time they came back it was the same site."

"We wanted a site that forced us to update it every two or three weeks," Mr Pilling says. But as he thought about it and talked to Pilot, the Leeds-based marketing company that handled ACDO's promotion, he realised an elaborate brandbuilding Web site could have other advantages.

First, it would give ACDO an opportunity to get leadership in a market where it has always been a minnow. "We just couldn't afford the telly," he says. "So we decided we'll try and get the biggest share of voice in new media." Second, a fun site should appeal to students, an audience the company had long targeted in an effort to keep up a stream of new customers. "Students are only students for a few years, and people tend to stick with the same brands," Mr Pilling points out.

The result, launched in April 1998, was the Bubble Soap Opera – a semi-animated cartoon produced in fortnightly episodes and featuring the adventures of the glamorous GloWhite, Dr Beckmann and assorted aliens. The soap opera, which uses the Flash plug-in (5.2.7), runs on the Web site – anyone who has registered receives an e-mail telling them when a new episode is out. So far, 1m people have visited the site.

This is not a cheap exercise – ACDO spends £50,000 a year on the site.

Because it is constantly being changed and updated (with new soap opera episodes always being made), this is a year on year rather than start-up cost. But ACDO is paying well below commercial rates, because Pilot saw it as an opportunity to create a showcase for its work, and agreed to subsidise the work. "It's a good shop window for them," Mr Pilling says. "And it was a challenge to take one of the most boring products and make it exciting in commercial terms."

Although the Bubble Soap Opera has built up a following since it was launched in April 1998 Mr Pilling is particularly pleased that the product finder and "Helen Why" question and answer sections on the site are at least as heavily visited.

Mr Pilling points out that although £50,000 a year is a tremendous amount for a small company to spend on a Web site, it is not outrageous when put in the context of overall marketing budgets for consumer products. Also, he says, "it's good fun to do."

www.acdo.co.uk

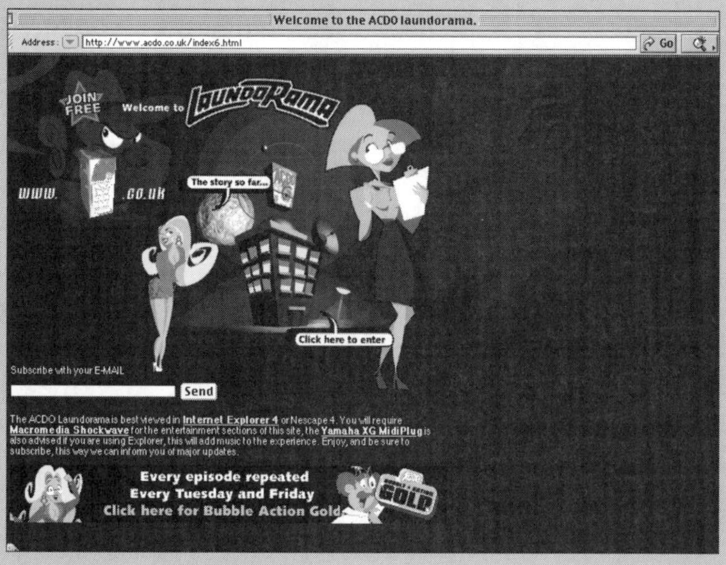

they tend to apply their brand building skills to their own sites. Wilson Associates is a Midlands-based agency that has created an extraordinarily elaborate site (www.waa.co.uk) that uses Flash plug-in technology to create a series of semi-animated cartoons with a Chandleresque theme. Wilson's home page gives "those with slower modems" a chance to skip the introductory sequence – if you choose to enter, you have to wait while the elements load, watching a private eye driving past road signs saying 10% loaded, 40% loaded etc. Music thumps away in the background to keep you amused, but there is still a danger that you will give up before the hero reaches his destination (Wilson's offices). If you are using this sort of technology, it is a good idea to give a chance to "bail out" at any point during the loading.

The trick with branding is to let your imagination range far and wide, and to look for inspiration wherever you can. Here are some big company sites that build brands well, along with short reviews taken from *Net Profit* in mid 1999. We cannot guarantee that the sites will still be as we saw them when you read them, but even the reviews may contain ideas you can plunder:

Teletubbies www.bbc.co.uk/education/teletubbies

Although not conceived as a brandbuilding site, that is what this is. Parents will be comforted by the lack of sell (hard or soft) and also by tips on how to use the site for education. Offspring, meanwhile, will pester them to be allowed to play the games on the site – and probably to buy a Dipsy or Noo-Noo too. What makes this different from most children's sites is that it is packed with things to do, rather than just look at. Tiddly children will be happy with the print-out-and-colour-in pictures, while the older ones will spend much time helping Noo-Noo do the cleaning, playing interactive jigsaws, or demanding that parents make them a robot costume.

Irn-Bru www.irn-bru.co.uk

An imaginative attempt to get adolescents hooked to the soft drink's online presence. The suitably garish, off-the-wall home page offers links to three pointless-but-fun features. "You've been blamed" enables visitors to send prank e-mails – such as "you've been spotted stealing a traffic cone" – to their friends. Victims are then encouraged to fill in a bogus form, after which they are linked to the Irn-Bru site – a clever way to generate new traffic. The talent show section displays users' own works of online "art". Viewers can express their opinions by "throwing" knickers (approval) or rotten tomatoes at the exhibits. Winning artists receive a prize. If visitors still have some time to waste, they can take part in a football game.

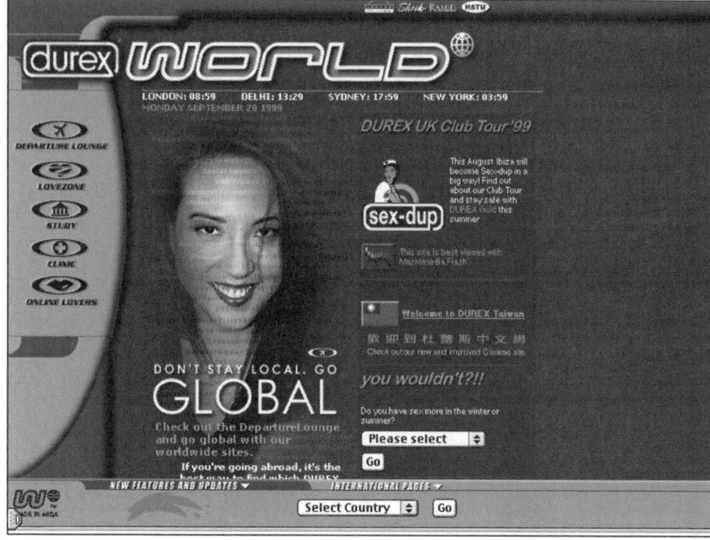

Durex
www.durex.com

Condoms have always been a sensitive subject, but Durex, through its advertising and particularly via this excellent site, has gone a long way towards breaking down taboos. That basic mystery for first time users – how to put one on – is graphically demonstrated on localised Web sites around the world, even on the Saudi Arabian one. The strength of the site is the way it wittily mixes fun elements – downloadable virtual lovers, Tony Mascapone's guide down the rocky road to love, an interactive guide to erogenous zones – with genuinely useful educational material. The site answers many of those personal questions you would not want to ask your mother, from advice on sexually-transmitted diseases to dispelling popular myths about contraceptive use. It is also an excellent resource for medical professionals, researchers and students.

Heineken www.heineken.com

An entertaining site with more than enough value-added features to keep visitors coming back. Users can chat online in six "virtual bars", each catering for a different language – ensuring pan-European appeal. The Planet Heineken section has a wealth of travel information – far more, in fact, than most dedicated travel sites. There are pages of information for destinations from Antigua to Zimbabwe. Geography, accommodation, emergency numbers, and nightlife are all here. You can submit your own personal travel experiences, or read others'. You can also send an electronic postcard, play a game, and download screensavers, desktop icons and animations. Most importantly for Heineken, the "glug, glug, glug" sound effect makes you want to go for a beer.

Persil www.persil.co.uk

Soap powder commercials only recently escaped from the "happy housewife" image – and they are still not associated with the most sophisticated brand-building. Which makes the Persil site quite a surprise. While not trying to pretend that detergents are funky, it has masses of useful and fun interactivity. The most useful bit is the stain guide, which tells you how to get rid of anything from candle wax to curry stain (use bleach because Turmeric is a clothes dye). The fun includes a kids section (make your own virtual stains), and for grown-ups a style and colour analyser. Put in details about the shape of your eyebrows, face, body etc, and you will be told what you should wear. If you are short man with a beer belly, avoid turn-ups and wear button-down collars.

JB Scotch www.jbscotch.com

An intoxicating site that uses sophisticated Web techniques to shed new light on an old brand. The initial hook is the 250th anniversary of the company, which is celebrated with some interesting history of the company's founder – a young Italian, Giacamo Justerini. But the main draw is the "Quest for the Rare" competition: an odyssey in search of 15 gold coins and an eventual prize. This uses a beautifully designed map, with links to various interactive games, including one where the aim is to stop thieves taking J&B barrels. On other brightly coloured islands, you can download screensavers, enter a quiz about movies the drink has appeared in, visit the J&B merchandise shop or, on Distillery Island, find out about how J&B is produced. Unlike most brand-building sites, the games are quite testing and are likely to make people come back for more. Another interesting diversion is the archive of old J&B advertising.

6.3 Creating a community online

"Community" is one of the marketing buzzwords of the Web. If people with shared interests can be persuaded to gather together online, they present excellent targeted marketing opportunities. BioMedNet (www.biomednet.com) is a library/club/shop for the biomedical research community. It finds companies wanting to sell to its members queuing up to take banner advertising space (see 6.5). Football clubs (see case study, page 176) are natural centres of community, and have been exploiting the opportunities, by selling advertising, and also through their online shops.

But if a company can create its own online community, it creates a powerful reason for visitors to return. If you can make visitors to your site feel they belong to a club, they will inevitably feel a certain loyalty to your company. One device, that has been used by online bookshops, is the forum where visitors ask and give advice on particular titles. Forums are easy to set up (see 5.2.7), but unless you have either high visitor numbers or a very specialist topic you can preside over, you should be careful. A little-used forum gives the impression, accurate or not, that your site is little-visited too.

One way round this is to create a password-protected members-only area. If, for example, you manufacture specialist equipment for the oil industry, you can create a closed area where people in your industry can swap ideas. People are more likely to contribute if they feel the whole world is not watching them, and the world cannot scoff if it cannot see how few people are using the facility. You can use the members-only area to make special offers, or to let them tap into specific information. Air Miles (www.airmiles.co.uk) has an area where members can find out what their balance is – it then tries to sell them flights or holidays that they can pay for with that balance.

6.4 Advertising

Banner advertising on the Web is big business – nothing like as big as mainstream media advertising, but running into billions of dollars a year. On hundreds of thousands of sites you will find long thin boxes with an advertising message in them. The vast majority are clickable – they take you through to the advertiser's site.

In theory, banner advertising can be more effective than any other form:

Case study: pulling fans together

Premier League football clubs are using the Internet to build closer relationships with their fans, opening up potentially lucrative merchandising opportunities. In late 1998 Tottenham Hotspur launched a product combining Internet service provision with other loyalty-building extras. CyberSpurs gives fans an "@spurs.co.uk" e-mail address, Web page space, Internet access, and a Spurs mouse and mat. The package is supplied by Cable & Wireless.

Spurs already had a Web site but, says mail order manager Phillip Rose, the package allows fans to get closer to their club. "The Web site is much more of a corporate site with club history and information about season tickets and so on. It became apparent that died-in-the-wool supporters wanted to have a closer relationship with the club, by having things like 'Spurs' in their e-mail address." Spurs created its site in 1996, but is the first to create an online community where fans can create their own Web pages. By pushing the community idea, Spurs is not only improving relations with its fans (albeit only those with a PC and modem) but is also building a valuable database of customers to whom it will be able to offer tailored products.

The launch of CyberSpurs comes as retailing on football-related sites is growing strongly. The success of the shop on the official 1998 World Cup site astonished the organisers, while Newcastle United, which launched its site in April that year, says sales have been rising "significantly". As with all the online club shops, the most popular items are still replica football kits, but fans can now also choose from lines that include Alan Shearer lampshades. Elsewhere, clubs such as Chelsea are even selling products not normally associated with football, such as vintage wines.

Mr Rose says Spurs has been pleased with the response to its site, particularly from outside the UK. "We have a different type of customer. Something like 45 per cent come from overseas, for instance. That's very exciting for us because we didn't reach those customers through other methods."

The popularity of Premiership Web sites is attracting the interest of advertisers. Companies including Ford, Budweiser, Sky TV and British Telecom have all advertised on the Newcastle site. It is the seventh Premier League site to be developed by Planet Sports, a division of Internet Service Provider Planet Online (which has also created eight Division One sites). The company says the Newcastle site is attractive to advertisers because of the type of Internet user viewing it. It claims that 55 per cent of these earn more than £25,000 a year – although this figure is likely to drop substantially as interest in the site grows.

Unsurprisingly, the slickest sites come from the bigger clubs and incorporate high quality graphics and up-to-the-minute newsfeeds from dedicated journalists. Almost all the sites have online shops. Many also offer live radio commentary, using "streaming audio" software. Attempts to extend this to video have however run into trouble, apparently because television companies are worried that even short clips could undermine their valuable deals. Fans can however watch clips of interviews with managers and players on sites such as West Ham's.

Spurs (www.spurs.co.uk)
Manchester United (www.manutd.com)
West Ham (www.whufc.co.uk)
Chelsea (www.chelseafc.co.uk)
Newcastle United (www.newcastle-utd.co.uk)

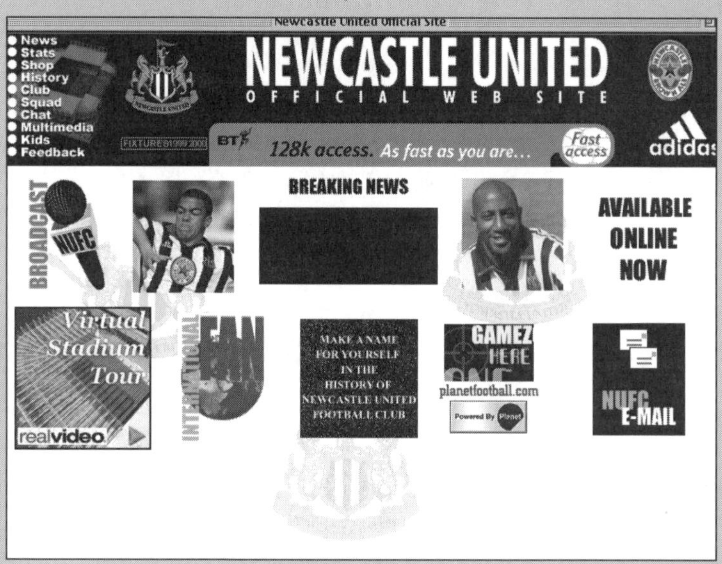

- It can be targeted, either by being placed on a specialist site or by using clever technology
- It can be adapted very quickly – a special offer or a new product can be added with a few strokes of a computer keyboard.
- An Internet marketer can see almost instantly whether his ad is working, by the number of people clicking on it. He can make adjustments to increase its effectiveness far more subtly than he can with any other medium.
- He can also see where the visitor goes once he has clicked through to the main site – so he can build profiles of users according the sites where they have seen the banner, and tailor future ads accordingly.

Internet advertising shows its strength

You want to fly from London to Boston and back. You know American Airlines flies the route, but you do not know its Web address. So you go into the AltaVista search engine (www.altavista.com) and type in "American Airlines". As the results come back, you notice a banner advertisement across the top of the page: "Book flights with us. Save time and money!" it says. You click on the banner and find yourself in TRIP.com (www.thetrip.com).

After giving up various details, such as your address, phone, e-mail and home airport (Heathrow) you are taken to a page where you put in your travel query – travel time and date, there and back, do you want to the cheapest or a business fare? You select cheapest fare, and are given three choices each way – one with American, one with United, one with British Airways. Click on American, and get the fare: $469.91. But there is a message – "We found lower fares using alternate flights." If you travel on United both ways, you can get there and back for $368.19. A few clicks and a credit card number later, you have booked your flight.

Two weeks later (and every two weeks after that), you get an e-mail from TRIP.com, telling you about special offers on flights from Heathrow.

This is Internet advertising at its most powerful – thanks to it, you have given business to a travel agent you had not heard of (TRIP.com), and to an airline you did not intend to fly on (United). What was happening?

The Internet's ability to target makes it more akin to direct mail, while its interactivity makes it more like the telephone, or even face-to-face marketing. It is as though a salesman can find out what each potential customer wants and make a tailored offer accordingly – to hundreds or even thousands of people a day. For an example of banner advertising at its most effective, see the box below.

That is the good news. The bad news is that there are 10m domain addresses on the World Wide Web. If there were 10m television channels or newspapers, would anybody take any advertising? This is why Internet advertising is still a minnow, and though it is growing fast it will never match main-

- TRIP.com has bought "keyword" advertising on the AltaVista site, so that whenever anyone typed in "American Airlines", the agent's banner would automatically appear.

- The banner offered cheap flights – why not go there, rather than to the specific airline site you were looking for?

- Once in TRIP.com, you could not proceed until you had given up quite a lot of detail, which TRIP.com could use to sell to you later. You also failed to click the box that would stop you getting the e-mail newsletter.

- TRIP.com is one of many sites that are linked directly to the airline's travel reservation systems. You are going into the same information database as a travel agent would, and are getting the same deals.

- The site is sophisticated enough to spot when you have not chosen the best option. The sort of intelligence that may well make you return when you next buy a ticket.

- The e-mail newsletter is sent out automatically, but is "personalised", in the sense that it knows where your home airport is. Once again, you may return to TRIP.com to book.

stream press or television levels. Online ad sales still account for only 0.1 per cent of the total UK advertising market, and question marks still hang over them. The vast majority of banner space remains unsold, which leads many people to infer that prices are too high. The truth is that Internet advertising can be effective, but you must be very careful how you use it.

Does banner advertising work?

Research suggests when people come to the Web for the first time, they respond well to banners. But as they become used to the medium, they click much less. This is bad news long term for the ad industry, because the supply of new and excited surfers will eventually tail off. The marketing director of a major online retailer is not alone when he says that "there is growing evidence that the public simply screens out most banner advertising".

The industry fights back by pointing out the underlying strengths of the medium – particularly the ease with which advertisers can measure response. But according to Dela Quist of Excite, a "portal" that earns its money from advertising, it is important to determine what you want to achieve from a banner campaign before you launch it. "There are two uses for banners: for branding campaigns, to generate brand awareness, and response campaigns, to provoke a direct customer reaction. The two rarely work well together," he says.

Where are banners most effective?

Large consumer groups use banners for brandbuilding. These tend to take the most expensive sites on the front page of a portal. But the great majority of advertisers are better putting specialist banners on specialist sites. The position of banners should be determined by a site's visitor profile, rather than the content of the site itself. "We found that a financial site was a great position for a sport-related banner, because the user profile was right," Mr Quist says.

Net Profit's own experience is that banners on smaller specialist sites are most effective – the problem with large sites is that a banner can simply get lost, which makes advertising fruitless unless you are able to take many slots.

Buying a keyword can be a good way of cutting costs – TRIP.com probably pays AltaVista about 5 cents every time its ad is displayed. This system works well for getting to tightly defined groups of customers. For example, a pharmaceutical company might buy the word "influenza" on AltaVista at 5 cents an impression (that is, each time the ad appears). If it is displayed 10,000 times, it has shown its ad to a highly-targeted audience for only $500. But unless you have quite specific keywords you can use, you are likely to be paying for banner displays that are rarely clicked on.

What should a banner say?

A study by Channel Four suggests that animation increases "clickthrough" rates significantly. Although you can spend tens of thousands on banners with amazing effects, or even a shop, it is not expensive to create a little bit of movement. The skill lies in the technical side, becauseit must not use up too many bytes (which will slow loading). Companies with a simple message can do well by eschewing subtlety. This is typical: "Look! Hundreds of CD-Roms for the entire family under $10. Click here."

Laura Steup, marketing manager at Emap Metro, publisher of FHM Online, says that banners have value as part of an integrated campaign. "When I conduct a banner campaign, I see a lift in visits to our site beyond the click-through rates on the banner itself." Because of this, she says, it is important to include the Web address of a site on any banner that advertises it.

What should a banner cost?

Anything from more than $100,000 a month – for a place on the home page of a big search engine – to nothing at all. You may be able to arrange "swaps" with other sites – if for example you sell gardening equipment, a gardening centre may put your banner on its site if you return the compliment. Link Exchange (www.linkexchange.com) is a free service that arranges banner swaps. Even better, sites that like your product may put your banner up without any obligation – look for those run non-commercially that could help you.

Banners are usually priced on "clickthrough" – how many people click on a banner to link to the advertiser's Web site. On the most attractive sites, banners can officially cost more than £50 per 1,000 clickthroughs. But many advertisers negotiate a much lower price. "Anyone paying more than £15 per 1,000 clickthroughs is paying over the top," says a large UK Web advertiser. There is evidence to support this claim. According to Fletcher Research, supply of banner advertising space is seven times greater than demand. UK sites sold only 15 per cent of their banner advertising space in 1998.

Advertisers can take advantage of all this unsold space by using a "blind buy" – paying rock-bottom prices from clearing houses. It is possible to buy a blind batch of banners at $3 per 1,000 clickthroughs. Banner Exchange (www.bannerexchange.com) and Flycast Network (www.flycast.com) both offer such a service. The gamble is that the buyer has no idea where the banners will be placed, and on a medium as diverse, unregulated and unpredictable as the Web, that is a big gamble..

6.5 E-mail marketing

E-mail is theoretically an extraordinarily powerful marketing tool because:

- it can be targeted.
- it can be personalised.
- it goes to the audience, rather than waiting for the audience to find it.
- it is very cheap – mass e-mails cost almost nothing to send out, and huge untargeted lists can be bought for a pittance. The going rate is about $1,000 for $10m addresses.

But the very ease with which it can be sent is also the source of its unpopularity. "Spamming" – named after the Monty Python spam song – is sending out untargeted junk e-mail. Most people with e-mail accounts get at least some spam. Here are two real ones:

*****AMAZING MELT AWAY FAT ABSORBER CAPSULES*****
*****WE GLADLY SHIP TO ALL FOREIGN COUNTRIES*****
LOSE 30 POUNDS IN 30 DAYS... GUARANTEED

Yes we do purchase uncollected Judicial Judgments!
If you, your company or an acquaintance have an uncollected Judicial Judgment then please call us and find out how we can help you receive the money that the court states you are rightfully due.

Not surprisingly, spam is unpopular with most Internet users because it clogs up their mail boxes. Some people even use anti-spam software to filter it out (see 2.1.3). This does not mean e-mail must *never* be used for marketing – but it does mean you have to be very careful not to upset recipients.

There are three groups to whom you can reasonably market by e-mail:

- Your existing customers, telling them about new products or services, or just to maintain contact. An e-mail newsletter is an excellent device for reminding people that you exist (see 9.1.1 – Keeping in touch).

- People who have expressed an interest in your product or company. One way of gathering names is through your company's Web site: anyone who has requested information online is a safe target for e-mail.

- People who you are quite certain are interested in your area - names you have gathered from a specialist conference, for example. Be very careful to make this clear at the top of the message: "As a delegate at the Peanut Butter Congress, we thought you would like to know about …"

The good news is that response rates on highly targeted e-mails tend to be high – it is easy for the recipient to send a quick "yes please" message, or to click across to your Web site for more information.

But the volume of names from these lists is unlikely to be great, which is why devices have been developed that allow companies to send targeted messages to tens of thousands of potential customers.

Mailing lists

One of the earliest manifestations of e-mail marketing was the mailing list of which, according to the list of lists at www.liszt.com, there are about 90,000. Mailing lists are e-mail newsletters and discussion forums to which anyone interested can subscribe, usually for free. See liszt.com for instructions on how to subscribe.

Lists, which can go out at any frequency, are used to circulate information on almost anything from marketing in India and horse racing to accountancy and farming. They can be sent in HTML (Web) format, or as text – there should always be a text option, because not all e-mail readers can understand HTML. Often a text list is linked across to an HTML version on a Web site.

You will first need to sort out the technical side. Lists can take up a lot of space on a server, so you will have to check that yours can cope. You will also need a program to handle a list. A popular one is Major Domo (see www.cis.ohio-state.edu/~barr/majordomo-faq.html). A non-technical primer on lists is at www.cnet.com/Content/Features/Howto/Mailing/index.html.

Marketers can benefit in two ways:

- By running their own list
- By sponsoring a list

Running your own list: a newsletter list is simply a matter of producing the editorial and sending it out (see 9.1.1). An example, covering Internet business matters in the UK, is Freepint (www.freepint.co.uk). People can sign up on your Web site, though you can expect your subscriber base to expand mainly through recommendation. Quality is therefore crucial.

Discussion lists are more complex. You will have to decide what the discussion group should be about – check with www.liszt.com on the competition – and whether it is to be unmoderated or moderated. A unmoderated list is unedited – people are allowed to say what they like (though if you run a list that contains a libel, you could find yourself held responsible). A moderated list is orchestrated by someone who is expected to chair the discussion, and make valuable contributions. If the list is successful it will gain a faithful coterie of industry-focused subscribers.

For examples of moderated lists covering Internet advertising and marketing look at Web Marketing Today (www.wilsonweb.com) or I-Sales Digest (www.mmgco.com/isales.html). These lists are moderated by a senior executive in a marketing company, who can subtly enhance the company's image by gaining a reputation for being an expert in the field.

Sponsoring: If you look at Freepint (below), you will see a short "sponsor's message" near the top of the newsletter, with a link to the company's page. These messages can be remarkable effective, because they are going to people who are interested in the subject, and who have requested the newsletter. Freepint charges about £200 to sponsor one edition of its newsletters.

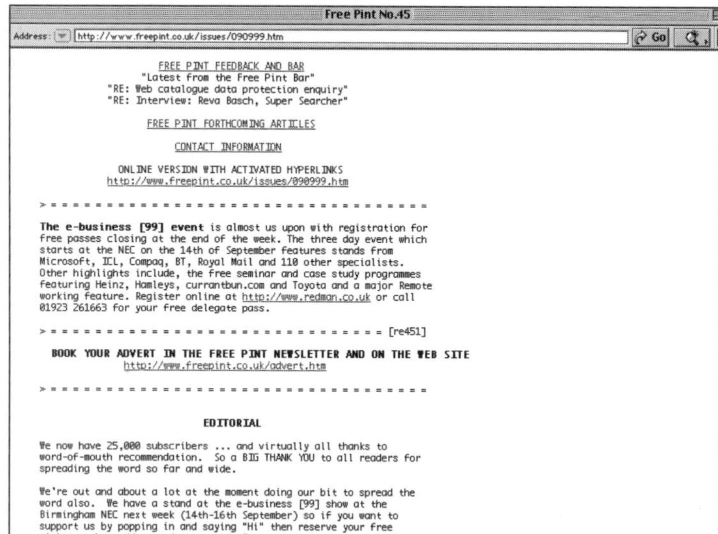

Free Pint No.45

Address: http://www.freepint.co.uk/issues/090999.htm

FREE PINT FEEDBACK AND BAR
"Latest from the Free Pint Bar"
"RE: Web catalogue data protection enquiry"
"RE: Interview: Reva Basch, Super Searcher"

FREE PINT FORTHCOMING ARTICLES

CONTACT INFORMATION

ONLINE VERSION WITH ACTIVATED HYPERLINKS
http://www.freepint.co.uk/issues/090999.htm

> =

The e-business [99] event is almost us upon with registration for free passes closing at the end of the week. The three day event which starts at the NEC on the 14th of September features stands from Microsoft, ICL, Compaq, BT, Royal Mail and 110 other specialists. Other highlights include, the free seminar and case study programmes featuring Heinz, Hamleys, currantbun.com and Toyota and a major Remote working feature. Register online at http://www.redman.co.uk or call 01923 261663 for your free delegate pass.

> = [re451]

BOOK YOUR ADVERT IN THE FREE PINT NEWSLETTER AND ON THE WEB SITE
http://www.freepint.co.uk/advert.htm

> =

EDITORIAL

We now have 25,000 subscribers ... and virtually all thanks to word-of-mouth recommendation. So a BIG THANK YOU to all readers for spreading the word so far and wide.

We're out and about a lot at the moment doing our bit to spread the word also. We have a stand at the e-business [99] show at the Birmingham NEC next week (14th-16th September) so if you want to support us by popping in and saying "Hi" then reserve your free ticket at http://www.redman.co.uk/. It promises to be a great show.

Free Pint (www.freepint.co.uk), showing a sponsorship message

Opt-in e-mail

This is an even simpler idea. Specialist marketing companies gather names of people who have said they would like to receive information on certain areas, and sell the lists to relevant companies.

For more on e-mail, see:

Everything E-mail	*everythingemail.net*
E-mail Today	*www.emailtoday.com*
Botspot	*www.botspot.com*

Marketing to children

The Web has many attractions to companies wanting to market to children. A 1998 survey by NOP found that one in three British children between the ages of seven and 16 has used the Internet at least once. In the US, the research company FIND/SVP reports that about 9.8m children under the age of 18 are using it. They conclude that kids with Internet access are "highly active" users, spending, on average, 4.3 hours a week online. Another survey, by Jupiter Communications, has revealed that a third of children under 13, and 40 per cent of US teenagers, claim they are watching less television because of the Internet.

US marketers in particular are excited by the potential power of the medium. "There is nothing else that exists like it for advertisers to build relationships with kids, nor a product or service like it in terms of capturing kids' interest," says Erica Gruen, senior vice president for Saatchi & Saatchi Advertising. "Marketers have an unparalleled chance to get kids actively involved with brands – brand characters, brand logos, brand jingles, brand videos … Advertisers can give kids public places to post these characters and also provide activities for them to do together. And all, of course, within the brand environment and using brand characters or other brand icons."

This aggressive – and controversial – approach to children's marketing on the Web is typical of US companies. In the UK there is less willingness to be quite so brash and intrusive when it comes to capturing children's mindshare.

Anthony Evans, head of promotion at Britt Allcroft, which hosts the Thomas the Tank Engine site (www.thomasthetankengine.com) and licenses Thomas merchandise, says that while product information might be directed at parents, the company resolved at the outset to ban direct selling, third-party advertising and personal data collection. "We don't believe it is right to force countless commercial messages down a small child's computer."

Britt Allcroft was one of the first UK sites to post marketing guidelines on its site, based on regulations formulated by traditional broadcast media. This, as it happens, was a far-sighted innovation as the US Congress has now decided to introduce legislation to limit the activities of US companies marketing to children on the Internet, and particularly the aggressive soliciting of personal data online.

About 70 per cent of visitors to the Thomas site come from the US and only about 10 per cent from the UK. Another 10 per cent come from Australia and New Zealand and 5 per cent from Japan. It is this global reach that has persuaded Britt Allcroft to spend more on its Web site than on any other single consumer promotion. The site features regular updates of Thomas TV programme schedules in the US and Australia and there is a rolling listing of regional Thomas events.

One of the great advantages of the Web is that there are no space restrictions, so there can also be areas for parents and teachers; and sites that are not necessarily child-focused can engage in "added value" marketing by creating special children's areas. One such site is belongs to the Yorkshire baker Elizabeth Botham (www.botham.co.uk – see case study, page 246). Mike Jarman, its managing director, wanted his site to teach young children about breadmaking "from seed to sandwich". Working with the University of Teesside, he created an interactive area based on National Curriculum guidelines. Botham's Kids Corner includes the story of bread, plus recipes, screensavers, and a game called Cake Swat and birthday cake pictures, both downloadable. It has proved so successful that Mr Jarman has introduced a bigger area for children aged 11 and older.

Mr Jarman is dismayed at the tactics employed by the more aggressive US firms, saying he would never carry sales messages or try to get personal data from children. "My intention is that kids should have fun and learn something," he says. With two in three children in the UK using the Internet for "education purposes" and 50 per cent using it for projects or homework (according to NOP), Mr Jarman's approach seems an effective way of attracting visitors and building goodwill.

A lot of companies that would benefit from special children's areas on their sites neglect the opportunity. Few sports sites, for instance, have catered for children, though surveys show that sports-related sites are among the most popular. An exception is Leicester City Football Club (www.lcfc.com), which has created City Cyber Kids with games, jokes, news, match reports, statistics, Q&As and family ticket offers.

Companies marketing to children should be very careful about gathering information. They should not follow the example of a US site aimed at young people that not only asks for name, postal address, e-mail address, gender and age, but also asks whether the child has been given stocks or cash, and whether the child's parents own stocks or bonds.

Chapter 7 Selling: the business issues

Electronic commerce has hardly started. This may seem a strange thing to say, but it is true: a tiny proportion of total trade is carried out over the Internet. This will change when businesses start selling online to each other, and to consumers, as a matter of course. Go to the US, and you will see that this is starting – for many business and individuals, the Internet has become as unremarkable as the telephone. But in Europe it is early days, which is why there are still plenty of worms for perceptive birds to catch.

International trade will grow sharply as a result, and so will competition. Companies will find themselves challenged by new rivals from other countries, from their own supply chains, and from completely different industries.

The good news is that they will be able to do some challenging too. Not all businesses will be affected – a minority in fact, because most service companies do not have a product that can be sold online. But if you have arrived here after going through Chapter 3, you probably belong to this minority.

Chapter 8 looks at the practicalities of selling online. This chapter looks at the business and planning issues:

- Why e-commerce will increase competition (7.1)
- Should you sell online? (7.2)
- Potential winners, potential losers (7.3)

7.1 E-commerce and competition

So why has e-commerce only just started? Because it is likely to reconfigure trade in two particular types of product – and it has hardly started work on either. They are:

- specialist products
- standard products that can safely be bought sight unseen.

Specialist products

Because the Web is a worldwide beast, it is ideal for selling specialist products. They include plum bread (see Elizabeth Botham case study, page 246), second-hand aircraft (see 7.3.2), specialised laboratory equipment (see Plade case study, page 160) and riot shields (see Civil Defence Supplies case study, page 166). What they have in common is that the Web has opened up a vast unexploited market, full of potential customers who simply did not know they existed.

Standard products

The epitome of the standard e-commerce product is the book. Books are appropriate for selling online because:

- people are happy to order them unseen: they can be sure that every copy of an edition is identical to every other.
- there are several million different books, and the Web is excellent at handling complexity. Customers can quickly locate a title using a search engine, or browse through categories, features or reviews until they find something they want.

What other products offer this combination of standardisation and variety? A huge number; for example:

- CDs, the second mainstream Internet product (see for example www.imvs.co.uk).
- stationery (order 500 window C4 envelopes, 1,000 yellow paper clips and a desktop fan. See 2.3 for sites where you can do this).
- tools (see Cookson's case study, page 206).
- software (from almost any software company's Web site).
- nuts and bolts, car spares, garden tools, sheet music, timber, standard components for anything from furniture to space rockets.

Computers are also standard-but-varied. If you go to Dell's site (www.dell.co.uk), you can "configure" a machine in hundreds of different ways (screen size, CD-Rom etc). Each computer is like a book in the sense that it is identical to every other machine set up in the same way. Insurance policies are standard-but-varied too. Go to Eagle Star Direct's site (www.eaglestardirect.co.uk), and ask for an online insurance quote – by answering a series of questions, you are "configuring" a policy just as you would a computer. Other financial service products are similar. So for that matter are cars (see 7.3.8).

Suppliers all over the world will be setting up Web sites to sell products that fit the standard-but-varied profile. The implications for business-to-business trade are particularly notable, because purchasing managers who have always sourced from half a dozen national or local suppliers will start buying from eastern Europe or Asia.

Even as traditional intermediaries are bypassed, new types of middlemen will emerge to make trade flow more freely: the opportunities for transport, distribution and logistics companies will be significant.

7.2 Should you sell online?

- What are the commercial benefits? (7.2.1)
- Do you have suitable products or services? (7.2.2)
- What are the risks of selling online? (7.2.3)
- What are the risks of *not* selling online? (7.2.4)

7.2.1 Commercial benefits

Selling from a Web site can save you money, for two main reasons:

- If you usually sell though intermediaries (eg shops, agents), you are keeping their margin for yourself.

- If you already sell direct, either as an end supplier or intermediary, the Web provides a new and low cost "self-service" channel. You save on phone-based enquiries, because customers can find all or most of the information they need on the Web site. You save on print, postage and administration costs. And you receive orders in a clear written form that reduces the chance of errors (see box on next page).

It can also increase revenue:

- It gives you worldwide coverage, with a particularly strong presence in North America.

- You will get incremental sales from people who have popped into your shop while wandering around the Web.

It should furthermore be easy to attract people to a transactional Web site. Rather than just being a window with nothing behind it, it is a full online shop, where customers can look around and buy. With reasonable publicity on and off the Internet (see 5.8), it should not be too difficult to attract visitors.

Cost cutting to the full

The full cost-cutting benefits of electronic commerce have yet to be visited on more than a handful of companies – but they will come.

1 When mail order companies go online, they initially raise their costs – because the Web is another channel that has to be built and run. Savings will build as costs associated with print are cut, but the real bonus comes when they abandon their printed catalogue. The only merchants that have so far managed this are IT-related. RS Components, which sells electronic components from www.rswww.com, hopes eventually to phase out its chunky printed catalogue – but recognises that it will be a while before it can afford to alienate its paper-loving customers (see case study, page 226).

2 If Web-based ordering is integrated with a company's own computer systems, costs can tumble. Because orders do not have to be typed in again, time is saved and rekeying errors eliminated. Electronic Data Interchange (see 9.2.2) offers "straight through processing" of this sort, but is rarely linked to the Web.

The few examples that are Web-based come from large companies. Online stockbrokers such as Barclays Stockbrokers (www.barclays-stockbrokers.co.uk) have taken the human out of the chain – when an

7.2.2 Are your products suitable?

These are the key questions you need to ask:

1 Are you selling to the right demographic, both geographically and by type of person (see pages 74-77)?
2 Can your products be delivered digitally, eg software, music, information, intangibles such as airline or hotel?
3 Can they be delivered by mail or courier?
4 Do you have products that can be sold from a Web site, even if they are delivered and paid for conventionally? (See 7.3.2 – selling big ticket items.)
5 Do they fit into the "specialist" or "standard-but-varied" categories (7.1)?
6 Do you have products that can be found easily by a search engine (ie with unusual names – see 5.8)?

investor buys or sells a share, the transaction is fulfilled entirely automatically. PC makers Dell (www.dell.co.uk) and Gateway 2000 (www.gateway2000.co.uk) have also integrated their systems. A buyer customises and orders a machine on the Web site; the order gets sent to a factory in Ireland, where it becomes the production schedule for that machine.

Will these cost-scalping practices spread? It seems eminently possible, as low-cost systems that link the Web "front end" with the company's own "back end" proliferate. Business-to-business trade could benefit particularly. A manufacturing director in Brazil could go on to the Web and check specifications and prices offered by several lathe makers. He goes into his chosen manufacturer's site and configures a lathe using a dropdown menu (exactly as we can configure computers on Dell's site). The order is fed straight into the factory's computer-aided manufacturing system. Payment will be made by conventional means (eg letter of credit) or perhaps by a Web-based trade finance system.

A warning from Gateway – unless a human is checking the orders, a consumer's mistake will go straight through to the production process. As computer people have it, garbage in, garbage out.

To decide on a go-ahead, you must answer "yes" to question 1 and to one of questions 2, 3 and 4. A yes to 5 increases your chance of success enormously, while 6 will be very helpful.

You should also ask these questions:

- Even if your products are suitable for online selling, are *you* the one to do it? Say you make paper clips, which you have always sold in bulk to wholesalers? Do you really want to encourage individuals to pester you for a few boxes – would it not be better if the wholesaler was pestered instead? If you are a publisher, does it make sense to sell your books direct from a Web site when customers will naturally go to the mega-retailers, where the choice is so much greater? Some publishers do sell online (eg HarperCollins at www.fireandwater.com), but they have to provide valuable extra content to lure customers into their sites. If you fit this category, consider a simple online presence to attract and service trade buyers.

- Do you *want* to sell online? It will take a lot of management time, and perhaps the establishment of a new-style delivery system. Should you not be sticking to your knitting? Before answering, read 7.2.4 on the dangers of *not* selling direct.

7.2.3 What are the risks of selling online?

They depend much on whether you are intermediary or an end supplier:

- Intermediaries (retailers or wholesalers) might cannibalise their own business (eg from their physical shops) by selling online, but are unlikely to upset anyone else. This is *channel conflict.*

- End suppliers that have traditionally sold through a distribution chain may be opening a can of worms when they try to bypass it online. This is *supply chain conflict.*

Channel conflict: Some retailers have held back from selling online because they do not want to damage sales from their physical outlets. This concern has tended to fall away as they have discovered:

- that online sales tend to add to existing sales, rather than replace them.

- that the volume of online sales is a tiny proportion of the total. Large retail chains have typically found that total Internet sales are equivalent to those from one store or less – this will change, but slowly. Although some specialist shops are seeing a much higher percentage of sales coming through the Web, these are almost entirely incremental (usually coming from outside their physical catchment areas).

Supply chain conflict: Unless a manufacturer or other end supplier already sells direct, it runs the risk of upsetting its distributors or retailers. Weigh up the pros and cons:

Pros:

- How much money will you save by selling and delivering direct?

- Can you open up new markets by selling online (eg by exporting for the first time, or exporting to new countries)? How much extra revenue could you hope to generate from this?

- What is the value of existing sales you would expect to redirect from traditional routes to direct supply? How much would you save by doing this (increased margin less extra fulfilment costs)?

Cons:

- What is the value of possible damage caused to existing relationships, both hard (ie distributors refusing to handle your products) and soft (goodwill)?

The balance is more likely to tilt towards the negative for large companies – they have distributors everywhere to upset, and few new markets to open up. That is why groups such Levi's (www.levi.com), Electrolux (www.electrolux.co.uk) and Lego (www.lego.com) have only recently started selling direct – and then only limited product ranges.

The happiest answer, at least in the short to medium term, is to keep your distributors happy while still selling direct. Here are some suggestions:

- Tell them of your plans early, so they are not taken by surprise.

- Point out that you are looking for extra sales from areas they do not cover.

- Stress that it is unlikely they will see more than a tiny effect on their sales, at least for a long time.

- Consider a joint arrangement. For example you could take orders from your site, but the distributor/retailer could deliver the product (suitable for white or brown goods). You could have a "mini-site" within the distributor's Web site, and give it a cut of orders taken there. If you are the originator of a financial services product, you might commit to channel Web site queries about non-standard products (which could not be fulfilled online) to brokers.

- Some companies give their major distributors a cut of all online transactions, to keep them happy. This is not likely to be a long-term arrangement, however.

- Consider what products you can sell without damaging relationships (at least as a start). Electrolux sells vacuum cleaner bags but not vacuum cleaners – because retailers are delighted to hand the low-margin high-volume bag business over to someone else, but have been promised they will not lose their mainstream sales.

At some stage, of course, your online sales may have become so significant, and so low cost, that you decide it is time to stop being nice to your distributors. At this point you can either use your new found clout to squeeze their margins, or bypass them altogether.

7.2.4 The risks of *not* selling online

You may find your market eroded.

- If you have decided that your products or services are suitable for selling from the Web, you can be sure that your rivals have noticed it too.

- Companies that you have never regarded as rivals will be sniffing around your markets. They will come:

a) from little-known and possibly low-cost parts of the world (eastern Europe will be a threat for many).

b) from within your supply chain – you could be cut out by your own suppliers, or find your wholesalers are using the Net to source from cheap rivals.

c) from completely different sectors. Who would have thought that British Telecom would get into paper clip supply – see the MarketSite case study on page 58. Blurred borders, as we have said, are a feature of electronic business, and everyone is trying to move into new patches.

- US companies are gearing up to move into Europe over the Internet. It is now commonplace to buy digital products – software, information etc – online from the US (customers may not even know they are doing so). Up to now physical distributors have preferred to stay within their own borders (few American companies are used to exporting), but that is changing. First, their home market is getting crowded. Second, they see Europe as an unexploited electronic fruit ripe for picking. Third, they will concentrate on the UK, because they do not need to bother with other languages – they may also have done their research and discovered that the UK is one of the most credit card friendly countries in Europe. Fourth, "fulfilment companies" such as GlobalFulfillment (www.globalfulfillment.com) are setting up warehouses and distribution chains specifically to allow online merchants to distribute abroad. Again, the UK is likely to be the first target (see 8.4 for more on fulfilment).

7.3 Potential winners, potential losers

Putting some flesh on these theoretical bones, which companies will be most affected by electronic commerce? The chart shows the balance between opportunity and threat. Opportunity means the chance to sell more. Threat means primarily the danger from increased competition, but also the risk of damaging established relationships. Appendix A, page 289, lists specific industries, businesses and trades by opportunity and threat – you should be able to find one or more that you can relate to.

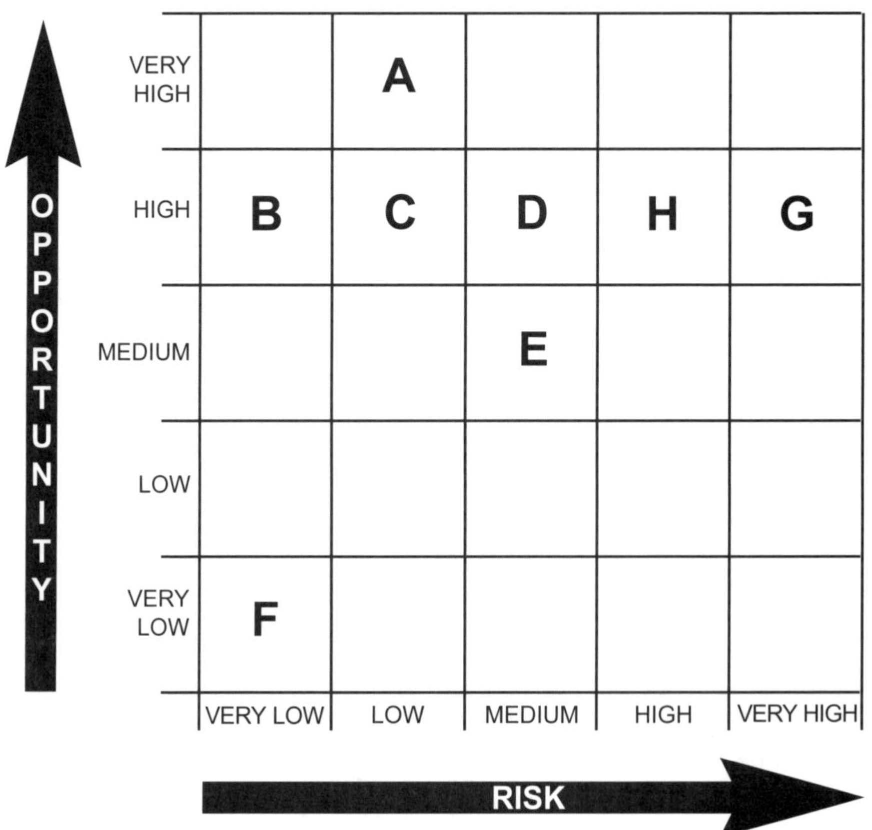

The chart shows the balance of risk and opportunity for different types of selling company.

Key – companies that:

A only sell direct
B have exclusive products that can be sold online
C can expand their market geographically
D can save so much money that it makes sense to disturb their distributors
E can sell online, but with difficulty
F cannot sell online
G are in the same areas as virtual players
H are at risk of being bypassed by end suppliers

7.3.1 Direct sellers

Companies that only sell direct (eg by mail order, or because they are in a very specialist area) should be able to move easily online. They are simply adding a new channel – the Web may cannibalise their telephone or printed catalogue sales, but this is good news because it is a cheaper channel. They are not upsetting anyone else, although they are by definition selling products that other people can sell online too.

The two main categories are:

- direct selling companies that have moved online.
- Internet start-ups.

Existing direct selling companies

These range from Dell and Gateway 2000, computer manufacturers that have always sold by phone or catalogue, to specialist intermediaries such as the Battersea Pen Home (see case study, page 200). On the business-to-business side they include RS Components (see case study, page 226), which already had a slick delivery system in place and was keen to cut costs. In services, companies that have already set up phone-based direct selling operations, such as Eagle Star Direct (www.eaglestardirect.co.uk), have gone through the process of soothing or ignoring intermediaries – for them the Web is just another channel. The low-cost airline Easyjet has always sold direct by phone – now it has painted its Web address (www.easyjet.com) on the fuselages of half its fleet (replacing the phone number, which remains on the other half).

Mail order retailers fit the bill too: one of the first companies to commit significant money to the Web was Great Universal Stores, whose Shoppers Universe site (www.shoppersuniverse.com) continues to grow. GUS had to overcome a problem of demographics. Its traditional mail order market was female C2DE, the least wired category, so it tilted its online presence towards (the much more male) sports clothes and equipment.

An interesting point here is that the small company (Battersea Pen Home) sees its benefit mainly in terms of increased revenues from finding new customers (especially in the US), whereas bigger organisations are driven much

Case study: Exports to write home about

Battersea Pen Home was set up offline in 1994 ago to market vintage pens by mail order. It attributes its real success to its move to the Web in 1996.

Simon Gray, a partner, says that previously orders would peak four times a year, after the catalogue was published. "We wanted to even out the peaks and troughs and reach out to a wider overseas market," he says. "Vintage pen collectors are a difficult market because there are only a few collectors in each country. We used to have 400 regular subscribers to our catalogue but we now have 1,200 to 1,500 visitors a week to our Web site."

To service the worldwide market better the company upgraded to two domain names – .co.uk and .com – and quoted prices in dollars. The site, which was self-built using a £90 version of Microsoft Front Page, has a simple online credit card facility from Mallpark (see page 239).

The Pen Home's turnover now stands at £250,000 a year, of which £150,000 is generated via the Web site. "Our biggest single purchase was an order from Belgium for several pens worth $16,000, but our average is about $500 an order," Mr Gray says. "We have had steady growth from the US where we have had great success, particularly in areas away from cities."

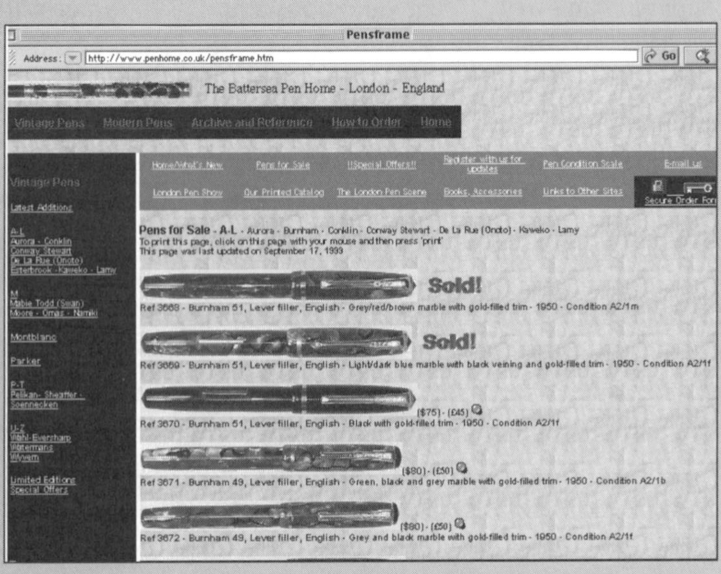

www.penhome.co.uk

more by a desire to cut costs. Companies that are spending a fortune manning the phones are delighted if they can switch to the "self-service" Web. The small companies are benefiting from lower costs too – but they hardly notice them amid the bumper bonus of export earnings.

Virtual start-ups

The companies that have made the headlines with massive market valuations are mainly Internet retailers: Amazon (www.amazon.com), and the online auctions e-bay (www.ebay.com) and in Europe QXL (see case study, page 266). These are companies that started with a good idea and a lot of venture capital, and grew mighty through careful planning and hard work. They are designed to be ultra low cost – anyone who can be replaced by technology will be – and in theory at least they can undercut rivals laden down with hefty labour and property costs. In late 1999 Europe's first Internet-only bank appeared. First-e (www.first-e.com) is following the American Netb@nk (www.netbank.com), which has used its low costs to offer high savings rates and thus suck business away from conventional players.

But for every Amazon there are dozens of failures – entry costs are so low that within months of someone launching a new flavour of virtual company it has dozens of competitors. Successful companies are marked out by the quality of their management – Amazon has moved surefootedly beyond books into other products, and into distribution. It knows that even with its famous brand, it is at risk from a deep-pocketed giant taking it on at its own game and outspending it.

That said, there are still opportunities for virtual start-ups. Europeans have the luxury of being able to watch what succeeds in the US, then copying the idea to the last detail. And it is possible to create a virtual business with high barriers to entry. House of Tartan (see case study, page 232) has something approaching a monopoly because it relies on sophisticated tartan-weaving software created by the company's owner.

Many managers have looked at their existing businesses and thought: "I can do this better online". Some have left to set up their own businesses. Others have turned their existing operations upside down. For now, most of the real excitement has been in the US, driven either by opportunity (see Nostalgia

Factory case study, below), or by need. Egghead, a large software retailer, closed its 80 shops and moved its entire operation onto the Web, saying it could not compete with online-only rivals.

There must be particular opportunities for business-to-business virtual only start-ups. Even in the US, these are few and far between.

Case study: shutting shop, opening online

In Boston, Massachussetts, the Nostalgia Factory gave up its expensive high street location to move to a warehouse, and now gets 90 per cent of its business through its Web site.

The store, which had been selling film posters and memorabilia for 30 years, was prospering but the owners, Barbara and Rudy Franchi, were finding it increasingly difficult to cope. "Our retail location was getting out of hand," Mr Franchi says. "We were open seven days a week, 12 hours a day and I spent huge amounts of time supervising a growing workforce. This was no longer fun and as the overheads were getting out of hand we made a decision to move our entire inventory of 12,000 products on to the Web. Once we had successfully created our searchable database online we decided to give up our high traffic retail location and move to another, low rent part of town."

The Franchis replaced their 2,200 sq ft store on Newbury Street and a 1,500 sq ft warehouse with a 5,200 sq ft two-storey building. In the process they managed to slash rent payments from $5,500 a month to $3,200. Staff have been cut back and the shop is open from 10am to 6pm, six days a week. Yet sales are up 30 per cent.

"Now our business is 90 per cent Net and 10 per cent retail," Mr Franchi says. "We also sell our merchandise on the eBay auction site (www.ebay.com) and have established a relationship with the Internet Movie Database (www.imdb.com). They have credits for over 150,000 films and we supply poster images in return for a link to our site."

www.nostalgia.com

7.3.2 Exclusive products

Companies with unique products or services that can be sold over the Web are in a happy position. They can expand their sales, but have no competitors. Examples are makers of interesting cheeses, owners of high-quality vineyards and sellers of one-off big-ticket items (see below). Companies with exceptionally strong brands should be comfortable too (see 6.2 for more on brands). Burroughes and Watts, maker of billiards and snooker tables, has an excellent combination of attributes – it is one of the few companies to make what it makes, and it has a name that resonates among lovers of the games (see case study, next page).

Very few companies have a total monopoly, of course – there will always be someone with a close substitute, and that substitute may well be available on the Web. But a very special product or a very special name will give you a big leg up.

Big ticket items

Companies that sell one-off high value items, probably to other businesses, can make excellent use of the Web. Sometimes their sites are more like marketing brochures – though these can have a remarkable effect on sales (see Plade and Eagle Machinery case studies, pages 160 and 162). Others list specific products and are therefore selling sites (though with price tags running from thousands to millions, few payments are made online). They include:

- Pavilions of Splendour (www.heritage.co.uk), a UK company that sells unusual or historic buildings, including follies and churches. It used its Web site to sell a cottage in Kent to a woman in Argentina (she bought without seeing it).

- Aircraft Shopper Online (www.aso.com), a site created by a US-based company selling second-hand aircraft at prices ranging from $50,000 to many millions of dollars. The company says that by posting full details of the planes online its sales team does not have to spend time giving them out on the phone – instead, it can get on with selling. This in turn leads to more rapid completion of sales.

- Aquatic Connection (www.aquacon.com), a Florida-based company supplying sharks and exotic fish to zoos and aquariums. It tripled its sales in its first year online. "When we started to enter chat groups and advertise online, we saw a huge pick-up in sales," said its owner, Ted Church.

Case study: back from the brink

One of the best-known names in snooker has used the remarkable success of its Web site to begin manufacturing top-quality snooker tables for the first time in 30 years. In 1999 the company saw turnover more than double, the first meaningful growth in decades.

Midlands-based Burroughes and Watts once bestrode the snooker and billiard world. Queen Victoria and Prince Albert were staunch advocates of its wares – delivered around the empire by the British army. The firm continued to make bespoke cues and sell the occasional restored table, but by 1998 turnover had dropped to barely £100,000.

Malcolm Jones, owner and managing director, credits one of the company's young fans with idea of a Web site. "A pool player who loved using our cues suggested our products were sufficiently rare and expensive to become a great seller on the Internet. There's lots of heritage in the Burroughes and Watts name and we thought it was evocative enough to advertise itself. We decided to tickle the memory banks of people out there. We also needed to show people around the world that we still existed. I think it surprised a lot of people that we were still in business."

Growth in turnover has been directly attributable to the Web site, which cost only £3,000 to set up. Cues, snooker and billiard tables and accessories can all be ordered online and delivered anywhere within six to eight weeks.

In the first half of 1999 the company has sold 22 restored tables including several for over £8,000. So far more than 50 per cent of Web sales have been in the UK, although overseas shipments have included several to Indonesia and the US, and a £4,500 restored mahogany table to Belgium.

The ability to tailor an order online is important. The new tables can all be

"The Internet is uniquely suited to our products because of their unusualness." Three orders have come from Moscow Zoo, totalling nearly $25,000; and a customer in Portugal asked for 30 sharks, each of which measured more than 40 feet.

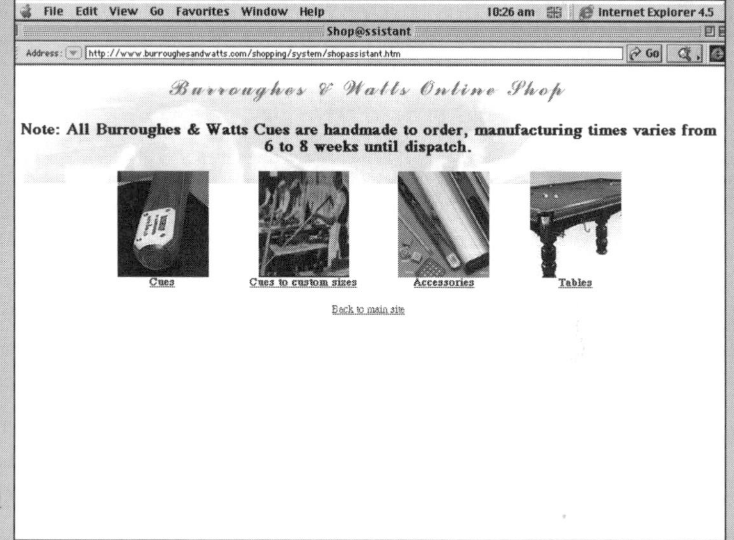

ordered bespoke online. Twenty-one types of ash and maple cues can also be adapted to the required size, and ordered through the secure transaction system.

The company has mainly relied on the brand name to push sales, but Mr Jones says that advertising and marketing are now playing a greater role. "Apparently snooker is very popular among the Asian population in California, so we will be advertising the Web site in the Los Angeles Yellow Pages. And our billiard tables would be very popular in Asia."

He says the company will not be resting on its laurels. "We used to be the biggest snooker enterprise in the world, but until the Web site was developed we were trundling along in a very small way, despite being at the top end of the market. Now we have a chance to share the history and heritage of the company with the global community. The immediate step is to get our name pushed further up the lists on search engines, and let everyone know that we are still in business."

www.burroughesandwatts.com

Case study: A regional retailer goes national

Cheshire-based tool retailer Cookson's was generating a third of its total sales through its Web site only six months after its launch. In late 1999 the company was forecasting that Internet sales would outstrip those of its physical outlets by the middle of 2000.

Cookson's has been running a retail operation in the north-west of England for the past 40 years. It employs 14 staff. Its architectural ironmongery branch employs another 14 people, and the entire group generated a turnover of £3m in 1998.

The company has 27,500 tools available online. The site, run by a separately formed company, cooksons.com, has grown exponentially. Tony Fletcher, marketing manager for the online operation, says Cookson's "saw very early on that the Internet would become the marketing tool of the future, and we knew we needed to be involved. We looked around at what worked on other people's sites, and from there assembled a spec of how the Internet could serve our business needs." The Web site was financed jointly by Cookson's, which contributed about £35,000, and a dozen of its suppliers, which provided a similar amount. Its effect, he says, has been to "expand beyond the north-west to the whole of the UK, and to attract a new and more varied customer base".

Mr Fletcher says the biggest challenge is "getting a year's work done in three months – every three months". Cooksons.com recruited three new members of staff, but the entire operation is designed "not to be labour intensive but fully automated". Spending was mainly on hardware and Web design and writing. The stock control and ordering systems that fuel the site were already in place, making it much easier to bolt on a Web "front end".

Cooksons.com suppliers share information via an extranet (a password-controlled Web site), so that products can be dispatched either from Cookson's or a supplier's warehouse. The transport companies involved all offer Web-based order tracking so customers can see when their products will arrive.

The breadth of Cookson's established customer base – from hobbyists to businesses and educational establishments – influenced the Web site's marketing. The company distributed 100,000 copies of a "hybrid" CD-Rom – holding a full copy of the company Web site and also allowing users to connect to the site – via *Woodworker* and *Industrial Equipment News* magazines, as well as trade shows and mailshots to existing customers.

Mr Fletcher is confident that the CD will eventually fall away. "We will be able to do everything cheaply on the Web in the near future. At the moment, browsing a 27,000 strong catalogue can clock up a terrible phone bill for our customers. We want to provide a more affordable option," he says. The main incentive for turning to the cooksons.com site is the pricing. "Prices on the site are considerably lower than in our stores," Mr Fletcher says. Because its system is fully automated, Cooksons.com can play with a large profit margin generated by reduced stockholdings. "We use tailor-made software to determine how far our range of discounts should reach – the average discount is about 20 per cent but can be anything up to 60 or 70 per cent."

The average shopping basket, at £90 to £100, is higher than in the physical stores – many online retailers find they receive bigger orders online. Repeat orders have mainly come from business customers, who make up 52 per cent of customers, against 40 per cent before the site was launched.

www.cooksons.com

7.3.3 Finding new markets

Companies that do not sell exclusive products, but that have limited their sales to a country or region, can expand without either upsetting existing distributors or hiring new ones.

Teddington Cheese (case study, page 222) is a specialist retailer that has created a model selling operation, and has also expanded its sales area enormously. Cookson's, a tool retailer in the north-west, has pushed out from its home region across the UK (see case study, page 206), while Mansfield Motors (case study, below) has boosted overseas sales of Land Rover spares. Stilwell's, meanwhile, has managed to "publish" in the US without ever going there (case study, opposite).

Case study: Spare parts fly abroad

Mansfield Motors is an Essex-based Land Rover spares dealer. It put its catalogue on the Web in early 1998 and already receives more than 20 per cent of its business via the Internet.

"As an independent we found that we were competing offline with established companies in the specialist Land Rover magazines," says managing director, Duncan Mansfield. "We decided the Internet could give us an edge and help us tap new markets." The company offers a searchable online catalogue of 4,000 parts with secure credit card purchasing. If the customer cannot find the part he wants, he can fill in a detailed e-mail enquiry form and the company will search its of 36,000 parts and reply within 24 hours.

"About 50 per cent of our orders are from the UK and 50 per cent of our export orders are from the US and Canada," Mr Mansfield says. "The rest come from all over including Malaysia, Borneo and Japan as well as regular orders from Brazil and Russia. We get bookings from embassy staff overseas for MOTs and servicing of vehicles that are due to be shipped out. We also receive about 10 enquiries a day via e-mail. All enquiries are followed up and about 10 per cent turn into orders."

www.mansfield-motors.com

Case study: Filling beds online

Stilwell's Publishing, based in London, produces printed guides to bed and breakfasts and holiday cottages. Tim Stilwell set up a Web version in February 1996 – business from it has grown steadily, though unspectacularly, with traffic tripling in the three years to early 1999.

Mr Stilwell believes he is still waiting for "take-off" and only then will he start making real money. "Looking at the bell-curve of the take-up of new technology, we are still at the very thin end," he says.

Although the site increases the appeal of the directory, because it broadens the readership (especially into the US), the only way he makes money from it is by charging to display photographs of properties. "That makes us a few thousand a year, which covers its costs," he says.

He has decided not to go for commission income by offering online booking. "We push our holiday cottages as being independent, so we don't want to act like an agency," he says. He does want to increase advertising income, but he believes the site still has a way to go. "If we get 1m hits a year, we will be attractive," he says, pointing out that the geographic searchability of the site makes it ideal for local advertisements.

www.stilwell.co.uk

7.3.4 Slashing costs

For some companies the temptation of selling direct is so great that they have set up in competition with their distributors.

The model has been set by the airlines. Web-based travel agents such as Travelocity and Expedia (www.travelocity.com or .co.uk, www.expedia.com or .co.uk) were the first to prove that air tickets were ideal for Internet sales. They were linked directly into the giant computer reservation systems (each owned by consortia of airlines), which meant they could give visitors access to information that was previously available only to travel agents. And the product was digital – just a confirmation that the ticket could be picked up at the airport. Airlines were quick to see that they could play this game too – every ticket sold direct saved a valuable chunk of commission. At first they were cautious about upsetting their agents too much – British Airways only made a selection of special offers available. But gradually they threw off caution and started selling aggressively.

Some US airlines are attempting to use discounts to wean customers from the phone to the Web (the direct selling UK airline Easyjet offers £1 off every ticket bought online).

More significant are the special prices airlines offer from their sites – they can offload last-minute seats at rock bottom prices rather than selling them through bucket shops.

Discounting has been taken to a high art: some airlines auction seats off, while American Airlines (www.aa.com) e-mails potential travellers with last-minute offers every Friday – matching unsold seats with the customers' location and known preferences (taken from a registration form).

Airlines may be leading, but other sectors are following. The music industry is being turned upside down by digital transmission. Why do bands and orchestras need publishers or retailers if they can sell directly-downloadable tracks through their Web sites? For now the turmoil is coming mainly from pirated music, but as technology is perfected we can expect to see the real benefits going to the originators, rather than middlemen.

Financial services can be sold online too; banks, building societies and insurance companies will increasingly sell their products online, bypassing the vast intermediary industry.

Then there are manufacturers. After several years holding off, for fear of upsetting its relationships, Levi has started selling jeans online – albeit only on its US site (www.levi.com) for now. Lego (www.lego.com) is selling some of its kits online – but this trickle must turn into a flood.

Manufacturers everywhere will be selling direct, and their distributors will have to look for ways to survive, or fight back (see 7.3.8).

7.3.5 Companies for which the Web is irrelevant

There are products that do not suit remote ordering. For example:

- tailored clothes (though the Web is ideal for repeat orders)
- high fashion
- food that must be examined before purchase (fresh fruit, bread and fish perhaps)
- works of art
- antiques
- very high-tech equipment

7.3.6 Companies that can sell online, but with difficulty

Many companies will have examined the suitability of their products, and decided they are not made for the Web. They cannot be delivered easily, they are non-standard, they have always been sold by human contact. Inevitably, though, there will be people selling those products – and if there is competition on the Internet, it is risky to ignore it.

Here are some examples:

- ***Fashion clothes:*** standard clothing has long been sold by mail order, and has made its way on to the Web via through mail order sites such as ShoppersUniverse (www.shoppersuniverse.com) and Hawkshead (www.hawkshead.com). Now we are seeing boutiques moving online. Fatface, a chain of shops specialising in fashionable outdoor clothing, has created a site (www.fatface.co.uk) that uses technology to get round the "I can't see what's it's really like" problem. By clicking on a picture, customers can zoom in repeatedly until they see buttons or other fine details with impressive clarity. See 8.1.1 for more detail.

- ***Fresh food:*** while some customers will not buy without seeing, others find the convenience of home delivery too great to ignore. Tesco (www.tesco.co.uk) and Sainsbury (www.sainsburys.co.uk) have home delivery systems that allow ordering through the Internet. Specialist home delivery companies such as the Fresh Food Company (www.freshfood.co.uk) and Food Ferry (www.foodferry.co.uk) in London also offer Web ordering. At

What price an Internet sale?

Pricing your products online can be a tricky business:

- You may be used to charging different amounts in different markets. This is much more difficult online because everyone can see your Web site. It is possible to set up different sites for different nationalities (with different domain names, eg www.smithjones.de for germany, www.smithjones.fr for France), or perhaps password-protected areas of one site. But the chances are you would be found out. Nor is the Euro helping, because it makes prices more transparent within Europe.

The answer for most companies must be to unify their pricing – or not to sell online to countries where they want to charge different prices. Currencies, of course, set up a whole new set of problems – see 8.5.5 for the practicalities of multicurrency pricing.

- The Web is undermining the concept of the fixed price. Increasingly products are being sold by auction (see QXL case study, page 266). At the moment these are nearly all end-of-line or refurbished, but we can expect to see mainstream products moving to auction soon. You can buy an off-the-shelf auction system to bolt on to your site. OpenSite's software runs from £3,000 to £31,000, or it will host an auction for you from £1,800 a month.

Airlines are taking the lead (see 7.3.4), both by auctioning seats off and by using Priceline (www.priceline.com). Priceline, which for now operates

some stage smaller retailers will join in – though this will not be big business until the idea of the "local Web" (see page 88) is established in the public's mind.

- *New cars:* cars are "standard-but-varied", which makes them in one way ideal for online selling. But they do need maintenance, and at the moment sale and maintenance are intimately linked through the dealer system. Expect that to change – the first manufacturer to start selling direct, at discount prices, will open the floodgate. The distribution network can expect to get drenched, unless it fights back (see 7.3.8).

only in the US, is one of the many Web-based systems that are blurring fixed prices. If you want to buy a ticket, you give Priceline the details and say what you are prepared to pay for it – it then scurries off to ask airlines and agents if they can match that price, or make a counter offer. The system also works for new cars (dealers receive requests through Priceline and respond to them). It sounds complex, but thanks to exceptionally careful navigation and instructions, it is easy to use – and very successful.

Many other online pricing mechanisms have been invented, mainly by Americans determined that the Internet should create a true free market, with prices set by supply and demand. Some are advanced haggling systems, others are automatic. It must be said that with a few exceptions (such as Priceline and the auctions), they have not been notably successful, probably because they are too complex. But the successes prove that it is possible, and we can expect to see the fixed price becoming less and less standard.

Other variable mechanisms (all US) include

- www.accompany.com, where the greater the amount of a product ordered, the further its price falls.
- www.bidnask.com, a "marketplace" where prices are negotiated on an electronic "floor" by buyers and sellers.
- www.emarketlive.com, where the price of a product rises and falls automatically according supply and demand.

7.3.7 Companies competing with virtual players

Virtual players are by definition intermediaries – so the existing companies threatened by them are too. The most aggressive virtual players so far have been in software, travel and finance – all deliverable online as digital products – and easily-deliverable products such as books and CDs. It is significant that the biggest single casualty of the Internet so far has been US software retailer Egghead (see 7.3.1), which closed 80 shops and moved to the Web. Does that mean conventional travel agents, insurance brokers, banks, bookshops and CD sellers will eventually pack up shop and move online too?

Not necessarily. Physical intermediaries are slowly realising that bricks and mortar are their greatest assets. When Dixons set up its Freeserve Internet Service Provider (see 1.3.4), its biggest advantage was that it could give away start-up CD-Roms in its shops. Waterstone's is using its physical shop to give reassurance, by telling online customers that they can return unwanted books to their local stores.

If pure Internet banks start offering savings rates other banks cannot match, because their costs are so low, the existing players will have to start fighting back by offering services that require a physical presence – real people offering real advice, for example.

As the world is depersonalised by electronic commerce, the human touch will become ever more valuable to those who can deploy it effectively (and cost-effectively). The local insurance broker *can* survive, but only by playing on the personal service it can offer.

We can expect to see cups of coffee, buns and children's play areas going

Case study: fighting back

Seaforth's, an Aberdeen-based business travel agent, is generating 20 per cent of its revenue from online booking. The company, one of the first agents to move online, did so to fend off the threat from direct booking with airlines and from the US-owned online travel agents.

Seaforth's Ticket Window system uses proprietary software, which can be downloaded from the Internet. Like travel agents' systems, it is linked directly to a giant booking system – in its case Galileo, which has data from 500 airlines and 30,000 hotels – but is far easier to use than the agencies' interfaces. Unlike travel agents' systems, it is specifically designed for the corporate user.

As well as finding flight times, the best fares, visa regulations and customs allowances, it lets companies monitor and control bookings. "Travel managers can use it to see who's going where, when and for how much, and why they are travelling," says Gary Hance, technical director of Seaforth's. "It can also restrict flights to certain airlines."

beyond a handful of US-style bookstores into even modest high street outlets. Virtual companies can't serve coffee.

7.3.8 Companies that could be bypassed by end suppliers

These are the potential victims of "supply chain conflict," the companies that are bypassed by the companies that have always relied on them.

- Travel agents
- Financial intermediaries
- Music publishers
- Many shops
- Many wholesalers
- Car dealers (but not yet)

What should these companies be doing? First, examine the threat and see how immediate it is. Second, look at ways of surviving and even flourishing if your suppliers do bypass you.

Mr Hance says businesses have not in general used it to reorganise their travel-booking arrangements. "We thought it would get distributed to desktops of all employees," he says. "But companies don't seem to have sufficient confidence to let that happen. It is still being used by secretaries and travel managers."

Mr Hance says the arrival in the UK of US-based online agencies such as Travelocity (www.travelocity.co.uk) and Expedia (www.expedia.co.uk) has added credibility to the market. "When we started showing the product at exhibitions, people really didn't believe they were booking a seat on an airline," he says. Seaforth's plans to launch Ticket Window Lite, which can be used directly from a Web browser. "We see the market dividing into two," Mr Hance says. "We're keen to develop the big corporate business with existing software but we believe Ticket Window Lite will be more for the casual user wanting to make business or leisure bookings."

www.seaforths.com

There are options:

- Provide such a good service that your supplier does not want to cut you out.
- Provide an online service that lives alongside your supplier's direct selling efforts (see Seaforths case study, page 214)
- Work out a joint venture, where for example the supplier takes the order and you supply and provides after-sales back-up (see 7.2.3)

The strange case of the estate agent

Estate agents are the ultimate intermediary – providing what seems to many to be a modest service for a substantial fee. Surely if the Internet does for any intermediary it will be the estate agent? After all, the Web is a great matching mechanism, so why can buyers and sellers not find each other without the help of a middleman?

So far, it has not happened and, if the experience of the US is a good one, it will not – at least not for a long time. There are two reasons:

- Estate agents spotted early that they were at risk of being "disintermediated" (cut out), and started to move online. Some, such as Ascot-based Chancellors (www.chancellors.co.uk) set up their own sites, which are updated with new properties every day. Others clustered together on one of the many affinity sites that sprang up (see 5.8.3 for an explanation of an affiliate site). Internet Property Finder (www.propertyfinder.co.uk) is run by ex-estate

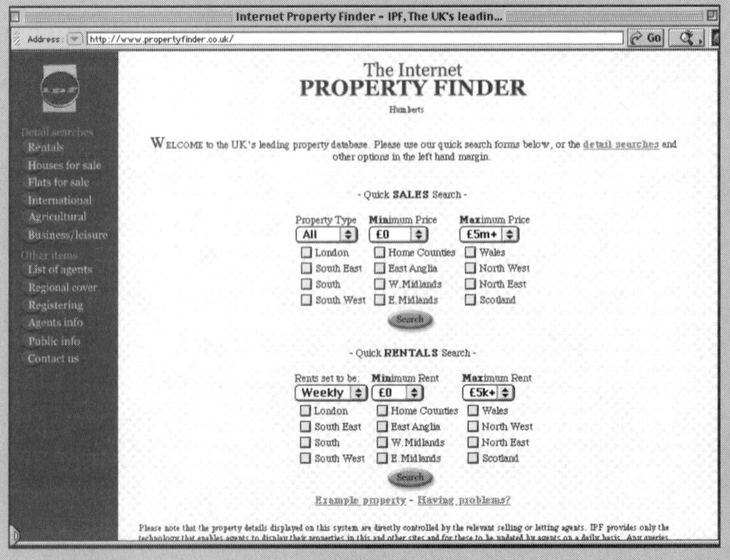

- Look for a new role. Consider what other services the customer will need, even if he does not buy a product or service directly from you. Can you deliver? Can you sell accessories? Can you offer financing? Etcetera.

agents from an office in Thurso, and includes many of the prestigious London-based groups.

These sites offer interactive searching. Specify location, bedrooms, price etc, and they will generate a selection of properties. Because of this, their success depends on the number of properties they can offer – they must be able to compete with a high street full of agents to be considered serious. Consolidation seems likely, with a handful of affiliate sites covering the country: in the US, one site alone (www.realtor.com) has1.3 m properties listed.

- Private sales over the Internet are growing, but not exploding. The US site Owners.com (www.owners.com) has 200,000 properties listed after three and a half years, even though agents' commissions are much higher there than in the UK. In the UK a handful of sites offer private sales: UK PropertyGold (www.ukpg.co.uk) has a sprinkling among its database of new houses, while Property Broker (www.propertybroker.co.uk) is growing fast, but in the summer of 1999 still had only 150 properties listed.

Will this change? The industry is certainly not sanguine. Property Broker has complained that newspapers refused to take its advertisements, and the estate agents sites are getting more sophisticated. In the US agents who act on behalf of the purchaser are finding a new role for the Web – they take a video of a property, and load it onto a Web site for their clients to view. Ultimately, though, the take-up of direct house sales will depend on the attitudes of the buying public. Perhaps we will decide we do like estate agents after all.

Chapter 8 Selling: the practicalities

There is no secret behind a good selling site – it is simply a matter of applying rigorous common sense, and great attention to detail (8.1). Because of the plethora of options, you need to think hard before choosing the right catalogue and payment software, and setting it up properly (8.2). How secure is e-commerce? See 8.3. The all-important fulfilment end is again a matter of good planning and getting the detail right (8.4). And if, as is likely, you expect to receive orders from overseas you need to be able to handle issues such as tax, shipping, currency and languages (8.5). Finally, don't forget that the Web is only one part of the Internet. A lively international trade takes place through newsgroups and other bulletin boards (8.5.6).

8.1 The Web site

Transactional Web sites should be easier to set up than non-transactional ones, because they have a clear job to do. But all too many sites make the process of buying so difficult or unappealing that potential customers turn round and, as it were, walk out of the door.

The process of building a site has been made much easier by the proliferation of electronic commerce software. These packages normally include a secure credit card payment system and a catalogue – a computer database that sits apart from the Web site and holds product, price and other details, including perhaps photographs. A few key strokes will allow you to change any information in the catalogue.

If you want to build a functional site as cheaply as possible, DIY packages are available from a few hundred pounds (competition is so fierce that there are real bargains around). They will include templates that allow you to create a utilitarian look, with the security you need, as well as a few bells and whistles such an automatic shipping and tax calculator. With a little graphical and technical skill, you can make them visually quite attractive.

More sophisticated packages, which usually integrate visually better into a Web site, will cost a few thousand pounds, plus a few more for expert installation. At the top end are tailor-made database systems that, for example, automatically update prices as customers add new options. These will cost tens of thousands or even more. See page 234 for available options and prices.

8.1.1 Getting customers to buy

The "purchasing area" will normally stand apart from the rest of the site, linked to it by buttons. But the whole site is part of your shop. Your aim should be to nudge customers towards a purchase, making them feel as comfortable as if they were in a physical shop. An example of a selling site that presses nearly all the right buttons is The Teddington Cheese (see case study, page 222).

- Take care with the navigation. Not only must it be intuitive, it should lead visitors towards a purchase. Give the customer access to all information, but make it easier to move in the direction that will lead towards the purchase point. Highlight the links that could lead to a sale – this is the equivalent of putting up arrows in a shop saying "This way please".

- Make sure links to the purchasing area stand out, using unambiguous buttons: "Buy online" or "Buy using our secure payment system." Make it clear on the home page that customers can purchase from the site (it sounds obvious, but it is surprising how many sites do not make this clear).

- As with any shop, there will be two main types of customer: the no-nonsense buyer and the browser. Make sure you serve both. The instant buyer needs to get straight to the shop from the home page, and to make his choice as quickly as possible. The browser can be taken around a themed area of your site, or a tour of the products (a "sales journey"), then nudged gently towards the shop. Make sure a "Buy online" button is always visible, so that he can nip into the shop at any point.

One of the most successful examples of a sales journey is Carphone Warehouse (www.carphonewarehouse.com), which uses an interactive questionnaire to help potential customers choose the right network, tariff and phone. They start by putting in postcodes where they spend most time – they are told the networks that will give them the best coverage. They then put in the number of minutes they expect to use the phone per day, whether they will phone mostly local or national numbers, and whether they want voice-mail. The best tariff packages are displayed, after which they say how important weight, price and battery life is, to generate suitable phones. Then they go to the shop – and buy online.

- Make sure that browsing customers know they are making progress: tell them what the next page will be, and when they get there, tell them what it is, perhaps thanking them for their interest. Some marketing sites benefit from having way-out or even slightly confusing navigation: this is never true of a selling site.

- You may be selling to distinct groups of customers: consumers and businesses, for example. Consider sending them off on different journeys by offering options on the home page. Many of the pages visited en route will be the same, but the emphasis given to them will be different. See Dell (www.dell.co.uk) for a site that pushes all customers to the same shop, but takes them there in a number of different ways.

- Reduce impediments to purchase. Here you should follow the general guidelines in Chapter 5, but note particular points about transactional sites:

- A survey in the US found that the main reason visitors left selling sites was that they were too slow to load. The trouble is, if you are selling a range

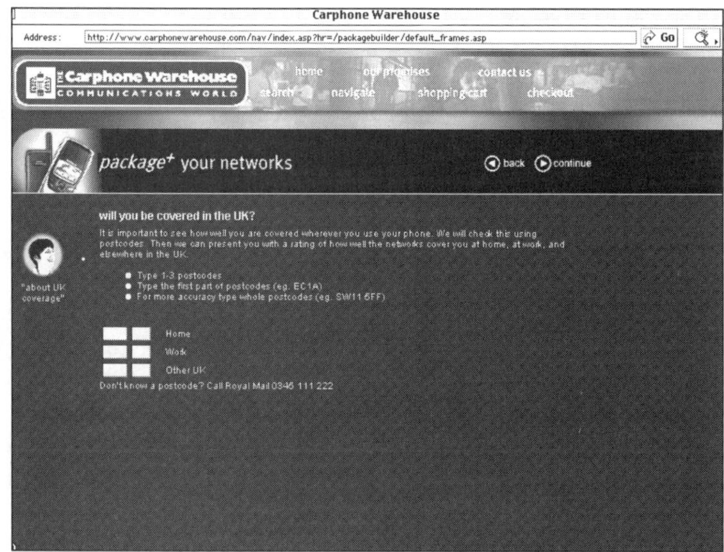

Carphone Warehouse's interactive chooser (www.carphonewarehouse.com)

of products, you will probably want to include many photographs. The answer may be to use "thumbnails" (small pictures linked to big ones – see 5.5). A high-tech version is used by Fat Face, the outdoor fashion retailer: its software allows you to zoom in on a detail of a garment – for example a button – until you can see it in remarkable detail. See www.fatface.co.uk, and for details of the software, called OpenPix Image Igniter, contact Hewlett Packard (www.hp.com).

- Make sure potential customers can get access to all the information they need, preferably without having to contact you. Include a page of questions and answers, if necessary repeating information about security, delivery etc. Space has no premium on a Web site, so you can add information over and again.

Case study: learn as you buy cheese

The Teddington Cheese started as a shop in Teddington, Middlesex, and moved into mail order in 1997. As well as using letters and catalogues, it commissioned a Web site, which was launched in October that year. It is a model of its kind: it cost £3,000 to set up, with a further £4,000 spent over the following 18 months and, the company reckons, it has increased annual turnover by 20 per cent, or about £100,000.

The site was built by the agency Axos and incorporates Shop Assistant e-commerce software (see page 237). Its home page uses a "newspaper" format to provide several short stories and titbits, with small but attractive photographs interspersed. Navigation is good, with the main site sections always in view along the top of the screen. Within the online shop, you can choose your cheese in a number of ways – the main classifications are by nationality, identified with flags down the side.

The site uses the Web's ability to store information to excellent effect with its "cheese encyclopedia". Click on the "eye" symbol next to a cheese, and you can read about its history, how it is made and what it tastes like. This makes the site a destination in its own right (unusually for a selling site): as the Encyclopaedia grows, it will be an obvious place to find out about cheeses.

- Make sure a clear e-mail address is always visible, so customers can contact you with pre-sales enquiries. It may be worth including a Call Me button – visitors type in their phone number, which is e-mailed to your office, and you then call them back. But do this only if you have the capacity to make that call immediately. Companies that use "call me" buttons include Barclays Bank (www.barclays.co.uk) and Legal & General (www.legal-and-general.co.uk) for mortgages, and KPMG (www.kpmg.co.uk) for graduate recruitment. For software, contact RealCall (www.realcall.com).

- Offer a choice of payment methods. Make sure customers do not have to put their credit card numbers over the Internet – give them the option of faxing, writing, phoning or pressing a Call Me button. Include an invoice option if appropriate.

The final (and perhaps most important) touch is The Teddington Cheesewire. This is a bi-monthly e-mail letter sent to anyone who subscribes (ie requests it) on the site. It contains a "cheese focus", describing a particular type of cheese, a recipe using the cheese, and another feature (eg on breeds of milking cow). The newsletter is interesting enough to print out and keep, and is an excellent way of keeping the retailer at the front of the consumer's mind.

www.tedding-toncheese.co.uk

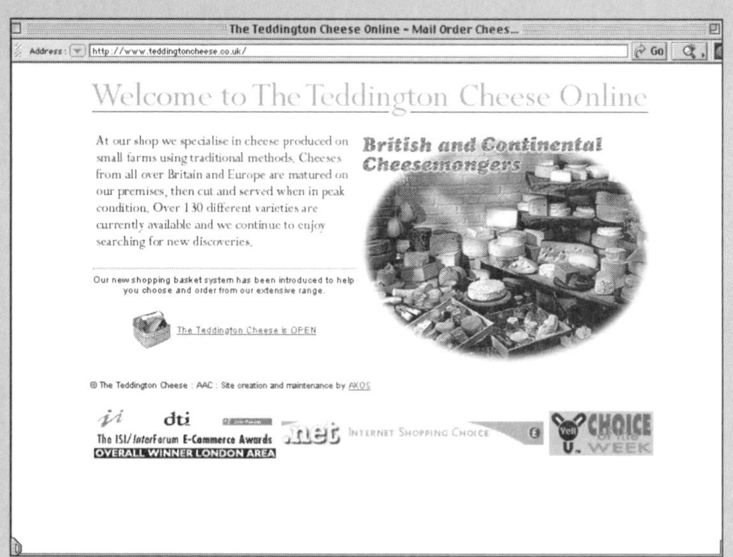

8.1.2 Inside the purchasing area

- Make sure the home page is easy-to-use and explicit. It should state clearly who are you, what products are for sale, what security system you use, and whether you deliver internationally.

- Make sure the site oozes with comforting signs. Create an "About our company" section, packed with information about your backers, turnover, background of directors etc. If you already have such a section, this is the time to expunge that photo of the finance manager drunk at the Christmas party, and replace it with an item emphasising his experience and qualifications. Put in plenty of contact details, including address, phone, fax and e-mail. Teddington Cheese (see case study, page 222) uses a pop-up window to give the company registration number, address etc.

- If you accept orders from overseas, make the site "foreigner friendly". Consider foreign language versions (8.5.4) and how to treat different currencies (8.5.5). Make sure the contact phone and fax numbers use the international dialling code (unless you want to discourage contacts from overseas). If you have a free phone number or FREEPOST address for UK customers, make sure the non-free versions are given as well.

- The order pages need more comfort yet. As well as repeating information about the security system, give delivery times, where customers can get support or complain, and what your policy on privacy and data protection is (see page 312). Include, either here or on a linked page, full shipping price and tax information – this can be complex (see 8.5.1), so make it clear. Repeat the contact details. Customers may never use your postal address or fax, but they want to know there is a "you" to whom they can complain.

- Allow enough space in the form for all possible details, including special instructions about delivery. Unless your product is being sent by post, ask where it should be left if the customer is out. And do not insist on being given nonsensical details: Londoners will only be irritated by forms that insist on the inclusion of a county (London is not in any county). A little thought here can make it much easier for you and your customers later on.

- Do not use the order page to demand additional information – it will irritate the buyer in a hurry. Limit extra questions to two or three, and do not make them compulsory (see 5.2.4 – Getting more detailed information).

- Put yourself in the position of the customers, and try to fulfil their every whim. Make sure they can send to other addresses. If your product is suitable, consider offering a gift-wrapping service (retailers such as www.amazon.co.uk provide pictures of different patterns).

- In the payment section, make clear what options you accept. Can customers pay by invoice as well as credit card? If you accept international orders, provide a way they can work out the price in their own currency (8.5.5). When they fill in the order form, make sure it does not insist on a particular format (see 5.2.4 – What should a registration form include?).

- Make it clear on the payment form how much tax customers will be paying, and what the shipping charge will be. Tax is particularly tricky. Typically you will be charging VAT to EU customers, but not to others. The shopping system should provide a box for non-EU customers to tick, so they do not get charged. Take care where there are complications, eg selling books (which have zero VAT in the UK, but not in other EU countries). And provide a link to the page explaining tax and shipping charges. See 8.5.1 for more on tax.

8.1.3 Business-to-business sites

The differences between business-to-business and business-to-consumer selling are far less obvious online than they are in the real world. The sites look similar, they list products on similar computerised databases and they have similar payment systems.

A corollary of this is that companies that have traditionally been trade-only are seeing more of their revenue coming from retail orders (eg RS Components, see case study, page 226).

These orders can be a nuisance because they tend to be smaller, but does this mean companies should actively discourage them? It is possible, certainly: they could demand VAT numbers, or sell only to companies that have set up

Case study: Components of business-to-business growth

RS Components, a subsidiary of Electrocomponents, is one of Europe's leading distributors of electrical and electronic components. In March 1998 it launched one of the first big business-to-business selling Web sites – it is still regarded as a standard for others to follow.

RS has an ideal profile for going on to the Web. First, it is a direct selling operation with a well-honed delivery system – orders placed before 8pm are despatched the same day. Second, it sells to a technical market where Internet penetration is very high.

RS's main channel has always been a printed catalogue, produced every four months and now listing 100,000 lines. To help customers cope more easily with this volume, it launched a CD-Rom in 1994: take-up was massive, which encouraged the company to look at the then-embryonic Web.

It was further stimulated by evidence of an emerging threat. "In 1996 we watched with growing interest and concern the growth of a new online service to industry called Industry.net," says Dave Sones, RS Components' technical director. "Customers could roam round the site, or use a search engine to locate specific products. Over the months Industry.net attracted many of the world's top manufacturers and distributors. It was around that time that a new word appeared: 'disintermediation'. It made us think hard about how the market might change."

After going to the US to examine the state of the art – which included consumer-facing sites such as Amazon and Dell – Mr Sones and his colleagues developed the site they thought they needed. "Our research showed that customers have a tendency to become familiar with only a few sections of the catalogue they use regularly," he says. To replicate this on the site, RS decided it needed to use "personalisation" software (see 5.2.5).

The site was launched in March 1998 and 18 months later had 100,000 registered users. Of these something under 5 per cent were end consumers, a market that had previously not been tapped.

The site's Broadvision personalisation system means that when customers enter for the first time, they are asked to register and fill in the types of products they are interested in. When they return, the site has been "personalised" – the home page has been geared towards these products, offering easy access to parts of the catalogue they are interested in, and perhaps making them special offers.

The site also carries 10,000 technical and other manuals in Adobe Acrobat format (see 5.2.7, formatting), which customers can download and print out. RS had to scan them in to the system to start with, but having done that has saved on the costs of sending out printed versions.

It has also been assiduous in its attempts to drive visitors to the site – in one campaign, people who registered were sent a letter (in the post) saying they would receive a free universal key if they made a purchase from the site.

RS believes it will eventually be able to drop its printed catalogue. Mr Sones said he could not predict when, but that "at some point we must come to an economic breakpoint where it is no longer feasible." He does however predict that the paper version will outlast the CD-Rom, which will lose its appeal when the Internet is fast enough to load graphics rapidly.

Although RS is aware that it could still theoretically be "disintermediated" by its suppliers selling directly online, it believes the structure of the components industry makes this unlikely. It has 1,200 suppliers, very few of which are geared up to sell online, and which would certainly not welcome a flood of small orders.

www.rswww.com
www.industry.net
www.broadvision.com

accounts, or they could set a minimum value or volume to orders.
But most companies have decided that an order is an order. And often they will be glad they did: many new customers will check a merchant out with a small order then, if they are pleased, come back with much bigger demands.

8.2 Choosing a payment system

When the first selling sites appeared on the Internet, their owners did not have to think too hard about the payment mechanism they used. There were no credit card encryption systems, so they had a limited choice: they could ask customers to send credit card numbers unencrypted by e-mail, or they could finish the order conventionally, by phone or fax.

Now a plethora of systems aim to get you selling online. The competition is good news for your wallet, but not for your brain. You will have to make several choices including

- what bank to use – the e-commerce support offered by banks varies, so you may find yourself moving away from your main clearer.

- what shopping software to use (this includes your catalogue and a credit card encryption system).

- whether to use a payment processing company to clear credit cards online, and if so, which one.

Here are a number of questions that should help potential merchants pick the right path – but do not settle on one element (bank, software, processing company) before you have decided all three. Some combination of banks, shopping software and processing companies work well. Others do not.

8.2.1 Do you want to take credit card numbers over the Internet at all?

It is generally accepted that whatever the potential risks of the Internet, the level of reported crime is minimal (see 8.5). But reality is almost irrelevant here – what matters is customer perception, so the real issue is a marketing one. If you are selling to a young audience, you must take cards online: buyers will think there is something wrong if you do not. But if your target is older (and the average age of Internet user is climbing steadily), it may be sensible to offer a phone or fax service.

You will certainly lose no business by offering a choice. Options include

- giving a phone number customers can ring. Few people are concerned about giving their card number over the phone, and they may want to ask extra questions before deciding exactly what to buy.

- providing a form customers can fill out, print and send by post or fax, complete with card number (or cheque).

- saying you will take the order by e-mail, but not the credit card details. You can then either ring the customer to get these details, or send a confirmatory fax, on which he can fill in his card number. He will then fax or post it back to you.

8.2.2 Do you already have an arrangement with a bank to take credit cards?

If so, you should be able to accept them through your Web site. But you may have to talk to banks other than your own. Not only are there very different levels of enthusiasm and understanding of electronic commerce among the clearers, the services they offer vary. Talk to your bank to see what services it offers – you will soon gauge both its enthusiasm and its ability to help.

Although you have an existing credit card merchant number, you will need an e-commerce or Internet merchant ID (this allows banks to track Internet transactions). There is a temptation, if you already have a “Cardholder Not Present” (CNP) arrangement, to forget about this – the bank cannot after all tell whether a credit card number on a CNP slip has come by phone, fax or Internet. But you may be breaking the terms of your merchant agreement, and be caught out when there is a query.

If you do not have merchant status, there are options. The best is to apply for it – you will normally have to fill out lengthy forms and wait a few weeks, though the industry is trying to make life easier. Ask your bank – it may well, by the time you read this, have a product that makes the process easier.

If merchant status is not approved (perhaps because you have not been trading for long enough), you will have to find someone who will take the risk on your behalf. Some organisations that are approved by the banks do this – though of course they charge you for the privilege. Netbanx, a payment processing company (see below) offers Bureau Merchant Status – it becomes the merchant and takes on the risk. You will have to pay Netbanx 5 per cent commission (on top of a bank charge of around 4 per cent), so you will have to work out if you can bear a near 10 per cent loss on each transaction. You will also get money from transactions monthly, rather than after three days. If you are talking to the other processors, or to a bank, ask if it has a similar arrangement (new products and services are appearingregularly in this field).

8.2.3 Do you anticipate low volumes of Internet sales, at least at first?

You will need "catalogue" software, which will let you take orders and receive credit card payments online. You should be able to clear these payments conventionally, by phone, so you do not need to sign up with a payment processing company (unless you are despatching products immediately – ie down the line. See the next section if you are).

Catalogue software combines ordering and payment functions, and can be used as the basis of a complete Web site. Some products are DIY – one claims you can get a selling site up and running within an hour. The more sophisticated catalogues will normally be installed by a Web design company or Internet Service Provider. Costs range from £200 to tens of thousands, once installation is included. See the box on page 234 for a description of some of the catalogues available.

Whatever the cost, catalogues offer the same basic functions, usually mimicking a physical shop. When a customer goes into your shop, he will click on an item he wants to buy. This will be added to a "shopping basket", which keeps tab of his purchases. When he has finished buying, he clicks on a button that takes him to the "check out". Here the shipping cost and tax will automatically be added. He fills in his name and address and, if he wants to pay by credit card, is passed through to a "secure area", where he fills in his card details. These are encrypted (see 8.5) and sent to you, the merchant.

Typically, the first you will know is when you receive an e-mail saying that an order (or a batch of orders) has been received on your site. You open up the catalogue's administration program, and take details of the order. The customer's credit card number will be now be "in clear", so you should delete it as soon as you have transferred the details. You fill in the credit card slip as you would for any "cardholder not present" transaction, ring merchant services for authorisation, ship the product and, in due course, pay the slip into your bank.

The catalogue software will also provide extra services to help your accounting – it will print out invoices and credit card schedules, for example.

8.2.4 Are you anticipating significant business online?

You should consider two areas. First, choose the right catalogue (see 8.2.3, above and box, page 234). A low-cost system may do the job, but you will get more flexibility from heavyweight offerings, for example those from Intershop. These will have more features than the low-end versions, and will also allow you more flexibility in what the site looks like. These are not normally DIY installations: they will be built into a Web site by a "partner", probably a Web consultant, Internet Service Provider or a specialist electronic commerce consultancy.

Second, you should talk to a payment processing company (sometimes called a payment solutions provider). These make life easier by authenticating credit cards as orders are made, so you do not have to clear the numbers by phone. They are essential if you are selling a digital product (eg information, music, software) that you want to despatch immediately.

Payment processing systems automatically link into one or more of the authorisation systems run by the banks, and check that the card is not reported stolen, and has an adequate credit limit. They are, in other words, just like the swipe machines used in restaurants. They do not provide complete pro-

Case study: Weaving a complex tartan web

The problems of making a selling site work properly held back a site that should, on paper at least, have been a perfect fit with the Web.

House of Tartan started selling kilts, shawls, scarves and hats, in 1996. Blair Urquhart, a photographer and tartan expert turned programmer, had already written software that could "build up" 17,500 tartans on screen, and realised he could use this as the basis for an Internet selling operation.

He believed that there would be great interest in the States, where millions can claim Scottish ancestry, and set about setting up his supply chain – consisting of a number of (very low tech) tartan manufacturers, who would make the tartans to order, and a delivery system outsourced to one of the big couriers.

Mr Urquhart did not go down the venture capital route, instead working hard to make a profit. And it was hard work. It took two and a half years before his numbers went firmly into the black, during which time he had do "quite a lot of streamlining," including moving to a smaller office. "It was slower to take off than we thought," he concedes.

The main problem was not customer take-up, but getting the site working smoothly. "We under-estimated the time it would take to put together the database and present it on the Internet." House of Tartan's database is complex, because it has to offer several products in 400 variations. "Getting all this stuff error-free is incredibly complicated," he says.

Although the site has been running since 1996, it was operated "manually" until last summer – that is, changes had to be made individually to each page. With 9,000 product variations, this was immensely time-consuming.

But after a year's work, Mr Urquhart's team managed to get the iCAT shopping catalogue system running smoothly. It is proving better for customers, who can now search for products using several criteria, and much better for the company, because so much of the process is automated and data needs to be entered only once. (The iCAT Publisher system, which was used, is no longer available, though the Intershop Merchant system [see box on catalogues, page 236] is similar.)

The success of the system is reflected in the fact that revenue has been increasing even though visitor numbers have been stable. Mr Urquhart says that an increase in product range seems to lead to an immediate increase in sales. “The more choice there is, the more customers can be satisfied,” he says.

Seventy per cent of his customers come from the US, and Mr Urquhart says he aims to provide the sort of personal service that is still found in some American shops. “It’s the kind that doesn’t exist any more here – where they sit you down and give you a cup of tea.” He says he has built up telephone and e-mail relationships with many customers – relationships that often start when a mistake is made on an order form that needs to be clarified.

www.house-of-tartan.scotland.net

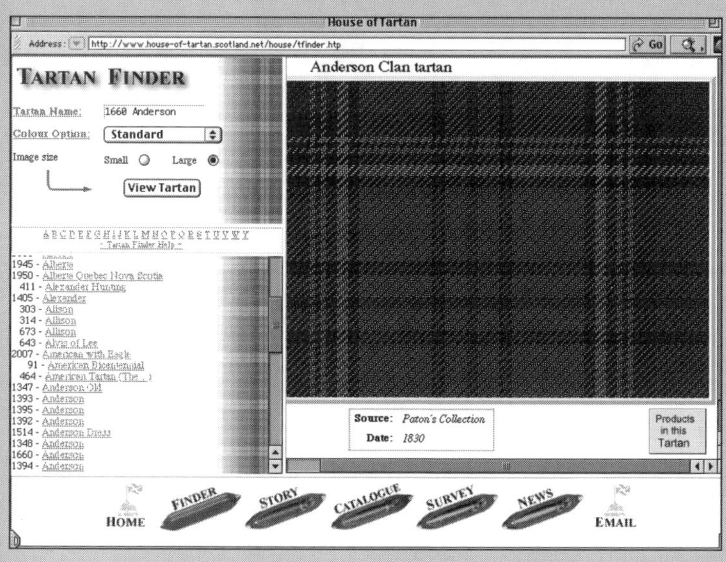

tection against fraud, because the card may have been stolen recently, and it is also impossible to stop users "charging back" the payment (see 8.4). But they are about as safe as any card checking system, and may well be enhanced by software that, for example, spots if the card has been used several times on the same site.

There is massive activity in the payment processing field, so new ones are likely to appear. In late 1999 the main ones are Netbanx

Shopping catalogues – the choice

It appears to be huge, but it is not quite as big as it seems. Many apparently new products are in fact rebadged versions of other packages.

If you are offered a package you have not heard of, ask what the underlying software is. And look at the software companies' Web sites – they will have demonstrations, and perhaps links to real users of their systems.

Nevertheless you should do plenty of homework before settling on a package.

Here are some questions:

- Has the package been approved by the bank you want to work with? Banks run security checks on all systems, and they may not have cleared them all.

- Will the package work with the payment processor you want to use? Check on the payment processor's site (see 8.2.4, above).

- Are you starting a site from scratch? Consider one of the "hosted stores" such as IBM HomePage Creator or Shop Assistant. These are easy to build and sit securely on a computer dedicated to such sites.

- Do you want to add a selling facility to your own site? See if your hosting company has an e-commerce system. But use it only if it suits your other needs. Otherwise choose one of the non-hosted systems.

(www.netbanx.co.uk), DataCash (www.datacash.com), WorldPay (www.worldpay.com) and ePDQ (run by Barclays at www.epdq.co.uk). If you are expecting substantial sales from overseas, check they allow you to offer a multicurrency option.

It is worth doing a good deal of research before choosing the right payment processor, because not all work with all banks, or with all catalogue software. The processors' companies' sites are full of useful information –

- Is the lowest possible price your priority? Choose a very simple DIY system such as IBM HomePage Creator (see below) or NetStart (www.net start-online.com).

- Is cash flow an issue? Some packages have an upfront price, others work on monthly payments. Don't forget that unless you do a DIY installation, you will have to pay a consultant or Web designer to install and integrate it.

- Did you build your own site? If so, you should be able to install one of the less complex standalone packages such as Actinic or ShopCreator. You should also be able to tweak packages to make them more visually attractive

- Do you want to do whatever is least troublesome? See if your ISP, hosting service or consultant has an arrangement to install a particular package. The advantage is that it will should work smoothly: .If a consultant or designer has a licence to install some of the more sophisticated packages, it should mean he has been properly trained. If you use a system backed by your hosting company, you can be reasonably sure there will be no glitches

- Do you want an online shop that can grow easily? Do not go for an option at the very bottom end. You will only have to start again later.

See next page for a run-down of the products.

Some of the better-known catalogues:

Intershop (www.intershop.co.uk)

Products include:

e-pages: ISPs will typically buy a licence and offer this system, which allows them to build up pages on set templates, to business clients. Prices range from £20 to £50 a month depending on the number of products and amount of Web space needed.

Intershop Hosting/Intershop Merchant: a sophisticated system for larger transactional sites. Intershop Hosting, where the site is maintained on an ISP's server, costs £250 per month. Intershop Merchant has a once-off price tag of £3,000 – you host and maintain it yourself.

iCat – Web Store and Commerce Cart (www.icat.com)

ICat Web Store is for companies without a site. You build one from scratch using one of its templates, add your own product information and logos, and select payment and shipping options from the ones accepted by the iCat system. The fee includes hosting on one of iCat's secure servers.

ICat Commerce Cart is for companies that already have a Web site, and want to add an electronic commerce facility. The commerce cart is hosted on iCat's servers, with links to your existing site. You maintain your site through a Web browser.

Both iCat packages start at £6 per month for up to 10 items displayed. This climbs to £155 per month for up to 1,000 items.

Beyond this, iCat will assemble a bespoke package for your company.

The package also includes "marketing" services such as order and tracking reports, and search engine visibility reports.

IBM – Homepage Creator (www.ibm.com/hpc/uk)

A do-it-yourself system that lets you build an all-in-one e-commerce package consisting of Web site, payment and delivery. You add your logos, pictures and product information. It will be hosted on an IBM server as part of the deal, and Parcelforce will deliver your products. You pay monthly, depending on the size of the catalogue. Packages start at £15 per month with a £15 set-up fee. This will get you a 12-item catalogue and 3MB storage space, hosted on IBM's servers. You can increase this to 500 items and 30MB storage, at which point you will be paying £120 a month. 30-day free trial available to download.

Shopcreator (www.shopcreator.co.uk)

Another hosted store system. Build your site from a template. Additional services include a daily updating with the search engines, so your site should be easy to find. Costs go from £10 a month for a 10-item store to £750 a month for 50,000 items.

Shop@ssistant (www.shopassistant.net)

Shop@ssistant fits into existing Web sites to create an online store that can carry any number of items. It includes in-built VAT and shipping calculators, and the ability to apply discounts and make special offers. A multi-currency version is available. It costs £199.

Actinic Catalog 3 (www.actinic.co.uk)

Actinic Catalog is a well-specified system that fits into a Web site and will also integrate with an existing product database. There is no limit on the number of products in the catalogue. It can be installed by a reasonably competent amateur, who can customise the template with his own design work. Actinic can use standard SSL security, but also offers a more secure Java-based encryption system (see 8.3).

including which banks and which catalogue software they can run alongside. The processing companies offer a variety of extra services. For example Datacash has a fast track merchant status application system, while NetBanx lets you build your own e-commerce site from scratch, using a service called NetStart. They will also build tailor-made catalogues for those who need something out of the ordinary.

8.2.5 What will it cost?

This is where you must get the calculator out, to work out the fixed and variable costs. There are three possible elements: the catalogue software cost, the payments solution provider charge, and the bank fee. The good news is that competition means they are more likely to go down than up.

Catalogues: costs range from £200 to several thousand pounds. Some are straightforward off-the-shelf packages. See box for guidelines – but don't forget to add designers fees. Catalogues can be very fiddly to install, and will take a good deal of work before they fit seamlessly into your site (See House of Tartan case study, page 232). Add £2,000 at least for installation of a medium-sized system.

Payment processing: tricky, because companies use different mixes of fixed and variable pricing. To show the complexity, these are the charges from DataCash, Netbanx and ePDQ (they may well have changed, so check):

DataCash: £600 a year, plus £100 a month for the first 1,000 payment requests and £75 for each additional thousand.

Netbanx: up to £500 a year upfront. Then three plans: 9 per cent of each transaction for the Bureau scheme (where you do not have merchant status); 1 per cent plus the bank charge, but with a minimum of £100 per month revenue for Netbanx (ie turnover of at least £10,000 a month); and a fixed rate of 50p per transaction, but only if transaction values are at least £50, and with minimum monthly revenue for Netbanx of £100 (ie 200 transactions).

Epdq: Set up fee of £500. Monthly fee of £40. Transaction fee starts at 3 per cent of the transaction, reducing to 1 per cent if business grows sufficiently.

Case study: two DIY selling sites

Proops Educational Packages

Stephen Proops of Proops Educational Packages built his own store using Shop@ssistant because he couldn't afford the fees, "which ran into thousands of pounds", quoted by agencies. Proops sells educational devices to schools – everything from hovercraft kits to gears, pulleys, motors and switches.

He is not particularly computer literate but taught himself to use Shop@assistant in a weekend. "For the basic design of the site I used Microsoft's Front Page product and 'cut and pasted' bits from other sites on the Internet – with the owners' permission, of course! It takes a bit of time to get your head around the structure but the helpline at Shop@assistant was brilliant. I'd recommend anybody to have a go themselves. It certainly saves a small fortune in agency fees."

www.proops.com

Battersea Pen Home (See main case study, page 200)

Having been quoted thousands of pounds by agencies, owner Simon Gray opted to do the initial design of the site himself. He chose Microsoft's popular Web design package, Front Page "which took about ten days to learn – and I'm not a techie." The overall set-up cost was under £1,000, which included the first year's Web hosting costs, registering a Web address and an e-mail account.

The site takes credit card details using a link to a secure server run by Mallpark Inc (www.mallpark.com) which hosts and stores order forms and credit card numbers securely for $120 a year. When a customer clicks on the order form button on the Pen Home site he is actually transferred to the secure US site. Gray retrieves the orders and credit card details every day and processes them offline.

www.penhome.co.uk

There are various deals bundling catalogues with a payment processing service. For example Actinic and Netbanx will cost £500 to set up as a package.

Bank: The charge depends on volume and the bank's view of your risk: between 2 and 4 per cent a transaction will be typical.

8.3 How secure is electronic commerce?

As we pointed out in Chapter 3 (page 94), electronic commerce fraud is only one of the risks associated with the Internet. We also noted that it is very difficult to say how widespread it is. The truth is, first, that security is still a big worry for the public. As IDC said in a report *Electronic Commerce in the UK* "the security of the Internet is the main issue that has held back electronic commerce development, particularly in the business-to-consumer market. The concern has to do with the transmission of credit card details and the potential for data to fall in the wrong hands."

Second, public concerns are not entirely misplaced. The Internet is by its nature insecure, because it runs over the public phone network. But a huge amount of effort has gone into making it safer, and it seems likely that much Internet fraud has taken place where basic controls have not been in place. This is probably a result of a somewhat devil-may-care culture in the US, where many online retailers still ask customers to send credit cards unscrambled. At the other extreme Scandinavians are very wary of giving card numbers online, while the Germans tend to shun plastic entirely. The UK is somewhere in the middle – we have a rather relaxed attitude to credit card security (how often does a shopkeeper scrutinise your signature when you hand a card over?), but few British Internet users are happy giving out their card numbers online without some protection.

Third, and most important for merchants, it is they - not the customers - who are the most likely targets of fraud. With care they can avoid losing money - but there is no shortage of people attempting to do them down.

Before getting onto the issues of encryption, it is worth noting that the Internet itself is only part of the security chain:

- Most security breaches take place within companies, by staff who take information from the network (this tends to be a big company problem, but is worth noting).

- If you take credit card numbers online, they will probably at some stage be stored "in clear" on one of your computers. Ideally this computer should be off the company network, and protected by passwords. It may still be at risk from hackers using the Internet to search its hard disk using cyberwoozles (see page 94), or even by pretending to be your Internet Service Provider. Most hackers do such things for the heck of it, but as the figures going across the Internet rise, it seems likely that genuinely criminal hackers (perhaps working for organised crime) will be used to pick as many fruits as they can.

- The best solution is to make sure credit card numbers are stored for the minimum time: erase them as soon as they have been given to your accounts people (whose computer should not be connected to the Internet or, ideally, to the company network).

If you set yourself up as an online merchant (or if you are buying online), these are the main risks:

- Confidentiality – has anyone seen the information as it travelled?
- Integrity – has the message been changed en route?
- Authentication – how do you know the person at the other end is who they say they are?
- Non-repudiation – what can you do if the other party denies having done a deal?

The first three are tackled by a standard set of "protocols" built into Web browsers and e-mail programs. These are called Secure Socket Layer (SSL) for the Web, and S/MIME for e-mail (a system designed to replace SSL, Secure Electronic Transaction [SET] has yet to get much momentum). The fourth, non-repudiation, is partly a technical and partly a legal problem. It is potentially the most tricky area (see below for more).

SSL and S/MIME use a system called public key/private key encryption to scramble the message, to check it has not been changed, and to make sure that only the right person (or rather computer) can unscramble it. Public key/private key means that the message is encrypted using one key (an algorithm or mathematical formula combined with a very long number), but can only be decrypted using a different one.

To see how this works, go into a Web site that uses SSL – an online retailer for example – and follow the process for buying something. At some stage you will be told you are about to enter a secure area. Before saying OK, look at the bottom of the screen: you will see an unlocked padlock (or perhaps a broken key). Click OK, and look at the padlock or key on the next page – it should have closed up. By moving your cursor over the padlock (or clicking on it), you should see the message "SSL 40 bit encryption" or similar.

What happens then? Your browser has been sent a copy of the merchant's "public key". When you fill in your credit card details, they are automatically encrypted using this key, and sent to the merchant over the Internet. His server holds the private key, which meshes together with the public key to unscramble the information. The two keys are derived from the same source using complex maths, in a way that makes it impossible to guess the one by seeing the other.

The clever thing about this is that the critical element in decryption, the private key, is never sent over the Internet – it sits on the merchant's server, protected by a "firewall" against hacking. It is as though a door can be locked by a key hanging by the door handle, but can only be unlocked by another key, which is kept in a strong box.
SSL and S/SMIME cover:

- confidentiality, because the message is scrambled
- non-interference, because the message can be checked for integrity when it arrives
- authentication, because only the right computer can unscramble it.

There are however potential problems:

Encryption strength: When you see a message saying the SSL strength is 40 bit, you know that a PIN 40 digits long is being used. If you were in the US (or using a US "non-export browser"), you would see a message saying it is

56 or 128 bit. That is because the US government wants to stop criminals or foreigners encrypting messages in a way that it cannot read: cracking a message encrypted at 40 bits would, according to one security expert, "be a lunchtime task for a cryptography class" (though this of course makes it quite impossible for the average criminal). The standard in US browsers, 56 bit, is vastly more secure, because each increase of one implies a doubling of encryption strength. It has been broken only by experts connecting to very high powered computers and crunching away. 128 bit encryption, licensed by the US government on a case by case basis to banks, is highly secure.

The level of encryption used depends both on the system installed in the merchant's server, and the customer's browser. Anyone outside the US using a Netscape or Internet Explorer browser will not, normally, be able to get more than 40 bit, regardless of the server's ability. The exception is if the merchant has negotiated a special arrangement with the US government. Washington's line on this has been softening gradually: it is already possible for non-US merchants to "step up" from 40 bit to 56 bit, and some non-US banks (including Barclays) are able to offer 128 bit encyrption, though they have to go through hoops to do so. If you are unhappy with offering 40 bit encryption, contact Verisign (www.verisign.com), which administrates "step up cryptography".

Should you be worried if you are selling products using 40 bit encryption? Not unless they are worth thousands of pounds – it just isn't worth a criminal's time breaking into a system that will yield a few orders at £10 a time.

Identification

Although you can be fairly sure with SSL that the right *computer* has opened the message, you cannot be sure that the right *person* has. If a small time crook steals someone's credit card, he can pretend to be that person and order goods online. The online crook has a more challenging task – to masquerade as a merchant by giving himself the same Internet Protocol (IP) address so that credit card details come to him. He can then send his own public key to the buyer, who sends a credit card number that can be unlocked with his private key. If you are the merchant, it is alarming to know that it is theoretically possible for someone to masquerade as you, and take money that should be yours. To gain real security, therefore, it is not the identity of the computer but that of the user that needs verifying. The answer should lie with digital certificates (see below).

Non-repudiation

Non-repudiation is not tackled by SSL or S/MIME, and is likely to become the big issue. Visa said in 1999 that an alarming number of transactions made using its cards were "charged back" – that is, the customer revoked the deal, and the card company took the money back from the merchant. Where it is a case of the customer's word against the merchant's, the card company will normally give the customer the benefit of the doubt.

This issue is going to get much more serious when big numbers start being transferred over the Net. While people are sending a few pounds over the Internet to pay for a book or a CD, it does not matter enormously if there is a misunderstanding (deliberate or otherwise) about whether the order was sent. But if they start placing big contracts, or buying large numbers of shares, over the Internet, non-repudiation becomes a major issue. Suppose you have placed an online order for £100,000 worth of sproggets with a Russian company – the sproggets do not arrive, and the Russians claim they have never received the order. What do you do? Or, suppose a customer claims to have placed an order you never received: you demand proof, but what can that be?

Some e-mail software (for example Eudora) can be set up to ask for a receipt: the message will arrive with a note: "the sender has requested you acknowledge receipt – click here." This is however weak proof if you are in a court of law, as you will not be able to prove the content of the message (see 2.1.5 for more on e-mail security).

An attempted solution is Secure Electronic Transactions (SET), which was developed by Visa and others, and which provides non-repudiation as well as a formidable array of security devices. SET has failed to take off in most of the world, mainly because it is too complex and therefore too slow. Also, it is relevant only for credit card transactions, when there is demand for security for all sorts of transfers (including e-mail messages).

SET includes a digital certificate, and it is this – stripped of the extraneous functions that makes SET so slow – that looks set to solve most security issues. Around 65,000 merchants use the digital certificate system offered by Verisign, the world leader. Combined with SSL encryption, it provides great comfort – not least proof that a particular transaction has taken place. If the customer denies that he has bought something, credit card companies are likely to charge the amount back to the merchant. If the merchant signs his messages with a digital certificate, he can offer "date-stamped" evidence that he sent a particular message at a particular time. Disputes of this sort have yet to be tested in the courts, but the certificate must at least tip the legal balance in the favour of the merchant (See page 315).

To run a digital certificate based service, online merchants must install the right software on their server (the computer where their Web site is based). They then select which certification authority (CA) they want to use. BT's Trustwise, based on Verisign, is available for a 14 day free evaluation from www.trustwise.com. The CA will check your right to use the name you give in your request – one check will be via your Dun & Bradstreet D-U-N-S number. You will also need a valid domain name. A few days later you should be authorised to use the system, and you can install a Secure Server ID.

In the next year or two we will be using digital certificates stored on smart cards, plastic cards with computer chips on them. But that is to look into the future: see End Note, page 287.

For an end user's guide to obtaining a digital certificate, see page 36.

8.4 Getting the fulfilment right

If you want to sell things through the Internet, you will soon find people taking a close interest in your back end. This, sadly, is simply the jargon for fulfilment of the order: the Web site, where the order is taken, is the front end.

It is usually more difficult to get the back right than the front, because there are no packaged "solutions" to help you when it comes acknowledging, packing and delivering the product.

The back end starts as soon as the order has left the Web site. When an order comes in, acknowledge it immediately, repeating the important details. And when the goods are despatched, send an e-mail telling the customer. Automated software can do this – but this is not necessarily a good idea. Elizabeth Botham, a Whitby baker (www.botham.co.uk), has a successful Internet sales operation based on personal messages sent by the managing director, Mike Jarman (see case study below).

You will in any event need staff who are detailed to answer queries and com-

Case study: what a little care can do

Elizabeth Botham, a baker's shop in Whitby, has earned useful extra income and immeasurable publicity from its Web site. Mike Jarman, the managing director and master baker, decided to set up the site in 1995. Because it was one of the first British companies to sell from a Web site, it attracted great interest – so much so that Mr Jarman has now diversified into Web site design through his company WebArt (www.webart.co.uk).

His site gets very busy before Christmas, and Botham's is kept busy sending bread, cakes and hampers all over the world. For the rest of the year there is a steadily growing stream of orders, "but I'm never going to go an expensive holiday because of it," Mr Jarman says. Most customers come from the US, followed by the UK, with a spread of customers from Japan to Qatar. "People will often make a small order which is hardly worth sending," he says. "But then they'll come back a couple of months later with a huge order."

Botham's site is interesting not for the huge revenues it generates, but for the loyalty it manages to generate with a little bit of care and attention. Mr Jarman sees every message coming in, and tries to reply personally. As a result, he is the pen pal of hundreds of people around the world. If someone mentioned that their mother was ill, for example, he would ask about her the next time they placed an order. "I like the customers to get the same service as they would if they popped into the shop," he says.

This low-tech approach means the service is very flexible. When *Net Profit* carried out a fulfilment test on the site, Botham's bent over backwards to be

plaints. Prepare them well and make sure they respond within a set time. On the high speed Internet, people expect high speed service – yet it is easy for employees to let e-mails fester while they attend to constantly ringing phones. Be prepared for high volumes of e-mails: they are so easy to send, people send them on the slightest excuse.

Take every precaution to make sure orders do not go astray in your computer system. It is easy to wipe computer information by mistake – do that with order details, and you have lost goodwill, face and probably money. This

helpful, making sure the delivery arrived on the right day.

Unlike most transactional sites, Botham's also has very strong content, in the form of an educational area. The section was designed by Mr Jarman and a local teacher, and aims to tell children the story of bread in a way that fits in with the National Curriculum. But perhaps the main commercial advantage of the site is the publicity it has generated. "I hear people going past the shop, and saying 'Look there's Botham's, like on the Web' – then they would come in," he says.

www.botham.co.uk

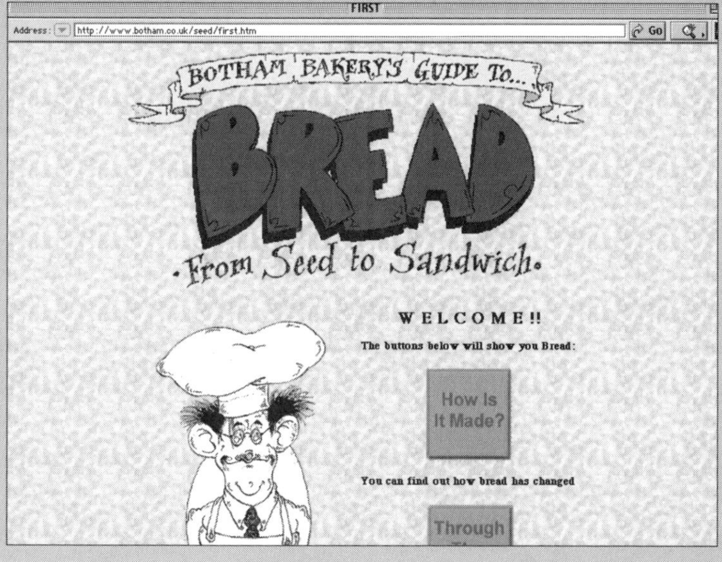

may sound obvious, but it is one of the most common disasters in electronic commerce: back up orders on disk and print everything out.

Delivery itself can be the easy part, and if you can send your product by post, it probably is. But think hard before you do this without at least offering a courier option. Because it is so easy and fast to order online, customers subconsciously expect delivery to be fast as well. “Allow 28 days for delivery” will not impress someone who has just ordered in 28 seconds.

This is particularly true if you are up against US competitors: consumer tests show that service is much better in areas such as CDs and books, where Americans compete in the UK, than in wine and flowers, where they do not.

The courier companies are gearing up to help e-commerce: they see it as an important part of their future (ironically partly because e-mail is likely to reduce their document delivery business). Parcelforce (www.parcelforce.co.uk) has joined up with IBM to produce HomePage Creator, the online selling package for smaller businesses (see page 237). Parcelforce offers the “physical” part of the package.

Federal Express (www.fedex.com) and DHL (www.dhl.co.uk) will handle more than just the delivery – they will warehouse, handle tax and carry out all sorts of services. Federal Express (www.fedex.com) takes the service furthest, offering to pack your products and even build a Web site for you (see www.uniquephoto.com for an example of this).

TNT (www.tnt.co.uk) and UPS (www.ups.co.uk) are the other big players.

If you find your online business growing, it may be worth coming to an exclusive deal with one of the couriers. For example QXL (see case study, page 266) has an arrangement with UPS that allows it to offer simplified rates, so that customers can easily see the shipping charge. Couriers all offer online package tracking – you can incorporate this into your own Web site or system, so that customers can see when your product is due to arrive.

How far should you “outsource” your fulfilment to a courier, or another company? If you are using a skilled operator like FedEx, you should get good service (though at a price). But be cautious. The Internet Bookshop (www.bookshop.co.uk) started off contracting out fulfilment to 25 bookshops. It brought it in-house when, the then chairman Darryl Mattocks said, "a customer ordered 60 books and two months later phoned rather crossly to say he had received only two." The problem was not so much the failure to deliver, Mr Mattocks noted, but that fact that no-one had told the customer what was happening. This underlines perhaps the most important point about

Case study: Delivering service

Online shops can offer lower prices than their physical rivals, but need to outshine them in terms of service and delivery. Capital Sound and Vision started out as a physical retailer 20 years ago, then moved into mail order. It has steadily lowered its cost base by processing more of its orders electronically, but also uses 100 suppliers dotted around Europe to get "the right price" for its goods and steal a march on its competitors.

"The hobbyist market is extremely price sensitive and knows when it is getting good value for quality goods," says Clive Swann, director of Capital Sound and Vision. "We only offer brand names that people can trust, and our prices are between 15 and 20 per cent lower than those on the high street. We also get in contact with them afterwards, to see if everything arrived properly. That's why people keep coming back."

Unbeatable offers to deliver anything in the UK within 24 hours. "We recently processed a £12,000 32-inch Plasma cinema screen over the Web site and delivered it to Wales the same evening," says Mr Swann. "We promise to deliver anything within a few days, and tell the person exactly when it is going to arrive."

This year the company is expecting turnover of around £12m, of which 12 to 15 per cent will be directly attributable to Web sales. Mr Swann expects this to increase to over 20 per cent in 2000, all of which will be "added revenue" created by the Web site.

Its next step is likely to be a foray into interactive TV.

www.unbeatable.co.uk

the back end – to have a properly trained, properly resourced customer service team (or at least person).

8.5 Exporting

When you set up a selling Web site, you will find yourself under pressure to export. That is simply because most users of the Internet are abroad, and sooner or later they will start asking for your products. You can of course politely decline to supply them (most US e-commerce sites refuse orders from outside North America) but the chances are you will be happy to be a "passive" exporter. You may of course want to be active – to use the Internet to push you into new markets at low cost. It can make a lot of sense: you do not have to set up an agent or distribution network, at least until you have hard evidence that a substantial market is waiting for you.

If you already export, you will be aware of the general issues surrounding

Web sites for exporters

- The DTI's site (www.dti.gov.uk) is excellent, especially its linked exporting areas (www.brittrade.com and www.tradeuk.com).
- Links to other sites around the world that can help exporters are at www.brittrade.com/emic/geolist.html.
- The Institute of Export has a database of exporters, as well as other information, at www.export.co.uk.
- The Chambers of Commerce Web site is at www.britishchambers.org: it has many useful links, and will direct you to your nearest chamber to find out about market research, documentation, languages for export. It also lists courses and seminars that may be useful.
- Business Link at www.businesslink.co.uk, has some international information, as well as details on how to contact its Export Development Counsellors.
- DHL has a section for UK exporters at www.dhl.co.uk.
- www.forworld.com has a phenomenal number of links to trade-related sites and bulletin boards.

overseas sales. If you do not, or you find yourself getting orders from unfamiliar markets, you can use the usual local channels, such as Chambers of Commerce, Department of Trade and Industry or Business Link, to get background information.

Issues for all exporters, passive or active:
- Tax (8.5.1)
- Payment (8.5.2)
- Delivery (8.5.3)

Additional issues for active exporters:
- Language (8.5.4)
- Currency (8.5.5)
- Stimulating export sales (8.5.6)

8.5.1 Tax

If you are exporting from your Web site, should you charge VAT, and if so how much? Governments are in turmoil struggling with this problem, partly because of the practicalities and partly because of ideology. Broadly, the US wants e-commerce to be tax-free, while everyone else wants it to generate tax revenue (there is healthy self-interest here: most of the companies that benefit from the growth of e-commerce are US).

In late 1998 the OECD countries, including the EU, came up with a general principle for electronic commerce – that where tax is charged, it should be paid in the country to which the product is delivered. This is designed to get round the particular problem of digital trade – how do you collect taxes on a piece of software or music being sent from one country to another?

But we should not make too much of this yet – with one exception (see 3, below), the guidelines are fairly clear, because they are derived from existing direct selling rules governing mail order exports. And for physical goods at least, most exporters will find they should charge VAT at their own home rate.

This guide draws heavily on information from Mark Dyer of Dyer Partnership (Dyer Partnership - Accounts thru Internet:

www.netaccountants.com. Tel: 01420 473473).

For VAT purposes, e-commerce can lead to three types of supplies. Each type has different tax consequences:

1 Supplies of physical goods to business or private customers: This usually involves a customer placing an order via the Internet for a product that is physically delivered, for example a book or music CD.

2 Business-to-business supplies of either services or intangible property: "Intangible property" includes "digitised goods" eg downloadable music, information or software.

3 Supplies from business to private consumers of services or intangible property.

1 Physical goods

If you are selling within the EU, you should charge VAT according to the "distance selling rules". When you start selling to a particular country, add VAT at your home rate. But if your volume of sales is sufficient to warrant VAT registration in that country, charge the import market's rate.

Where the sale is to a VAT-registered customer, the transaction usually qualifies for zero rating. You do not have to charge VAT, but you must obtain the customer's VAT number and keep documentary proof of the export of the goods.

It is important to monitor the volumes of business undertaken with each EU country. As soon as they exceed the thresholds for VAT registration, you must register, and can be punished for not doing so. You must also make sure you have administration systems capable of charging VAT at the correct rate.

If you are selling outside the EU, you do not have to charge VAT – the tax is the responsibility of the importer (though you must put the value of the shipment on the packaging). There is usually a value below which no duties will be charged – some online exporters break their shipments up in an effort to keep each below this threshold. If you want to be sure that your exports are going through the proper channels, you can ask a courier to handle the tax for you – it will do all the paper work and make sure the correct amounts are collected. You should also make clear on your Web site that the product may be subject to import tax in the customer's country.

2 Selling intangible goods to a business customer

It is almost impossible to know where a digital import has come from – but the authorities want to find someone to tax, so they look to the importing country. If you, the exporter, are registered for VAT in the target market (ie you already do a lot of business there), you will be expected to add tax at that country's rate (as with physical goods).

If you are not registered, the "reverse charge" procedure comes into play. That means it is your customer's responsibility to report the transaction, entering on its VAT return the amount that you would have charged had you been based in his market. Because the customer is VAT-registered, this will not normally mean he actually pays extra tax. If you are selling digital goods outside the EU, it is not your responsibility to add tax, and there is no realistic way the importing country can monitor it.

3 Selling intangible goods to customers who are not VAT registered

If you are registered for VAT in your customer's country, you should add VAT at the rate ruling in the customer's country (as above). But if you are not registered, the tax authorities have a problem, because private customers cannot be expected to declare and pay VAT on their purchases under the "reverse charge" procedure. A few countries have tried this – but with little success. The EU and other OECD countries are continuing to try to find a solution, but in the meantime no VAT is being collected from transactions of this sort.

As with selling intangible goods to a business customer, it is not your responsibility to add tax for sales outside the EU.

Useful reports:
Electronic Commerce UK Policy on Taxation Issues, Customs & Excise (www.coi.gov.uk - use search engine to find it)

1998 OECD conference on e-commerce tax (www.oecd.org/daf/fa/e_com/ottawa.htm)

Other useful sites:
Customs and Excise (www.hmce.gov.uk)
Irish Revenue (www.revenue.ie)

8.5.2 Ensuring payment

If an order comes in from overseas, how do you know whether to trust the buyer? The most privileged form of seller here is the one who does not ship the goods and products in one go (for example a newsletter publisher). Here, the risk is restricted, because if the buyer does not pay, the supply can simply be turned off. At the other extreme, if you are offering digital material (music, software, information), you need to know immediately whether you will receive payment.

There are more problems with credit card payments from overseas – chargeback levels (ie the customer cancelling the transactions) are high for some regions, including Russia. Your bank may load much more of the risk onto you, or may insist that you carry out checks before accepting a card payment from abroad. You may able to run a credit check on the buyer online (see 2.2.6).

If you are accepting payment by invoice (open account), the risk is just as though you were shipping conventionally. If the transaction is significant, you should talk to your bank about protected payment schemes, such as letters of credit. Trade procedures are moving online – it is for example possible to open letters of credit on the Web with some banks (including Royal Bank of Scotland – see www.rbs.co.uk/pcm/trade).

It seems likely that wholly new systems will gradually take over, replacing the byzantine world of letters of credit and bills of lading. TradeCard is a system that allows every participant in an international deal – exporter, importer, bank, insurer, freight forwarder – to keep track of it on-screen. It is not Internet-based, but runs instead on a private network (see www.tradecard.bm).

In principle, Internet-based digital certificates (see 8.3) should also banish uncertainty. They are specifically designed to ensure that correspondents can trust each other. Within the next few years, they are likely to become key to the trade financing system. But for now you should be extremely careful: do not celebrate that bumper order from Kazakhstan until you see the money in your bank account.

8.5.3 Delivery

If you are selling low-value goods, you can use the mail. But most online exporters use courier companies, because they will handle much of the administrative work – coping with customs and tax declarations for example (see 8.5.1). See 8.4 for a list of couriers.

If your export volumes to a particular market become significant, you can either appoint a conventional distributor, or you can investigate the new breed of e-commerce fulfilment houses. These are just setting up, and are mainly aimed at US companies wanting to sell abroad – but they may eventually be able to help. They will handle orders taken on a Web site, organising transport if necessary, and also storing and distributing products in the importers' market. See for example www.globafulfillment.com.

8.5.4 Languages

The days when it is acceptable to offer English only on an e-commerce site are drawing to a close. Given that you should make everything as easy as possible for your customers, it must make sense to talk to them in their own language. The home appliances giant Electrolux is busy providing its site in 20 languages, because it does not believe it can sell vacuum cleaner bags or fridges unless it goes local. What is true for Electrolux is true for most online sellers – the only exceptions may be those that sell to high technology markets where English really is universal.

See 5.9 for the issues surrounding foreign language sites.

8.5.5 Currencies

As with languages, so with currencies. If you want to sell to an overseas customer, make sure you are quoting a price he understands. Does that mean you should offer to take payment in any number of currencies? And if so, what?

The answer is – it depends. Here are some pointers:

- The dollar is dominant on the Web, because so many e-commerce players are US. But it has another advantage – everyone knows the conversion rate between their currency and the dollar.

- Sterling is not widely understood, so sterling-only pricing is a mistake.

- The Euro is more widely used in e-commerce than anywhere else – but it is still far from being common.

- Software is available that will translate your prices automatically into many currencies, and you can link into a multi-currency payment system that will show prices in 150 currencies.

- If you are charging by credit card, the payment will in any event be converted into the customer's own currency.

The main choice is whether to offer indicative foreign currency prices or actual ones. This may sound like nitpicking, but it is crucial. If you are providing only an indication, you know how much you are going to receive, and the buyer takes the risk of the exchange rate moving before the payment goes through the credit card company. If you are providing an actual foreign currency price, you take the risk. There are legal as well as marketing issues related to this.

These are the choices:

- You can keep prices in your own currency, but add foreign currency equivalents.

- You can offer a link to a currency converter, which gives exchange rates updated daily. Emphasise that this is a rough conversion, to avoid complaints later.

- You can give visitors a choice of seeing prices in different currencies, updating them daily through your catalogue. Again you should stress that the rates are approximate.

- You can offer true multi-currency pricing. At the moment this will involve using a payment processor connected to NatWest's merchant services division. Datacash (www.datacash.com) and WorldPay (www.worldpay.com) offer this service – customers can see prices in anything from Peruvian News Sols to Finnish Markka, and you can be paid in any one of 17 currencies. The rate is frozen at the time of the transaction, so both you and the customer know how much they are receiving.

If you are receiving good income in a particular currency, consider setting up a bank account in that currency and using it to pay overseas creditors. It may make particular sense to establish a Euro account, because you can use this to pay in most EU countries.

8.5.6 Stimulating export sales

The Internet is the world's biggest bazaar – wandering around, you may well find a completely new outlet. But because it is so large, you can never guarantee that you have covered all possibilities. Here are four possible paths you can explore, starting with the most "respectable" and ending with the Wild West of the online bulletin board.

Government trade leads

The DTI's TradeUK (www.tradeuk.com) has three main services.

- A directory of UK exporters, so that potential buyers can find you.

- An online catalogue. You can put your products into a standard shopping catalogue, and buyers can click to order. Buyers can normally opt to pay by credit card or invoice. Alternatively, you can link the catalogue entry direct to your Web site.

- A sales lead section. This has leads fed in by British embassies, consulates and other sources, and is highly sophisticated. You put in search criteria (ie oil valves, any country), and are given brief details of the lead. You will only receive contact details if you have signed up with the service – so that overseas exporters do not find the service too useful. You can also subscribe to an e-mail service, which will alert you to suitable leads.

Web-based markets

A number of Web sites have been set up to act as both "portals" and marketplaces for different industries. Though they tend to have a strong US bias, and to be somewhat chaotic, they are packed with information and also have buying and selling areas – in some these are more like classified ad sections, in others more like newsgroups (see next section). For links to these and more, see www.forworld.com.

They include:

- *IndustryNet (www.industry.net).* Claiming to be the world's biggest source of tools, you can list your products and company details, and see if you generate interest. This is the site that alarmed RS Components when investigating the Web (see page 226).

- *Heavy Equipment Exchange (www.point2.com).*

- *MachineryNet (www.machinerynet.com)* for the metalworking industry

- *Interstone (www.interstone.com)*, for buyers and sellers of "dimension" stone, such granite and marble.

- *PharMatch (www.pharmtrade.com).* Part of the giant pharmaceutical site PharmTrade, this allows wholesalers and importers to make offers to each other online.

- *Interxchange (www.interxchange.com)* for the meat industry.

- *www.metalsite.net* for metals and metal products.

- *www.timberweb.com* for timber and wood.

- *fastparts.com* for electrical components.

- In Europe the paperback/CD-Rom service URL2 Directory links you to 1,300 buying and selling sites. See www.eceurope.com, tel 020-7903 5378 or e-mail info@eceurope.com.

Newsgroups

Although most newsgroups (see 1.4) are non-commercial, some are specifically designed as marketplaces. A good way of searching for a suitable group is via www.deja.com.

Here are some extracts from the newsgroup *alt.business.import-export*:

We are one of suppliers of Tapioca Chips in Indonesia, and looking for importers. The tapioca chip is in starch min.68% and moisture 14.5%. Please do not hesitate to contact us if u have any querries.

PT. BOMA INTERNUSA
Attn. Mr.Poernomo

DEAR SIRS,

WE ARE LOOKING FOR THE MEAT BONE MEAL (MBM); SOYA BEAN MEAL (SBM) AND WHITE
POLAR FOR ANIMAL FEED.
PLEASE REPLY TO ththk@inode.in
Best Regards,
Kho, Jan Suwandi

Dear sir,

We are looking for the Tin ore which it have to Tin content of about 70%
May I think that the largest Tin Supplier is existed in Indonesia, Brazil etc......
Because that country have a lot of the Tin mine.

Anyway, If you can supply to us, Pls. send that how much you can supply to Tin and Specification (Tin content) for your Tin ore.

Best Regards,

H. J. Min / R.O.K

Tradeboards

These carry very similar offers to the newsgroups above, but most are industry or country specific. They are even more difficult to locate than newsgroups, but are worth investigating. Try putting the word "tradeboard" into a search engine, and see if any that are listed are suitable. Alternatively you may find a link through www.forworld.com. Look at the buying and selling areas to see if they are well-used – some have very light traffic.

Here are some tradeboards:

www.tradeboard.co.uk	general import/export
www.trade-board.com	general import/export
www.melakatoday.com.my/etrade/main1.htm	general import/export
www.tradecourt.com/chemhouse	chemicals
mcontainer.com/tradeboard	containers (drums etc)
blankcd.com	recordable CDs
bubu.com	Indonesian tradeboard
www.yurdal.com	Turkish tradeboard

Chapter 9 Stretching the medium

The uses of the Internet are almost limitless – or rather they are limited more by imagination than by technology. So far companies have expended most mental energy on marketing and selling – which is fine, but these are only a part of the picture.

As we point out in Chapter 3, the most immediate benefits of the Internet come from cutting costs. Most of the ways of "stretching the medium" we describe in this chapter are likely to do that – though they have other benefits as well. Exploiting the Internet for customer service (9.1) can both save you money and make your customers even happier. If you are a member of a supply chain, you may already be noticing the effects of a shift to low-cost Internet communication (9.2). Recruitment (9.3) provides the one single reason why any company should have a Web site – to improve the quality of new employees. Then there are the "death of distance" companies, which are changing the way they work because of the Internet: providing services for customers who were previously beyond their geographical reach, tying staff together with the new medium, and saving on costs by running "virtual organisations". Is this the way forward for you? See 9.4.

9.1 Customer service

Customer service has become an online battleground. With customers only a mouse click away from their rivals, companies have sought to build up loyalty by offering soothing and efficient service on their Web sites, and by e-mail. The really good news is that they are, or should be, saving themselves money at the same time.

In most areas of online business, smaller companies spend their time pretending to be big – they are helped by the slick facade the Web can provide. But in customer service, the advantage is with smaller firms. Large companies are constantly attempting to duplicate the friendliness of the corner shop, but rarely succeed. Companies with relatively low volumes of business can, by contrast, provide a surprisingly personal service on the impersonal Internet.

9.1.1 E-mail

Handling queries

For companies handling a large number of customer enquiries, e-mail can dramatically reduce costs while providing a better service overall: they can be processed more quickly than phone calls, especially if a set of standard replies has been prepared.

But it is a mistake simply to add an e-mail address and assume your current systems can remain unchanged, because you will almost certainly have to deal with many more enquiries than you did before. People who cannot be bothered to pick up the phone will be happy to send an e-mail query. The Entertainer, the British toy shop chain, started selling from its Web site (www5.red.net/entertainer/index.html), but found its staff was spending an inordinate amount of time answering enquiries. A particular menace were US collectors of Beanie Babies and Star Wars figures, who scoured the Web looking for rare characters. The enquiries were often so specific – down to the last detail of a character's dress and colouring – that the time taken to deal with them was disproportionate to the revenue generated. "We have to have one person answering e-mail all day," says marketing manager Barry Eldridge. "We get thousands of e-mails a day, but very few sales."

The issue here is not necessarily how to discourage communication, but rather how to manage it to maximum effect. Companies that receive high volumes of queries have started to use software, such as Brightware (www.brightware.co.uk), that attempts to understand e-mails and either route it to the right person or to send back a suitable prepared reply. The system can respond automatically to between 50 and 80 per cent of e-mails, and is claimed to have 95 per cent accuracy.

Such systems will be appropriate only for companies that get hundreds of e-mails a day, and probably service their customers through a call centre. But even for organisations that get dozens of enquiries, or fewer, there are potential complexities:

- Incoming e-mail is easy to ignore. If an employee has a choice between picking up a ringing phone and opening an e-mail, the phone will always win. The answer is to set targets – e-mails must be answered within a certain time, say 12 or 24 hours. It is still quite rare to get consistently prompt e-mail responses. When *Net Profit* carried out tests on 20 large organisations in 1999, five – two supermarkets and three airlines – did not reply within a week. As e-mail often arrives within minutes, this is unacceptable.

- The best service in our response tests came from Internet-only companies. They know that they will only maintain loyalty as long as they give excellent customer service. But they also set standards that other companies should aim to match.

- Internet-only companies make heavy user of "auto-responders"; these are not intelligent, like Brightware, but simply acknowledge that a message has been received and assure the customer it will be dealt with. Auto-responders are however worse than useless if the promised "real" response does not follow quickly.

- The best service of all comes from small companies that really make an effort. Although e-mail is usually impersonal, it need not be – a quality exploited by Mike Jarman of Elizabeth Botham (see case study, page 246) when he sends chatty messages to regular customers.

- Some companies do not give an e-mail address, believing that customers can get all the help they need on the Web site. This is acceptable only if alternatives are provided (one is to allow e-mail, but only after customers have trawled through a good Q&A section – see below).

- Having said that, you must be ruthless about dealing with enquiries that are not worth following up – as experienced by The Entertainer. Send a polite "We are not sure we can help you but we will get back if we can."

Keeping in touch

E-mail can be used to keep customers in touch, and therefore loyal. The Teddington Cheese (see case study, page 222) sends out a bi-monthly newsletter, with good features about a "cheese of the month," and the like. It offers a Web version on its Web site, and gets customers to subscribe to the e-mail letter on its site. The aim is periodically to bring the company back into customers' minds – if they are sufficiently charmed by the newsletter, they will click across the Web site and order something nice and smelly.

E-mail newsletters should not be too long (2,000 words maximum) or too frequent. Ideally you should have an HTML version with pictures, and a text one for subscribers without the right sort of e-mail reader. Ask subscribers which they want when they sign up. If in doubt, product a text-only version – an HTML newsletter will be almost unreadable to some of your subscribers. Incidentally, the word "subscribe" normally implies that something is free on the Internet – a challenge for companies trying to sell paid-for subscriptions.

9.1.2 The Web

The Web is the ultimate low-cost customer service tool. If companies can answer every conceivable query on their site, there is in theory no reason why customers should contact them by phone, e-mail or pigeon post. That does not mean you should stop people contacting you (see 9.1.1) but the more information you put on your site, the less time your staff should spend answering queries. Customers can benefit too: if the information is well presented, it is quicker and cheaper to obtain than by phone.

Here are some of the ways you can provide customer service on your site:

- Include a question-and-answer page. Technology companies call this an "FAQ" (Frequently Asked Questions). Better for most companies to give it a friendly tag: "Your questions answered" or "Q&A". Start off with all the questions you can think of yourselves, then add new ones as they come in from customers.

- Provide back-up literature online. RS Components (see case study, page 226) provides 10,000 manuals and other documents that can be downloaded and printed out, using the Adobe Acrobat plug-in (see 5.2.7). Milacron, an Ohio-based manufacturer of machine tools, has gone a step further on its site (www.milpro.com), giving smaller customers access to aids that only work on the Internet (including an interactive calculator that lets users choose the correct drill bit). Not only are these useful services in their own right, they bring customers back to the site – where they may even buy something else.

- Some organisations use the Web to replace specific tasks carried out offline by allowing customers' direct access to their databases:

  - Courier companies (eg www.dhl.co.uk, www.parcelforce.co.uk) let customers track the progress of their packages online – they are bypassing the call centre agent they would have rung, and are tapping straight into the couriers' computer databases. The result: better service for the customer and cumulative savings of millions of pounds for the carriers.
  - Hotel chains such as Marriott (www.marriott.com) give similar access to their databases – this time to let potential guests see whether the rooms they want are available.
  - Telecom companies encourage business clients to report faults on the Web – they can also track the progress of repairs.
  - Utilities such as Scottish Power (www.scottishpower.co.uk) let business customers see their invoices and payment history.
  - Barclaycard (www.barclaycard.co.uk) lets customers see their statements and pay off their credit card bills, using debit cards.
  - Most UK banks offer Internet banking, where customers can see their statements online, and manipulate them.

In each case the company is replacing either a phone call or a piece of mail with a "self-service" on the Web. These systems are expensive to set up but as software is standardised and streamlined, it is likely that direct database interrogation will come within the reach of smaller companies. If, for example, you were a parts distributor and your client could check online whether you had a part in stock, he would be getting better service – and you would be saving money.

9.2 Supply chains

The least-noticed but possibly most important commercial role of the Internet is in supply chains. It has two main functions:

- **Matching:** Bringing companies together that would never previously have known about each other. Whether they are buying or selling, their choice of partners is massively increased (this includes freight, distribution etc as well as goods and services).

Case study: Customer service worth millions

QXL was due to be floated towards the end of 1999 for around half a billion pounds. It claimed to be Europe's largest online business, and was certainly the dominant online auction house on this side of the Atlantic. For a company that did not exist two years previously, and that had never reported a profit, this was quite an achievement.

Much of its success has undoubtedly been due to the high quality of customer service it attempted, and often succeeded, in providing.

QXL, which used to be called Quixell, was founded by Tim Jackson, a journalist, in late 1997. He was following the model that was already working in the US with companies such as e-bay and OnSale – offering companies (initially computer companies) a way to sell off their surplus or refurbished stock at a reasonable price, while giving consumers a chance to buy equipment cheaply.

Having studied the US auctions closely, he concluded that the secret to success lay in excellent customer service. He arranged a special deal with UPS, the courier company, so that customers would get simplified and reasonable delivery charges (there are four shipping bands for the UK, depending on weight and size). Customers would be kept constantly informed by e-mail.

During the auction itself they would be told if they had been outbid. They would be told if they had won. And they would be sent an e-mail telling them that the product was on its way and giving them a "tracking number" so they could follow its progress on the UPS site.

The first few weeks after launch were "a nightmare," Mr Jackson says. Traffic was low and there were constant operational problems.

A shift from weekly to daily auctions, after two months, triggered an explosion in business. Business started doubling every week, and his big problem became keeping service levels up to standard. Quixell hired support staff as quickly as it could, but there were still hiccups. Some customers did not receive products they had won because the computer "lost" them.

He knew his job was to convince customers that the mistake was genuine, so that they came back. “A lot of customers started off not knowing if we were rip-off merchants, so we paid special attention to factors that would convince them, such as being able to return a product for any reason. One guy bought a computer that didn’t work. We gave him speedy technical support and he has made 85 bids since.”

QXL, which has now launched operations in Germany, France and Italy, has found it difficult to keep its service level up to the initial high standard. There are hiccups. But when it works, it works very well indeed – customers comment in particular on its habit of offering five days delivery, then delivering in two or three.

It is worth looking at QXL’s customer service section for tips on handling shipping, guarantees, returns policy etc.

www.qxl.com

- **Integrating:** Bringing down the cost of a streamlined all-electronic supply chain. A level of integration that was formerly possible only among wealthy companies is now available to every member of a supply chain.

9.2.1 Matching

Companies are increasingly using the Internet to look for new suppliers of standard parts and products, casting an electronic net further than ever they did before. The results can be spectacular: GE Lighting claims to have brought its average purchasing cost down by 20 per cent, simply by asking for quotes by e-mail from more suppliers. After years in which companies have tried to reduce the number of suppliers, they are suddenly increasing their lists dramatically.

This is a double-edged sword for potential suppliers. On the one hand they will find prices squeezed by the competition. On the other they have the opportunity to win contracts they could never have previously contemplated. And every supplier is also a purchaser – they too can save money by buying online.

New mechanisms that allow buyers and sellers to get in touch with each other are appearing:

Brother's procurement pages (see page 269)

- Firms are posting requests for tenders on the Internet. Groups such as Sony (www.sony.co.jp/soj.BizPartners/Procurement/index.html) and Brother (www.brother.com/E-procurement) have set up their own procurement Web sites with the aim of finding cheap, good-quality supplies. Brother has posted detailed specifications of components, such as transformers and electronic wires, and asked suppliers to quote estimates on mock shipments.

- Companies have begun to use electronic trading communities that link buyers and sellers online. In addition there are hundreds of sites where people post purchase requests or advertise their goods (see 8.5.6 for details on how to find them).

- Purchasing managers scour the Web looking for particular items. If you are trying to interest them, it is essential to make your site as attractive as possible to search engines (see 5.8.1). We can expect to see business-to-business "bots" appearing to join the many retail offers (see page 55, also www.internet.bots.com for more on the way this technology is developing).

- If you make or sell "standard-but-varied" business products (see 7.1), such as stationery, desks or components, you should make sure your products are available via large companies' intranets. You can contact purchasing managers direct, or seek advice from the Institute of Purchasing and Supply (tel: 01780 756 777). It will also become increasingly valuable to be on the approved database of companies such as the Cost Reduction Partnership (www.cost.co.uk), which helps companies get the best deal on purchases. See also the CRP's Web site (www.buy.co.uk) and page 55.

- Companies do not just buy products – they also buy services. Hertfordshire-based Road Tech has created a Web site for hauliers, called Roadrunner Online (www.roadrunner.uk.com). Within it is a service, Backloads, that aims to match spare capacity on trucks with companies wanting to fill it, at a discount. Hauliers (who pay £1 a day subscription) can advertise available capacity, giving the type of vehicle, date and route. Companies can advertise their loads for free on the service.

It is early days in the matching business. Some companies that attempted to bring others together have found the market was just not ready. One of these was Womex, which tried to link purchasing managers in Western department stores with general goods manufacturers, mainly in Asia. It found the demand was not there (among the buyers, rather than the sellers). But as managers become more used to using the Internet, we can see an explosion in business-to-business matching systems of this sort.

9.2.2 Integrating

Electronic linkage of members of a supply chain has been growing for the past 20 years. Electronic Data Interchange (EDI) is a set of standards that allows standard documentation such as invoices and purchase orders to pass up and down the chain. Its big advantage is that messages do not have to be rekeyed when they arrived – they flow straight into the recipient's ordering or finance system. If a supermarket's stock control system is connected via EDI to a confectionery supplier's production system, the right number of bars will be manufactured without human intervention. This saves time and also cuts rekeying errors.

The problem has always been that EDI had to run over privately run networks (Value Added Networks, or VANs). These were expensive, which is why only larger companies could use them. And EDI was often seen as unfair – the buyers benefited most from it, but the suppliers had to pay to use the VANs.

The Internet has changed that by providing a low-cost conduit across which EDI messages can run. But that is just a start. Companies in supply chains are starting to use the Internet to bring a far higher level of openness and collaboration.

There are signs that the Internet is becoming a condition of trade. A 1999 NOP report found that 30 per cent of large UK corporations insisted that smaller companies have Internet access, e-mail and PCs before they start trading with them. A further 30 per cent said they plan to make similar demands in the near future.

Internet EDI

Companies that are already using VAN-based EDI systems are unlikely to drop them, at least for while (VANs can have advantages, including better speed and security). So systems have been developed that allow other members of the supply chain to link into the VAN with standard Web technology.

Using GE TradeWeb, companies can complete documents on a Web browser. The data is automatically translated into EDI format and fed into a customer's VAN. Many large companies, including Dixons, have asked their smaller suppliers to use the system. They can sign up on TradeWeb's site (www.getradeweb.com), follow an online tutorial, and plug straight into the system. There is a sign-on fee of £30; the cost then varies depending on how heavily businesses want to use the service: £260 a year, £28 a month or £3.50 a document.

Collaboration

EDI is efficient at sending specific items of data up and down the supply chain. But there is a trend to use the Internet for far more – to let members see more information about each other than they ever could before, to collaborate to an unprecedented degree. The advantages are partly hard financial ones – manufacturers see how well a line is selling, for example, so they can gear their production accordingly. But they are also soft – great openness between business partners means they should be able to operate almost as though they are one company.

Various Internet-based systems have been developed to improve information flows. H & R Johnson has created its own (see case study, page 274), while Sainsbury's is busy transferring its smaller customer from a fax to a Web-based ordering system (see case study, below).

Many supply chain systems are based on extranets. An extranet (see glossary for a definition) can give suppliers access to a customer's computer system via a Web browser. Typically, they will get into a special area of the buyer's site using a password. At the moment systems of this sort are most widespread in the motor and retailing sectors – but they are likely to spread.

Bentalls, the department store chain based in the South-East, used to use VAN EDI to link up with suppliers such as Levi-Strauss – but the system was limited to suppliers that could afford the hefty set-up costs. "What we found during our first sortie into electronic commerce is that only 100 sup-

Case study: Sainsbury's switches to the Web

J Sainsbury is hoping to transfer 1,000 of its small suppliers from a fax-based to an Internet-based ordering system. In mid 1998, before it launched the Xtra-Trade system, it was receiving 75,000 monthly invoices on paper from the 60 per cent of its suppliers which were too small to invest in traditional EDI.

By using Xtra-Trade, developed by Manchester-based software company Kewill Systems, it hopes to cut this number dramatically, while speeding up processing and reducing errors. Suppliers go into a password-protected area of Sainsbury's site, where they can view and acknowledge new orders received from the group, raise invoices and enter delivery information, and a view a variety of historical information.

Domain Boyer, which imports Bulgarian wine for Sainsbury's, is one of many small suppliers using Xtra-Trade. The company's Mark Taylor says it has brought many benefits. First, he has a better understanding of the needs of businesses further up the chain. "We understand Sainsbury's needs much better, so that if we need to make extra provision, we can do," he says. Also, Domain Boyer tends to be paid more quickly, because there are fewer disagreements about what has left the factory and what has arrived at the other end.

Sweet Port, a supplier of Italian desserts for Sainsbury's, is another user. Lyndon Stacey, UK marketing developer, says Xtra-Trade has improved workflow and has made Sainsbury more approachable. Before the introduction of the system, he says, he would often waste time trying to contact the person who would deal with a problem ("and once you'd find him, he would be on holiday or away from his desk"). But now he can contact people directly via the system, and can take advantage of a full technical help section and online newsletter.

www.kewill.com

Sainsbury's Web ordering manual for suppliers is at www.meadowhouse.co.uk/SAINSBURYS/manual.pdf

pliers, the really big guys, could trade on EDI. We thought 'what about the other 2,400?'," says Sarah Roper, operations director. So it set up an extranet system that links the company with its suppliers, allowing each end to view product catalogues, orders, invoices, and sales information. Bentalls charges its suppliers between £21 and £55 a month to use the system, depending on their size.

9.3 Recruitment

If there is one reason why a company should have a Web site, it is to increase the quality of its recruits. School leavers and graduates will naturally turn to the Web to find out about a company they have seen advertising a job – if it does not have a presence, or has a poor one, they may not bother to apply.

But there are also active ways in which you can recruit:

- through a special section on your Web site.
- through online classified ads.
- through an online recruitment operation.

Through your own Web site

Most large companies have recruitment sections on their Web sites. Some are specifically aimed at graduates, and offer repackaged online versions of the material they distribute to universities and colleges. Others use the medium to advertise specific vacancies. One of the problems some face is that these efforts are too successful – they are overwhelmed by unsuitable applicants from all round the world.

Any company that needs to recruit regularly should consider setting up a special area. It need not be elaborate, but should describe the "ethos" of the company, the sort of people you are looking for, and the limitation on those you can accept. Unless you are looking for a real specialist, discourage non-EU applications by pointing out the difficulty of getting a work permit.

Culpeper, a Cambridge-based retailer specialising in aromatherapy and

Case study: Tilemaker looks up and down the chain

If enough information about stock levels and manufacturing schedules were available online to suppliers, manufacturers could do away with the need to raise purchase orders altogether, according to a Stoke-on-Trent tile manufacturer, H & R Johnson Tiles. That is the reasoning behind its development of an Internet-based 'virtual supply chain' that goes both up and down the supply chain.

The first stage of the system was to link into its distributors, allowing them to enter orders electronically, check stock levels and track the progress of their orders. One of its features is that they can bring up a 'personalised shopping trolley' so they do not have to key regular items in repeatedly. The system can also be integrated into distributors' own databases so that there is no ambiguity about what is being ordered. "We might use a number for a product code whereas the distributor would use a description such as 'pink bathroom tiles'," says Johnson's Ken Packwood.

The system is so successful that a substantial proportion of trading with its distributors is now conducted online. One distributor has even given every member of staff an ISDN connection so that they can all use the system. It plans to provide a similar system for its customers in Europe.

The company is now developing a system to streamline relationships with

essences, has used its Web site (www.culpeper.co.uk) to recruit, in a gentle way. Its "Latest News" section contained a piece saying it was looking for young textile and art designers and Web site developers. It also announced the opening of a new shop in Leeds and asked if anyone would care to work or even manage the new outlet.

An advantage of recruiting in this way is that visitors will already be interested in the company. So you may find you get applications from people who are not actively seeking for a job, but are attracted by your company. In Culpeper's case the wording was carefully chosen to present the company as "upwardly mobile", so that the right sort of person would be likely to apply.

its suppliers. Mr Packwood says one of the biggest headaches for manufacturers is the "unreliable" paper chain that is created when raising an order for materials with a supplier, and the difficulties in matching up the original order with the final invoice and the goods that are received.

"So many things can change between the initial order and receipt of the final invoice that the disparity in the paperwork is often the biggest headache any admin department faces," he explains. "We are looking at a prototype system for the Internet which will let our suppliers know exactly what our stock levels are at any one time. They will also be able to see our manufacturing schedules and, armed with this information, they will be able to supply us with the necessary materials on a just-in-time basis without the need for a purchase order. Computerising the whole process will not only speed up the supply cycle, it will also reduce the amount of errors caused by conventional administrative paper-trails."

The key to successful online supply chain management, says Mr Packwood, is the quality of the information provided, particularly the accuracy of the information. "Whatever we give out on the Internet must mean the same to the trading partner as it does to us."

www.johnson-tiles.com

Classified advertisements

By advertising in your local paper, you may also be advertising on a Web site. The advantage is that you are also getting to people who live outside the paper's physical catchment area, but want to work near you. A site that brings together more than 20,000 classified job ads from several hundred local papers is Jobhunter (www.jobhunter.co.uk). You can place an ad by contacting individual papers through the site. If your area is not covered, see if your paper has a Web site. For links, see www.yahoo.co.uk/Regional/Countries/United_Kingdom/News_and_Media/Newspapers/

Recruitment operations

The Internet is an excellent matching mechanism, which is why so many specialist Web and e-mail based companies have been set up to bring together potential employers and employees. Many use the Web and e-mail in tandem, alerting job-seekers or companies if a suitable "match" appears. Until recently they were overwhelmingly focused on IT jobs – now they cover a much broader spectrum. In late 1999 there were already more than 130 general recruitment firms and dozens more specialist sites.

Some are online-only operations; others are run by established recruitment companies. Some cover specific job types, others are more general. A few are free, such as Gisajob.com (see below) and even those that are not charge only modest fees. Here are brief descriptions of six of the better-known:

- **www.jobserve.com**: a successful IT-only operation that relies heavily on e-mail. It costs between £4 and £15 to post a single advert on the site – £4 will buy a single line of text and last for a week. You can also buy a "package" of 30 adverts, which you can use at any time.

- **www.jobsite.co.uk:** one of the oldest recruitment sites specialises in IT, engineering and sales. It will created tailored mini-sites in which individual companies can place their ads. This service starts at £75 a week.

- **www.monster.co.uk:** Monsterboard is owned by marketing and advertising company TMP Worldwide, and specialises in IT, engineering, finance and sales. The cheapest advertisement is £250 – for this you receive an A4-sized display that lasts for 60 days.

- **www.taps.com**: owned by a consortium of recruitment companies, TAPS covers IT, marketing, sales finance and graduates. Companies can create their own area on the site for £1,700.

- **www.topjobs.net**: Topjobs, one of the first Internet companies to advertise on television, covers most areas, including legal, media, travel, marketing. It offers a big range of advertising options, from £6,000 to £100,000.

- **www.gisajob.com**: Gisajob has 70,000 jobs on offer from more than 1,300 agencies. Job adverts can be posted on the Web site for free (for now at least) and anyone can subscribe to a free, tailored, job notification service. It is much used by graduates and a specialist job search is included, although the site is heavily weighted toward IT.

9.4 Reorganising your business

Much has been written about the death of the office, how we will all become teleworkers, and how the nature of work and jobs will change fundamentally. There is hyperbole, and many people will be working in offices as they are now for decades to come. But some companies will be able to spread themselves far and wide – thanks very largely to the Internet.

With an Internet connection and a phone, mobile workers can have access to all the information and all the people they need (9.4.1). Companies can save money by telling their staff to work from home (9.4.2). Others can work globally without leaving the office (9.4.3). Others yet can be truly virtual, working in a way that would have been quite impossible before the Internet arrived (9.4.3).

Recruitment sites

www.aft.co.uk	Appointments for teachers
www.appointments-plus.com	*Telegraph* jobs site
www.ask4.co.uk	Accountancy and finance
www.barzone.co.uk	Hospitality and leisure
www.biomednet.com	Biological and medical research
www.careersinconstruction.com	Construction careers
www.cityjobs.com	Finance, IT, media and legal
www.coolwebjobs.co.uk	Web-related
www.corporateskills.com	Computer jobs in Ireland
www.cvserve.com	CV database with a vacancy board
www.cvstore.net	IT and Internet
www.disabilitynet.co.uk	Part of the Disability Web site
www.journalism.co.uk	Editorial
www.e-job.net	Advertising, marketing, PR and sales jobs
www.education-jobs.co.uk	Educational recruitment
www.eurojobs.com	Job vacancies around Europe
www.gaapweb.com	Accountancy and finance
www.get.co.uk	Graduate recruitment specialists
www.gisajob.com	*See main text*
www.goldensquare.com	Secretarial
www.gradunet.co.uk	Graduate recruitment
www.grapevine.bris.ac.uk	Social science research
www.foodanddrink.co.uk	Appointments section of *The Grocer*
www.gti.co.uk	Graduate recruitment
www.jobsunlimited.co.uk	Appointments section of newspaper site
www.netlink.co.uk/users/erol/hljobs	Health jobs
www.high-flyers.co.uk	Accountancy
www.internetjobs.co.uk	Internet-related jobs
www.jobclub.com	IT
www.jobhunter.co.uk	Vacancies in regional press
www.ifi.co.uk	Environmental
www.jobmart.co.uk	General, SE England
www.jobpharm.com	Healthcare and pharmaceutical

www.jobsearch.co.uk	General
www.jobserve.com	*See main text*
www.jobsgopublic.com	Public sector and charity appointments
www.jobsintelecoms.com	Telecom
www.jobsite.co.uk	*See main text*
www.londoncareers.net	Appointments from *Ms London, Midweek, Girl about Town* and *Nine to Five*
www.marketing.haynet.com	Appointments from *Marketing* magazine
www.milkround.com	Graduate recruitment
www.mipmap.com	Games and multimedia recruitment
www.monster.co.uk	*See main text*
www.mrweb.com/framejob.htm	Market research appointments
www.onesite.co.uk	Legal
www.overseasjobs.com	Overseas from the *Overseas Job Express* magazine
www.pharmiweb.com	Pharmaceutical
www.peoplebank.com	CV database with a vacancy board
www.personnelnet.co.uk	Healthcare
www.planetrecruit.co.uk	Covers most industries
www.recruitmentscotland.com	Scottish vacancies
www.sciencejobs.com	Appointments from *New Scientist* magazine
www.spacelinks.com/SpaceCareers	Space industry
www.taps.com	*See main text*
www.appointments-plus.co.uk	Appointments section of newspaper site
www.topjobs.net	*See main text*
www.wcn.co.uk	Worldwide graduate recruitment

9.4.1 Mobile working

There has been a tendency to pull people back from physical visiting, to concentrate information in a central database, and to use a call centre to disseminate it. The argument has been not only one of cost, but also that remote salespeople or engineers do not have access to the customer or product information they need.

That need no longer be true. By linking a laptop computer or other mobile device to the Internet or the company intranet (see glossary), staff on the road can gain access to the latest information. Sales and marketing people can call up the most recent prices and full customer histories, and can also demonstrate their company's products on its Web site (they can store this on their hard disk, so they do not need to dial up). Engineers can tap into databases of any size to solve a problem (the full workshop manual for a jumbo jet is available through Boeing's intranet). And everyone can look up internal phone numbers and send messages to colleagues.

All this, of course, depends on having some way of tapping into the Internet:

- The favoured device is the laptop computer. If your staff on the road are likely to be near fixed phone sockets, they will do best plugging the cord from their modem into this. (The modem for a laptop is a PC Card, which slots like a fat credit card into the side of the machine.) An ordinary phone line is likely to give the fastest and most reliable connection. The ability to cadge sockets is an important skill for the mobile worker.

- It is possible to link a laptop computer to the Internet via a mobile phone. This will need a data card (different from a modem) and a phone capable of carrying data. These can work from almost anywhere and so give great independence. But for the moment they run at only 9.6 kbps, or possibly 14.4kbps, against the 28 or 56kbps that is the standard for fixed lines. Fine for e-mail, but slow for normal Web access (tip: turn off the graphics in the browser). Most intranet content is free of graphics, so should load in reasonable order.

- A "cardphone" incorporates a mobile phone into a PC Card, so you do not need an external phone at all. The Nokia CardPhone costs about £100.

- Tiny computers can now dial into the Internet. Some are mini-PCs (running the Windows CE system), others have their own software (like the Psion or Palm Pilot). Their advantage and their disadvantage is their small size: they are difficult to type on, while the Palm Pilot does not even have a keyboard. But they are increasingly powerful, and can store plenty of information.

- The Nokia 9110 (www.nokia.com/phones/9110/index) is a hybrid mobile phone/computer. It looks like a large phone, but opens up to reveal a small screen. Watch out for similar devices.

- The next generation of mobile phones will allow Web access in their "windows". The windows will be larger than they are now, but the information they display will obviously be limited. The good news is that the Internet connection will be much faster than current mobile data rates. See End Note, page 287.

9.4.2 Teleworking

Teleworking – working at home or other places away from an office – is growing in the UK. In 1998 there were 1.1m teleworkers in the UK; almost 5 per cent of the UK workforce. In 1999 a CBI survey found that 10 per cent of UK employers in the private sector use teleworkers.

Teleworking has a number of advantages:

- Every employee working from home reduces office space costs.

- The elimination of commuting saves considerable time. A 45 minute journey to work takes up seven and a half hours per week – almost an entire working day.

- Teleworking employees can work flexible hours – suiting, for example, those with families or other personal commitments.

- Employers recruiting teleworkers are not restricted by geography – a remote employee in Lands End can work for a firm based in John O'Groats.

Case study: a man in touch

Mike Davenport is a typical "road warrior", one of the growing band of corporate wanderers who spend most of their working lives out of the office.

He is a marketing executive ostensibly working out of Hewlett Packard's laboratories in Bristol but in practice travelling throughout Europe three or four days a week. One week a month is spent working from his home in the Lake District.

Mr Davenport never leaves home without his electronic kit. This includes a mini video camera, a palmtop computer with modem and a digital phone. Wherever he is in the world ("I've only ever had a connection problem in Albania during the protests") he can communicate with colleagues, customers, suppliers and family.

He can use his portable communications centre to send and receive e-mails, research prospective clients' companies on the Web and hold video conferences with colleagues or his family. If he wants to create a customised sales presentation on the fly he can pull slides from his personal Web site. He also uses the site to store large documents that he can download as needed.

At home a desktop PC, scanner and ISDN link to HP's intranet enables him to grab information from the company's internal network and to tele-conference using a shared "whiteboard", which allows two or more people to work on the same document on screen at the same time.

But it also has disadvantages:

- Working from home can be an isolating experience for workers.

- Teleworkers miss out on day-to-day information-sharing within an office. This can limit their knowledge of company activities, and thus reduce the value of their intellectual and creative contributions to a firm. It is therefore important for teleworkers to meet with colleagues as regularly as possible.

- Teleworkers can find it difficult to separate work from domestic distractions.

- Teleworking can complicate issues such as computer support – if a computer breaks down, an IT technician may have to travel long distances to fix it.

The tools for teleworking

E-mail is the standard tool, allowing the transfer not only of text but also of spreadsheets, graphics, drawings and photos. It is even possible to send sound and video files. To make this technology work, it is essential that computers at each end are powerful enough, and ideally run the same versions of the same software (see 2.1.2, on attachments, for why this matters).

Unified messaging services, such as Freeserve's Telserve, enable workers to access and forward faxes, e-mails and voice messages from any phone or Internet connection (see page 33). These systems will make it much easier for remote workers to organise their lives.

Intranets: many large companies now have intranets – "private Internets" that integrate Web technology and a company's own computer network. Staff on an intranet can open up their Web browsers and have access to a mass of company information – the phone directory, memos, health and safety regulations, product information, the company newsletter etc. Not only does this save money on printing, photocopying and distribution of paper, it has the potential to make the company culture more open. In some intranets employees are encouraged to "publish" their own information, so that their colleages know what they are up to, and can perhaps avoid reinventing the wheel.

Although an intranet is normally available only to members of a particular company, it can be opened up to chosen partners – usually suppliers or partners. This makes it an "extranet" and it allows partners to have access to selected parts of the host company's internal information – product details for customers, for example, or products needed for suppliers (see supply chains, 9.2).

What has this to do with teleworking? Any company with a Web site can set up its own intranet, and use it to share information with remote workers. A lot of new software, including Microsoft's latest word-processing, spreadsheet, database and presentation products, can be saved as HTML – that is, in the language of the Web.

The company needs to create a special area of its Web site, which could either be protected by a password or could simply be unpublicised (ie with

Case study: blown along by e-mail

A Northern Ireland-based company providing training for competitive sailing is using the Internet to connect a global network of trainers to an international client base. "We conduct 60 to 70 per cent of our business over the Internet," says James O'Callaghan, business development manager at SailCoach. Yet the communication tool they selected to generate this business is the simplest on the Internet: e-mail.

Visitors to SailCoach's Web site can find information on the company's products and a range of services – from sailor training camps to people who work as specialised coaches. Users can click on a chosen e-mail address to start negotiations with one of the members.

As well as attracting customers, the site has been used to build up the company's portfolio of coaches around the world. "Our industry is a truly global one, and our Web site is a conscious effort to meet the need to operate internationally," says Mr O'Callaghan.

SailCoach has taken on three more staff to deal with increased business since the site was launched, even though the only communication option is e-mail. People interested in the company's sailing books and coaching packages in Europe, North America and Australia must e-mail a member of SailCoach to order them.

Sailors can also e-mail the site requesting a coach with particular expertise. SailCoach then uses e-mail to put that sailor into contact with an appropriate expert. The company has agents in Canada, Australia, India, Germany and Scandinavia, all of whom can be contacted via the Internet.

an address such as www.netprofit.co.uk/private). The HTML documents can then be uploaded to the server (see page 105), and viewed by anyone with a Web connection and knowledge of the right address/password.

This is of course the most basic level – it is not very secure, and many companies would want to add extra levels of sophistication. But it does show just how simple intranets can be.

"The system is faster, more flexible and economical than mail, fax or telephone," Mr O'Callaghan says. The use of a Web site as a "shop window" – with e-mail as the link between clients and independent coaches – is proving to be a vital component of the company's business infrastructure.

It is so vital, indeed, that the smooth running of the operation depends on it. "Put it this way," Mr O'Callaghan says, "our computers crashed earlier, so I am having a terrible day."

www.sailcoach.com

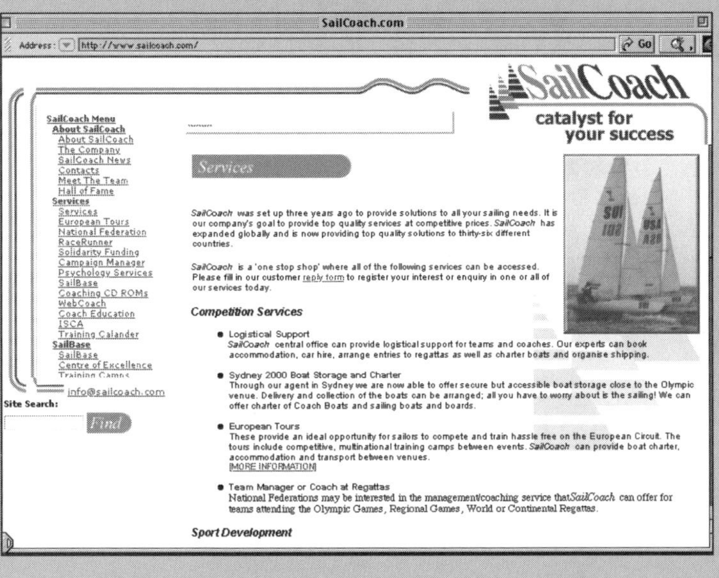

9.4.3 Truly virtual

The companies that have made best use of the Internet are those that have concentrated on the commercial potential, not the technology. Sailcoach (see case study) is a Northern Ireland company that could not exist without e-mail. Accountants Thru' Internet is similar.

Mark Dyer, who runs The Dyer Partnership in Surrey, set up Accountants Thru' Internet in 1995. His Web site (www.netaccountants.com) has plenty of practical information for UK owner/managers. But the company's real secret weapon is e-mail. Mr Dyer has customers all over the world, and communicates with many of them by e-mail alone. His most intriguing client is a company that makes wind farms in the Ukraine. "The managing director saw us on the Web and asked us to handle the company's financial affairs," Mr Dyer says. "We act as its financial department providing accounts, collecting debts and supplying weekly management reports by e-mail. We've met once in 18 months. He travels around Russia, Europe and the US and just plugs in his portable wherever he happens to be if he needs a financial update."

End Note Things to watch out for

It is often said that an Internet year is three weeks. And it is true that technology, if not take-up, is moving at a dizzying rate.

This book was finished in the autumn of 1999. Although it is always dangerous to predict the future, various saplings are sufficiently well developed to guess the rough shape of the trees that will mature over the next one to three years:

- Internet take-up among consumers will continue to grow very rapidly. It was given a huge boost during 1998 and 1999 by the rapid spread of free Internet access services. We expect free phone calls to provide the next jolt, with telecom companies making revenue in other ways – perhaps from a cut of online transactions.

- Business-to-business use of the Internet will grow even more sharply, with an acceleration in take-up by small and medium-sized companies. The cost-cutting potential of the medium will be the main driver.

- There will be a proliferation of "purchasing communities", which give access to all sorts of products at low prices, and also to online marketplaces. Web-based systems that have so far been targeted at consumers, such as auctions and price comparison "bots", will spread into the business-to-business world (see page 55).

- The "local Internet" will become established. We will be able to order take-aways, find the cheapest petrol, book a doctor's appointment, recommend a plumber – all from local sites (see page 88).

- Possible negatives could come from fall-out from the Millennium Bug, and a sharp drop in stock prices. The disappearance of "Internet fever" on the US stock markets would have a knock-on effect on the way the medium is regarded. But any general economic slowdown should stimulate electronic business (because it has so much cost-cutting potential).

- The spread of interactive television in the UK will have some effect. If it fails to capture the public's imagination, the Internet will continue to grow as before. If it takes off, consumer-facing companies will start to put their money into TV, rather than the Web. The two technologies are however closely linked, so the Web industry will simply start working for television.

- Internet-enabled mobile phones will arrive in a big way. Services that are now of interest, but little more, on a PC will become very valuable: the ability to see whether a train or plane is on time, stock prices etc. We may be able to buy products from our mobile phones by punching in a code given in a newspaper ad. Two developments will bring us high-speed Internet access on mobile phones. The Wireless Application Protocol (see www.wapforum.org) is a standard for "Internet-enabling" mobile phones and other devices. The Universal Mobile Telecommunications System (www.umts-forum.org) is the successor to the GSM mobile network system, and will allow very high speed data transfer. WAP-compliant devices are being launched during 1999, while the first UMTS services start in 2002.

- The security of electronic commerce will continue to be a significant issue. On the positive side, digital certificates will be widely used, giving a much higher level of comfort (see 8.3). Smart cards – plastic cards with computer chips embedded in them – will allow us to carry our digital certificates around with us. On the negative side, organised crime may turn its attention to the "problem" of cracking the Internet. There will be scares, but it seems likely that the "goodies" will win.

- Privacy issues could become problematical. The amount of private data floating around on the Internet is a press scandal waiting to happen. Be very careful to obey the Data Protection Act (see page 312).

- You will find you are offered help by all sorts of unlikely people. Do not be surprised if your bank offers to build a Web site for you, or the post office says it wants to assemble your product. Everyone is looking for a new role in electronic business.

Appendix A: Opportunities and threats

This appendix consists of a selected list of industries/trades, divided into manufacturers and services. The aim is to provide at least one with which you can "relate," so that you can see what the possible benefits of the Internet are to your business, and what dangers might lurk if you do nothing. Note that these ratings have been drawn up in autumn 1999, and relate to the conditions that we see during 1999/2000. It is possible they will change – for example, we have given a fairly low rating to local marketing opportunities. That is because there is little momentum so far behind local Internet use. But we believe that, sooner or later, will appear (see page xxx)

Some points to explain the ratings (see chapter 3 for more):

- Cost-cutting opportunities are rated as highly as revenue-generating ones.
- Opportunities in non-marketing areas such as supply chains, recruitment, customer service are rated as highly as marketing possibilities.
- Normally, the greater the opportunities, the greater the threats.
- The exception is where a product/service is unique (eg cheesemaker, stately home owner), where there are big opportunities but few threats.
- Opportunities for sales are linked closely to “deliverability” (can a product/service be sent digitally or by post/courier), and the demographics of the target audience (geographic as well as age, gender).
- Business-to-business selling/marketing opportunities are potentially huge, but it depends on the "wiredness" of the sector (See page 75)
- Intermediaries may be threatened in one way (ie being bypassed by end suppliers) but have opportunities in others (eg geographic expansion)

Legend:

Excellent opportunities	*****
Minimal opportunities	*
Heavy threat	*****
Negligible threat	*

MANUFACTURER	OPPORTUNITIES	THREATS
Academic journal publisher	***** Opportunity to obtain subscriptions and circulate journals online saving on print/production costs. Archived material can be searched online and pay per view facilities introduced	** Each journal is unique, but may find itself rivalled by online publications in the same field.
Aerospace component manufacturer	**** Low cost supply chain. Technical manuals online. Opportunity to widen market with showcase Web site.	** Threats from online competition for less specialist products.
Aggregates company (quarry)	*** Online prices and stock list. E-mail communication with customers.	** Some increased competition.
Aircraft dealer (secondhand)	**** Opportunity to widen market with showcase site. Posting pictures, specs and history gives enquirers better info, making phone selling more effective	*** Increased competition.
Blind manufacturer	**** Direct-to-consumer selling, finding new distributors, and e-mail links with existing ones.	** Increased competition
Book publisher	**** Opportunities to sell direct and widen market plus provide added value information. For specialist publishers opportunities to cut costs by selling electronic texts online ("e-publishing").	***** Readers' choice vastly expanded by online bookshops.
Brewery	**** Opportunity to market brands, sell merchandise, and for specialist brewers to sell direct and find new distributors.	*** Greater competition, though the more specialist the beer, the lower the threat.

MANUFACTURER	OPPORTUNITIES	THREATS
Brick manufacturer	*** Opportunity for low cost links with suppliers and distributors. Can market by displaying range online.	** Currently, low. But, for all core building supplies/ raw materials much depends on growth rate in Europe of US style online 'exchanges' where organisations put out contracts for tender on the Internet.
Car component maker	**** Low cost communication (CAD etc) with suppliers and customers. Opportunities to bid for contracts in countries where you have no presence. Smaller companies can benefit most.	**** Car manufacturers/ first tier suppliers will increasingly expect their suppliers to be integrated into their e-mail/Web systems. Pressure increased as they look for new suppliers using e-mail/Web
Cardboard box maker	*** Low cost brochure/ price list Web site could save costs, expand market. Opportunity to provide online customisation of designs and e-mailed quotations and/or automatic pricing mechanism.	** Pressure increased by new competitors using Internet to market.
Cheese maker (specialist)	***** Excellent direct selling opportunities, using attractive Web site.	** Low, especially for the most distinctive cheeses.
Chemical manufacturer	**** Opportunity for cutting costs with online supply chain cutting out expensive paperwork. Brochure Web site could widen market - particularly overseas.	**Increased competition.
Clothes maker	**** Low cost e-mail communication (patterns, orders etc) with suppliers and customers. Web site could expand market. Possible direct selling opportunities.	*** Competition from low cost suppliers increased, though domestic suppliers could benefit by offering fast-response Internet-based tailoring service.

MANUFACTURER	OPPORTUNITIES	THREATS
Contact lens manufacturer	*** Opportunity to allow opticians to order from Web site, reducing costs and errors.	** Pressure from competitors doing the same.
Crystal glass manufacturer	**** Opportunity to widen market and direct sell using attractive Web site as showcase. Also low cost supply chain management using secure, password protected 'extranet' for suppliers and distributors.	*** Pressure increased by international competitors-especially in eastern Europe?
Cycle manufacturer	**** Direct selling opportunities, or finding new markets/outlets with content-rich Web site. Bespoke manufacturers can take tailored orders online.	*** Pressure increased by new competitors using Internet to market/sell.
Firework manufacturer	**** Opportunities for finding new outlets, using attractive Web site. Possible direct selling opportunities.	*** Pressure increased by new competitors using Internet to market
Fresh pasta manufacturer	**** Opportunity of expanding market with attractive Web site and possible direct selling.	*** Supermarkets will be able to find and manage new sources using the Internet.
Garden gnome manufacturer	****Opportunity of expanding market and possible direct selling. Quirky enough to attract lots of interest if promoted well.	*** Pressure increased by competitors using Internet to market.
Jewellery maker	**** Opportunity to widen market and direct sell with attractive e-commerce site.	*** Pressure increased by competitors using Internet to market.

MANUFACTURER	OPPORTUNITIES	THREATS
Musical instrument maker	**** Opportunity to showcase products and reach wider audience with sound samples and background on production methods, history etc. Opportunity to sell direct.	** Increased online competition.
Newsletter publisher	***** Opportunity to widen market and cut costs with electronic delivery. Free sample copies can be posted on Web site and online subscriptions taken. Intranet versions of the newsletter can be updated via the Website.	***** Greater competition, though very specialist publications should be protected.
Pallet manufacturer	*** Opportunity to cut paperwork using online delivery management system, and e-mail links with supply chain.	** Other operators could take business with online presence.
Plastic extrusion company	*** Opportunity for reducing costs with online supply chain cutting out expensive paperwork. Informative Web site could widen market - particularly overseas.	*** Other operators could take business with online presence.
Printing firm	**** Opportunity to widen market with Web site. Examples of work and details of capabilities can be shown as well as added value information such as advice and tips on print methods, submitting artwork, etc. Online supply chain can cut costs and speed transfer of artwork, text, fonts, etc.	*** Threats from online competitors.

MANUFACTURER	OPPORTUNITIES	THREATS
Signmaker	***** Web excellent for displaying examples. Customers could choose sign from Web site, adding words, or e-mail their own graphic.	*** Pressure increased by new competitors using Internet to market/sell.
Speciality chocolate maker	***** Excellent opportunity for widening market and direct selling - particularly mail order gifts - using attractive Web shop.	*** Threat from online stores. Gift market is particularly strong on the Internet so threat is from other gift suppliers as well as other confectionery makers.
Steel fabricator	*** Low cost e-mail communication with suppliers and customers. Expand business with low cost brochure Web site.	** Pressure increased by new competitors using Internet to market. Emergence of online 'exchanges' where suppliers bid for contracts could increase competition.

SERVICE	OPPORTUNITIES	THREATS
Accountancy practice	**** Get non-local business. Carry out business by e-mail.	** Other operators could take your business with online presence.
Acupuncturist	** Local marketing. Putting appointments system online. E-mail appointment reminder.	* Negligible.
Advertising agency	*** Awareness building. Recruiting. Private areas for each client (extranet).	** Higher competition for best recruits.
Agricultural supplier	**** Low cost communication with farmers, with easily updateable price lists.	**** Farmers could turn to competitors' sites to seek lower prices. Auction sites and 'exchanges' could fuel competition and create bidding wars.
Airline	***** Big savings to be made by selling direct, and managing seat sales very finely. "Cyber specials" etc can be used to offload seats at last minute. Excellent opportunity to widen consumer and business market and provide added value information. Also to create community of regular customers online.	***** Becoming fiercely competitive. This and greater transparency provided by the Web is likely to drive prices down.
Air conditioning supplier	**** Put technical details on the Web to help customers choose systems. Cut costs with downloadable technical manuals.	** Some manufacturers will sell spare parts and complete systems online.
Antique dealer	***** Expand your geographic buying and selling area at low cost. Use online auctions to increase margins.	**** Not going online means you could miss out on the development of a mainstream buying and selling tool.

SERVICE	OPPORTUNITIES	THREATS
Architect	**** Marketing: displaying portfolio. Low cost communications with clients (e-mail and extranet).	*** Other practices could take business with online presence.
Asbestos removal company	*** Expand market geographically. Opportunity to become useful Web "resource."	** Possible increased competition.
Auction house	***** Excellent medium for extending market with online auctions, while costs can be saved by publishing catalogues online.	**** Threats from online competition, although established auction houses will still continue to attract live audiences.
Bank	***** Opportunities for online 24-hour banking and to use Web to explain portfolio of financial products. Direct individual and business access to databases will cut customer service costs. Potential to develop products and services such as certification, smart cards and digital money. Costs on wholesale side can be cut using Internet/intranet based integration.	***** Opposition from competitors and low cost Internet start-ups. Easy to compare rates and offers online, while allegiance is eroded by widening choice from non-banks. Traditional role of banks - moving and storing money - undermined by non-banks and eventually by the Internet itself.
Bath re-surfacer	** Local marketing.	* Negligible.
Book shop	**** Opportunity to extend market reach with online bookshop. Physical shops offering exemplary customer service can make inroads, especially if the physical and online elements can support each other. .	**** Online stores are gaining ground, while e-publishing - selling downloadable texts - will erode specialist book sales.

SERVICE	OPPORTUNITIES	THREATS
Bookbinder	**** Expanding geographical market. Opportunities for attractive and informative Web site.	** Other operators could take business with online presence.
Butcher (retail)	** Low, owing to high cost and logistics of mailing perishable food from a small local outlet. But as domestic Internet usage grows might be opportunity for home delivery service locally.	**** Home delivery offered by supermarkets and Web-based mail order operations will have to be held off by personal service.
Builder	*** Local marketing. Opportunity to provide added value information - clients, references etc. Communicating with suppliers by e-mail.	** Low, but watch out for industry umbrella sites which recommend local builders such as the Federation of Master Builders.
Car dealer	***** Opportunity to sell volume cars online, so sales people concentrate on high margin work. Use site for customer service, eg e-mailing MOT reminders, and build loyalty with newsletter. Selling spare parts online.	***** Threats from other dealers online, as well as from car auction and classified sites. The ease of comparing prices on the Net will put pressure on dealer margins. And manufacturers are preparing to sell direct.
Card shop	* Difficult to market low-priced items online.	*** Threats from large number of sites offering free and low-cost 'electronic' cards sent via e-mail.
Carpet cleaning service	** Local marketing.	* Negligible.
Catering equipment supplier	**** Opportunity for widening market with attractive Web shop and, perhaps, broadening base by offering consumer range.	*** Threats from competitors online.

SERVICE	OPPORTUNITIES	THREATS
Charity	***** Excellent opportunities for fund raising online and awareness raising campaigns. Also good for research and communicating with donors, creating discussion groups and forums etc.	**** Many charities are already active online with high profile sites.
Chemist (retail)	*** Local marketing for individual shops but opportunities for direct selling online for larger organisations.	*** Threats from large-scale direct sell operations online.
Civil engineering consultant	**** Opportunity to widen market, and provide added value information - eg client list, examples of work undertaken, internal contacts with cvs. Also opportunity to use Internet for communicating with workers in the field by transmitting CAD drawings, measurements etc online. Likewise for communicating with suppliers and customers, online recruitment and product sourcing.	** Threats from competitors online.
Clothes shop	*** Opportunity to get customers into shop using gimmicks such as "virtual sizing aid" or "colour swatches". Possible online sales.	*** Competition from direct-selling retail Web sites and, now starting, from manufacturers. The higher the fashion, the lower the threat.
Commercial vehicle dealer	**** Opportunity to broaden market and generate leads. Also, to provide customer service. Selling spare parts online.	*** Competition from other dealers, auctions and, eventually, manufacturers.

SERVICE	OPPORTUNITIES	THREATS
Computer retail chain	***** A Web shop offering high quality back-up service and competitive prices has opportunities to sell both to consumers and businesses. Online auctions can be mounted for used, refurbished and end-of-line items. Opportunity to add value with online support, software downloads and spare part ordering.	***** Massive competition from entrenched online stores - including manufacturers selling direct at very keen prices. Low cost software is increasingly sold online. Risk of cannibalising physical sales with Web-based ones.
Corporate entertainment company	**** Opportunity to generate leads with informative Web site and even online booking. Communicate with business clients using e-mail.	**** Increased online competition.
Courier service (motorbike)	*** Opportunities to provide fulfilment for products ordered online. Local marketing.	***** Delivery of valuable documents, artwork etc will be largely undermined by secure e-mail systems and ability to download material from Web sites.
Dating agency	**** Opportunity for widening market and using "profiling" to match suitable people. You will not need an excuse to produce a fun site.	***** Being bypassed. In many ways the Internet is itself a huge online dating agency with its chat rooms and meeting places for virtual strangers.
Delicatessen	**** Opportunity for widening market via mail order with online shop as showcase. Particularly high priced gifts and hampers. Also possible move into corporate gifts. Local home delivery service.	**** Competition from online operators offering home shopping and gift delivery.

SERVICE	OPPORTUNITIES	THREATS
Diamond merchant	*** Opportunity to reach wider market overseas. Stock and price list plus e-mail communication and ordering.	* Negligible.
Direct mail fulfilment house	**** E-mail communication with clients now standard. Also to provide downloadable samples of design work, addressing formats etc. Could also use Web to expand services - eg sale of envelopes, e-mail marketing etc.	*** Increased competition, and danger that physical mailshots will be reduced as e-mail marketing increases.
Doctor's surgery	**** Info such as surgery hours. Online booking. Dealing with reps online.	* Negligible.
Dog breeder	**** Opportunity to widen market with informative Web site. Dog care advice, e-mail enquiry line and Frequently Asked Questions can help add value.	* Negligible.
Double glazing installer	** Local marketing.	* Negligible.
Dry rot firm	*** Opportunity to widen market with Web site, give added value information on causes, treatments, prices, guarantees etc.	** Threats from online competitors.
Electrical goods store	**** Use Web site and e-mail to increase service levels with eg downloadable manuals, technical support. Offer home delivery for products ordered from manufacturers' sites.	***** Transparency of prices on the Web makes this a volatile sector. Competition will come from large online retailers and manufacturers.

SERVICE	OPPORTUNITIES	THREATS
Estate agent	***** Opportunity to widen market and provide added value information such as virtual tours of properties, and details of local facilities. Downloadable property details can save on printing and distribution while site can be used for communicating with clients via e-mail.	***** Threats from online competitors, especially on sites that gather many estate agents' portfolios together. Watch out for growth of private sales, bypassing agents.
Flower shop	***** Home delivery business should increase through orders made through eg Interflora site.	***** Threats from competitors, including supermarket home delivery services.
Freight forwarder	**** Link into all-electronic shipping systems, saving paperwork. Offer downloadable forms and advice for shippers and importers. Widen market through Web presence.	*** Threats from online competitors, and danger that Internet matching systems will make freight forwarders less necessary.
French polisher	** Local marketing.	* Negligible
Garage owner	* Local marketing, with possible online booking.	* Negligible.
Garden centre	*** Opportunity for mail order/home delivery with attractive, informative site.	**** Competition from online suppliers of equipment and plants.
Graphic artist	***** Prospective clients can be directed to Web site for initial assessment of work saving time and cost of travelling/couriers. E-mail for low cost communication, transfer of design roughs, finished artwork etc. Can work wih remote clients (even overseas).	**** Increased competition.

SERVICE	OPPORTUNITIES	THREATS
Hairdresser	** Local marketing. Online booking facility. E-mail appointment reminder.	* Negligible, unless your rivals are using the Web effectively.·
Holiday cottage rental company	**** Opportunities to put properties on Web site, greatly increasing audience.	**** Cottage owners will use specialist rental sites to bypass intermediaries.
Home sitting service	* Local marketing.	* Negligible.
Hot air balloon company	**** Low cost marketing aid with opportunities for exciting Web site. Could include online booking.	*** Other operators could take business with online presence.
Hotel/guesthouse owners	**** Low cost marketing, especially to Americans	** Other operators could take your business with online presence.
Independent financial advisor	*** Online support from product suppliers will provide valuable marketing and communication aids. Demand for IFAs who can provide the most sophisticated advice will increase - they can market online.	***** End suppliers will increasingly sell direct, using the Web's interactivity and ability to handle complexity to help customers choose even quite advanced products.
Instant print shop	***** Online ordering, design and proof checking can cut costs and attract new business. Opportunity to create online templates - business cards, letter headings etc - which can be completed online by customers.	**** Competition from online print shops.
Interior decorator	*** Opportunity to widen market reach and show examples of work online with attractive web site.	* Negligible.

SERVICE	OPPORTUNITIES	THREATS
IT recruitment agency	***** Perfect match with the Internet. IT people worldwide are connected. If your recruitment agency is not on already you probably don't exist.	***** Hugely competitive online with some entrenched market leaders.
Kindergarten/nursery	** Local marketing.	* Negligible.
Landscaper	*** Opportunity to showcase work and reach wider market with Web site.	* Negligible.
Language school	***** Opportunity to widen market, particularly overseas. Internet can be used for distance teaching and downloading course materials. Also used for booking courses and data gathering including assessing prospective students' language skills.	***** Threats from online competition offering distance teaching facilities.
List broker	**** Opportunity to widen market and cut costs by posting list catalogue online. Added value features might include advice about mailing techniques, online selection and purchasing lists plus sale of items such as envelopes.	*** Threats from online competition.The entire list broking process could be automated by companies with enough resources.
Local authority	***** Web site provides a platform for communicating with local residents at low cost. Specific information, eg planning permission requests, can be supplemented by feedback forms, forums and online advisory services. Potential for placing tenders online and recruiting.	* Negligible.

SERVICE	OPPORTUNITIES	THREATS
Local newspaper group	***** There is an opportunity to create new business models including local "interactive" community sites, person to person auctions replacing conventional classified ads, local directories and up-to-the-minute local news services. Opportunity to link with other regional groups to provide national coverage for classified ads. Site could be used as "portal" for local businesses wanting to market and sell.	***** Threats from online competitors, particularly free classified sites and person to person auction sites which threaten to erode local paper revenues. Also free local guides, business directories and entertainment listings are usurping the local paper's traditional role and eating away at their niche audiences. Few papers can yet contemplate abandoning the print version, so the Web just adds costs.
Machine tool repairer	*** Opportunity to widen market and communicate at low cost with clients.	* Negligible
Magician	*** Opportunity to widen market with entertaining Web site. Online bookings could conjure up new business.	* Negligible
Marina operator	**** Opportunity to expand market and demonstrate facilities with attractive visuals, prices and services on Web site. Also direct selling of boats and chandlery.	*** Threat from online competitors particularly for the sale of boats and equipment.
Model agency	**** Excellent opportunity to cut costs and widen market by putting model portfolios online in attractive Web site. E-mail communications with models and clients.	*** Threat from online competitors.

SERVICE	OPPORTUNITIES	THREATS
Music store	**** Local shops can use Web site and e-mail newsletters to keep customers loyal. Personal service and idiosyncratic knowledge will help provide an edge. Specialist music can be sold online, or at least samples offered.	***** Threats from online competitors dominating the market and offering vast choice and keen prices. Downloadable music and online ordering of customised CDs emerging as a threat to traditional retail shops.
Off licence	*** Home delivery service. Opportunities for content-rich Web site to raise profile.	*** Direct-to-home mail order and supermarket services expanding fast.
Oil rig maintenance company	*** Opportunity to widen market and to reduce costs by trouble shooting online. Technical information, manuals and updates can be posted online while a 'live' customer service link via real-time chat can help sort out problems remotely.	** Increased competition.
Old peoples' home	**** Opportunity to cut costs and widen market by showing facilities and services online. Website can have virtual tour of home plus Frequently Asked Questions section. Can provide e-mail contact with relatives for added 'comfort factor'.	*** Threats from online competitors.
Optician	** Local marketing, or for chain, direct selling opportunity for eye-care items. Added value advisory pages and Q&A forums to encourage visitors. Online booking.	* Negligible.

SERVICE	OPPORTUNITIES	THREATS
Orchestra	**** Opportunity to market orchestra with pictures and sound samples. Web site can include news and profiles of players and guest performers. Also, fundraising, schedules of up and coming concerts and sale of recordings, tickets and merchandise.	* Negligible.
Photo library	***** Opportunity to put catalogue online and provide digital delivery of stock saving on processing costs and reaching global market.	***** Threats from online competitors, particularly start-ups offering downloadable, copyright free stock.
Photographer	**** Widening market by exhibiting portfolio online. Online booking/enquiry forms. Use of Internet to transfer images remotely.	*** Increased competition.
Plant/tool hirer	*** Potential for widening market and cutting catalogue costs by providing full range with specs and advice on safety etc online. Could provide online booking, though this is not yet a "wired" market.	** Possible increased competition.
Plastic surgery clinic	**** Widening market by demonstrating expertise online: profiles of staff, questions and answers about treatments, impartial advice and e-mail queries.	** Some increased competition.

SERVICE	OPPORTUNITIES	THREATS
Public relations company	**** An essential tool for communicating with journalists, clients and media. Press releases and lengthier, in-depth background briefings can be sent via e-mail. Site can be used for promoting company to new clients and recruitment.	**** Clients can carry out their own PR more effectively online.
Restaurant	**** Opportunities for extending market reach, particularly to incoming tourists (notably US) searching for eating places. Menus, special promotions etc online plus entry in plethora of online restaurant guides. Online bookings.	** Competitors using online restaurant guides to attract overseas visitors.
Restaurant (pizza takeaway)	**** Opportunity for local marketing and home delivery with online ordering.	*** Increased competition.
Road haulage company	*** Opportunity to promote services to reach a wider - including international - market. E-mail communication with clients. Online freight tracking. Opportunity to subscribe to 'consolidation sites' which allow haulier to advertise spare capacity.	** Increased competition.
Security guard company	*** Opportunity to provide details of services, clients, prices etc and to field online enquiries.	* Negligible.

SERVICE	OPPORTUNITIES	THREATS
Shot blaster	*** Put technical details, prices etc on Web site. Opportunity to expand market.	* Negligible.
Solicitor	**** Opportunities for cost cutting and reducing office space by providing virtual services for clients and partners. Web site can provide added value advice about specialist legal matters, links to partners plus downloadable forms for wills, standard contracts etc.	*** Increased competition.
Sports complex	*** Opportunity to display facilities, opening times, prices etc. Online booking.	* Negligible.
Stately home owner	**** Expanding market, especially to the US. Opportunities for good looking site.	* Negligible.
Storage company	*** Opportunity to sell spare capacity over the Internet through Web site.	** Some increased competition.
Surveyor (quantity/land)	***** Using Internet for rapid transfer of data, drawings etc from site to office and clients. E-mail communication. Widening market reach with Web site.	** Some increased competition.
Taxi company	** Local marketing, and possible online booking	** Some increased competition.
Tea importer	**** Opportunity to use e-mail to liaise with customers and suppliers.	** Some increased competition.

SERVICE	OPPORTUNITIES	THREATS
Television repair shop	** Local marketing. Buying and selling online of secondhand TVs.	* Negligible.
Ticket agency	**** Opportunity to sell tickets online via Web site and extend market reach.	**** Threats from online competition. Already an active trading area on the Web.
Tour operator	***** Opportunity to sell direct via attractive Web shop with lots of added value information on destinations, hotel facilities, currency convertors, weather etc. Last minute bargains can be posted and even auctioned on-site. Opportunity for interactivity and capturing data on customer preferences to tailor-make holiday offers.	***** Highly competitive. Web makes it easy for customers to compare prices and offers. Also easy for customers to chat online and compare notes about holidays, operators etc. Cut price airlines and ease of finding accommodation online means users can customise their own holidays.
Trade association	***** Huge opportunity to provide added value information for members and save costs on closed site eg legal advice, discussion forums, downloadable publications etc. and to promote association and its members generally on public site.	*** Competing associations could provide added value services online and poach members.
Tyre sales (local)	** Local marketing. Special offers online.	* Negligible.
Vet	* Local marketing; booking appointments.	* Negligible.
Waste paper merchant	*** Opportunity to trade online	* Negligible.

Appendix B: Legal issues

Anyone doing business on the Internet must be aware of the legal implications of doing so. There are areas of immense uncertainty, partly because of the nature of the technology (and the fact that law never keeps up with technology) and partly because the Internet has no respect for national boundaries. Up until autumn 1999 no legislation had been enacted with the Internet specifically in mind. The situation changes however in late 1999/2000 with the arrival of the UK Electronic Communications Bill and the European Commission's e-commerce directive. These pages give a broad guide – you should consult a lawyer (see list from page 315) for specifics.

Setting the rules

If you are selling online, you should include a terms and conditions section (for an example, see www.qxl.com/TermsAndConditions.shtml). Among other things, this should state what law disputes should be heard under – for example QXL's auction sales are covered by English law, even if products are bought from one of its foreign language sites (eg www.qxl.fr).

This could however run into conflict with the new country of destination rule, announced in 1999 by the European Commission, which says that consumers making a remote purchase can sue traders in their local courts.

If an international deal is carried out by e-mail, or from a site without an explicit statement, both the jurisdiction and the governing law may be unclear. It is up to the person bringing the case to choose the jurisdiction. Normally he will choose his own national law – but not always. For example a continental company may opt for English jurisdiction, because it will get its costs covered by its opponent if it wins – which it would not under civil (continental) law.

Contracts

Contract law applies to all forms of electronic commerce, including trading carried out via e-mail as well as through a Web site. When employees use the Internet to order stock, negotiate contracts or sell company goods and services, they may not be aware that they are committing the company to a binding contract. If a contract dispute arises from an e-mail transaction, companies need to be sure they understand the legal ramifications of this, so they can prove who did what, when and how, and what the intentions of the parties involved were.

Although contracts involving telex and telephone are entered into at the time and place where the acceptance is received, no UK law courts have yet dealt specifically with e-mail contracts. The problem is that e-mail differs from the telephone in not being instantaneous. There may be hours or even days between the message being sent and it being received, so the two parties might not agree on the time the contract was struck.

The "where" part of the equation cannot be assumed either, because an e-mail address relates to a person, not a place. The message could be received in whichever country the recipient happens to be at the time when he logs into his mailbox.

The Internet also makes it difficult to produce evidence that a contract has been agreed. Disputes often revolve around the record of the details of the contract and its transactions, so a permanent record of the communications making up the transaction is essential. The problems of proof are greater in electronic trading because computer-recorded information is generally regarded as more suspect than written records. This may change with the UK's electronic commerce bill.

These problems should be largely overcome by digital certificates (see 8.3) – they allow a company or individual to show not only that a particular message has been sent at a particular time, but also that it has not been tampered with. Their legal validity will have to be tested in the courts, or settled by the EC's directive.

All this gets more complex when the contract is between parties in two countries. Although every country has contract law, courts in civil law countries could interpret a contract differently from those in the UK, which has common law. So the question of jurisdiction could be crucial to the outcome.

Privacy and data protection

When the London Business School analysed the most serious and long-term barriers to the growth of electronic commerce in 1998, it decided that data protection was one of them. One of the great commercial benefits of the Internet is that it can be used to extract information from individuals, the better to target marketing (see 5.2.4). That means that there is a mass of private information on computers connected to the Internet, which can either be misused by the company that holds it, or can be extracted by hackers and quite possibly published in the open areas of the Web.

This was highlighted in mid-1999 when Microsoft's e-mail system, Hotmail, had to be closed down temporarily because hackers had published a key on a Web site that allowed anyone to get into the e-mails of its 40m members.

It seems likely that the privacy issue will become a hot one in the press: a few major leakages will be enough to get investigative journalists very interested indeed. It is therefore vital for companies that are gathering personal information via the Internet to protect themselves against prosecution or public embarrassment.

The EU's Data Protection Directive aims to harmonise European laws to allow a free flow of personal data within Europe. The UK passed its own Data Protection Act in 1998 to implemement this directive – it is expected to come into force in March 2000.

The 1998 UK act is a strengthened version of the original 1984 Data Protection Act. This stated that any personal information used by a company (which must have registered with the Data Protection Registrar) must be processed fairly. In other words, companies could use and supply personal information in any way, as long as they were not outside the law. The 1998 Act is more stringent, and has particular relevance to the processing of personal data on the Internet. It says that "unambiguous consent" has to be given to a company by an individual stating that it can process their information in particular ways.

The best approach is openness:

- Have a clear privacy policy stating how information gathered online will be used. The principle of data protection in UK law, that information should be "freely and lawfully obtained" must be observed. Under the 1998 legislation, you must get active assent to use information in a specific way. So instead of a box saying "tick here if you do not want this information to be used in certain mailings", it might say "tick here if you are happy for this information to be used in third party mailings."

- Give visitors a choice whether to provide information, and make it clear what benefits they will receive if they give it. These could be in the form of access to extra information or personalisation of the service. Be explicit about the bargain that you are offering. The Internet industry seems to be moving in this direction with the estblishment of two standards, the Platform for Privacy Preferences (P3P) and Open Profiling Standard (OPS), codes embedded in the Web site that declare the privacy policy. Users will be able to negotiate to release information in return for something valuable (access to a special area, or air miles, perhaps).

- Cookies (5.2.7): even though these are not actively extracting information, it is necessary to warn visitors that they are being used.

- You could sign up to a service such as TRUSTe (www.truste.org), a sort of electronic commerce ombudsman. You publish your TRUSTe-approved privacy policy on the your site, giving a link to a section of TRUSTe's site where customers can register complaints if they believe you have violated your own guidelines. TRUSTe will then act as a liaison between you and the customer to try to sort out the dispute. See QXL's privacy policy at www.qxl.com/pr/privacypolicy.shtml for an example of a TRUSTe-backed policy.

It is important not to fall foul of other countries' privacy legislation, especially the US's. However, the European attitude to data protection is generally much tougher than the American one, so you are unlikely to get into trouble if you obey EU and UK rules.

Consumer protection

In May 1999 the European Parliament reached agreement to harmonise national regulations on consumer regulations. The aim is to make sellers obey the same rules wherever they are, and to stimulate cross-border purchases by giving consumers a minimum level of rights.

One regulation designed explicitly to protect EU customers is the "distance selling directive", which is supposed to be implemented by June 2000. This deals with sales concluded by telephone, e-mail or fax, and therefore deals with contracts formed over the Internet. It states that a trader selling goods ordered by mail or phone has to give the consumer the following information before any transaction is made:

- A description of products and their function
- Their price, inclusive of delivery cost
- Delivery arrangements
- An address to send complaints

Customers will also be given the right to withdraw from a distance contract (meaning any delivered product) within seven business days of receiving the goods, and to cancel a transaction in the case of fraudulent use of a payment card. However the supplier is still entitled to charge the customer for the direct cost of returning the goods. The only goods that allow no right of withdrawal are perishable and custom-made goods, as well as periodicals, magazines and audio or video recordings, or computer software that has been unsealed by the customer.

Domain names

To have a presence on the World Wide Web a company needs to register a domain name (see 4.7). As each domain name has to be unique, problems have arisen when companies have discovered that the name they want has already been registered by someone else. There are two main reasons for this:

- Two organisations have an equal right to the name. Here, the one to register first will normally be able to keep it. Prince, a UK company, registered www.prince.com with Network Solutions (the US company that administers .com domains). An American company, also called Prince, demanded the domain on the grounds that it had the US trademark. At first Network Solutions agreed, but after a battle in the High Court in London, the British group was allowed to keep it.

- Someone has registered the name of a well-known company in the of selling it to the company. This is called "hijacking" or "land-grabbing". In every case that has come to court the "rightful" owner has been given the name.

The domain name registrars in most countries have also set up arbitration procedures to sort out disputes without bringing them to court. For .com names, see www.networksolutions.com/legal/dispute-policy.html. For .uk names, see www.nominet.org.uk.

Advertising

Online advertising will be covered by existing legislation on advertising, as the Internet is simply another distribution mechanism. Companies are, however, advertising globally and must (at least in theory) take into account the national rules relating to advertising in all the countries in which their products or services are being advertised – that is, almost every country in the world. It may be illegal to advertise certain products such as contraceptives or prescription drugs in particular countries – the usual answer is to put a note on the home page of the Web site.

Companies may also have a problem with conflicting trademark registrations – they should consider the rules in all large markets, and if necessary add a disclaimer: "This product is not for sale in Germany" for example. But if every authority claimed the right to apply its legislation to every Web site advertisement in its area, the Internet would soon be in trouble. In theory at least Chinese political censorship and Middle Eastern mores should be combined with the French insistence that the site be in French. But in general governmental views are more pragmatic – what is carried on one Internet Service Provider (ISP) is available on every other Internet service and you cannot block them all.

Security

Electronic signatures (see 8.3) will have to be legally recognised if they are help online business develop. The UK is currently drafting legislation concerning the legal recognition of electronic signatures and the voluntary licensing of Certification Authorities, which issue digital certificates.

The European Union has issued a Draft Directive that will require any legislation on electronic signatures to "only cover minimum technology". This means that it would cover technologies that have not yet been developed. The draft directive should be adopted at some point in 1999, and member states should have implemented it by 31 December 2000.

It seems likely that electronic signatures will be given equivalent status to handwritten signatures in specific circumstances. But full equivalence is thought to be unlikely as each member state has its own way of concluding business contracts.

Specialist Internet lawyers
Lawyers everywhere are eyeing the electronic commerce market with increasing interest. At the moment the market is developing in the British fashion, with courts making decisions as and when disputes arise. The problem with this process is that new decisions often become square pegs for existing round holes: the likelihood of a new Internet law, on data protection perhaps or digital signatures, fitting in seamlessly with the existing legal status quo or the expectations of both businesses and consumers may be low. Add in possible conflicts between national, EU and US law, and extraordinary complexity can emerge.

Lawyers have not been slow to spot the potential. Some large London-based companies have built up specialist teams, while many smaller ones have at least one professional with some expertise. See the company's Web sites for more on the issues.

Internet/e-commerce law specialists

Ashurst Morris Crisp (www.ashursts.co.uk)

Mark Lubbock – Head of team	Tel: 020-7972 7762 mark.lubbock@ashursts.com
Chris Coulter – Technology	Tel: 020-7972 7989 chris.coulter@ashursts.com
Louise Krosch – Commercial/IP	Tel: 020-7972 7657 louise.krosch@ashursts.com
James Perry – Financial Services	Tel: 020-7972 7214 james.perry@ashursts.com
Richard Palmer – Tax	Tel: 020-7972 7289 richard.palmer@ashursts.com
Charmian May – Data Protection	Tel: 020-7972 7283 charmian.may@ashursts.com
Ian Starr – Litigation	Tel: 020-7972 7454 ian.starr@ashursts.com

Bird and Bird (www.twobirds.com) Tel: 020-7680 6800
Jeremy Landau jeremylandau@twobirds.com
Graham Smith grahamsmith@twobirds.com
Graham DeFries grahamdefries@twobirds.com
Mark Haftke markhaftke@twobirds.com
Sian Morris sianmorris@twobirds.com

Jeffrey Green Russell (www.jgrweb.com)
Stuart Russell Tel: 020-7339 7000 / 0171 339 7001

Clifford Chance (www.cliffordchance.com)
Nick Elverston Tel: 020-7282 7000

Cameron McKenna (www.cmh.co.uk)
John Armstrong Tel: 020-7367 3000

Law firms with staff with a working knowledge of Internet law

Firm	**Town**	**Contact name**	**Telephone no**
Bevans	Bristol	Keith Gandy	0117 923 7249
Bhatia	Nottingham	Ash Bhatia	0115 950 3231
Birketts	Ipswich	James Austin	01473 232300
Bishop Longbotham and Bagwell	Trowbridge	Terry Bishop	01225 755656
	Bath	David Morrison	01225 462871
	Swindon	Rod Powell	01793 615 011
	Bradford-on-Avon	Guy Bagnall	01225 866541
Bremner Sons and Corlett	Liverpool	David Berry	0151 227 1301
Bullock Worthington and Jackson	Manchester	Tim Kendall	0161 833 9771
Burges Salmon	Bristol	Simon Coppen	0117 939 2000
Clarke Wilmott and Clarke	Taunton	Marlford Harris or Chris Taylor	01823 442266
	Yeovil	Nigel Lindsey	01935 401401

Firm	Town	Contact name	Telephone
Digby Brown Solicitors	Glasgow	Fraser Ewing	0845 273 2323
	Edinburgh	ditto	ditto
	Dundee	ditto	ditto
Edge Ellison	London	Caroline Egan	0990 134441
	Leicester	ditto	ditto
	Birmingham	ditto	ditto
Elliott Duffy Garrett	Belfast	Damian McFarland	01232 245034
Ensor Byfield	Southampton	Fiona Harte	01703 483200
Fawcetts	Walsall	Neil Fawcett	01922 640424
Fidler and Pepper	Sutton	Mark Slade	01623 451111
	Mansfield	ditto	ditto
	Kirkby	ditto	ditto
Fox Hayes	Leeds	Ian Coupland	0113 249 6496
GAH Lockharts	Antrim	Alan Lockhart	01849 462636
Gillespie Gifford and Brown	Dumfries	William Coulthard	01387 255351
	Castle Douglas	ditto	01556 503744
	Kirkcudbright	ditto	01557 330539
	Dalbeattie	ditto	01556 611247
Gregory Abrams	Liverpool	Lynn Evans	020 7236 5000
Guildford Chambers	Guildford	Richard Moore	01483 539131
Hegarty and Co	Peterborough	Tim Thompson	01733 346333
	Stamford	ditto	01780 752066
Hilliers Solicitors	Bedford	Paul Hillier	01234 840044
Hugh James	Cardiff	Hugh James	01222 224871
Hughes Paddison	Cheltenham	John Hughes	01242 574 244
Julian Bloom and Co	Watford	Julian Bloom	01923 231235
Marcus J O'Leary	Bracknell	Marcus O'Leary	01344 303044

Firm	Town	Contact name	Telephone
Marshall Hall Levy	South Shields	Keith Turnbull	0191 455 3181
Merriman White	Guildford	Chantal Brace or Jeremy Wolff	01483 574466
MJF (Services) Ltd	Knutsford	Mike Farrell	01925 757887
Morgan Cole	Cardiff	Michael Lindsey	029 2038 5385
	Swansea	Tony Hughes	01792 634634
	Oxford	Alison Farsfield-Hall	01865 262600
Charles Morgan	Newcastle	Charles Morgan	0191 222 3344
Stephen Nottridge	Loughborough	Stephen Nottridge	01509 217770
RH Solicitors	Andover	Stuart Ranson	01265 351533
	Salisbury	ditto	01722 328871
Richard Reed	Sunderland	Brian Puesh	0191 567 0465
Rollo Davidson and McFarlane	St Andrews	Jeremy Russell	01334 477700
Rosleys Solicitors	Nottingham	John Rosley or Roseann Kane	0115 958 0584
Rothera Dowson	Nottingham	Richard Hammond	0115 910 0600
Shadbolt and Co	Reigate	Zoe Shaw	01737 226227
Shepherd and Wedderburns	Edinburgh	Liz McRobb or	0131 228 9900
	Glasgow	Paul Carlyle	0141 556 9900
Shoosmiths	Reading	Paul Giles	0118 965 8765
	Fulham	Jacqueline Wilson	01489 881010
Silverman Sherliker	London	Jonathan Silverman	020 7749 2700
Sylvester Mackett	Trowbridge	Nick Guinness	01225 755621
Thorntons WS	Arbroath	George Dunlop	01241 872693
	Dundee	Nick Barclay	01382 229111
	Forfar	Elizabeth Barr	01317 466886
	Perth	Graham Harding	01738 621212

Appendix C: Web and new media design and consultancy companies

This list has been assembled from a questionnaire sent out in late summer 1999. A constantly updated version can be found on *Net Profit*'s Web site: see www.netprofit.co.uk.

Sites for which the companies are responsible are in italics.

Berkshire

Goring

Entranet
Tel: 01491-878 787
Fax: 01491-878 700
Web: www.entranet.co.uk

Richmond Event	*www.stayintheloop.com*
Verso	*www.versomortgage.co.uk*
The Co-operative Bank	*www.cooperativebank.co.uk*

Newbury

Hiway Communications
ISP providing Web service including e-commerce
Tel: 01635-573300
Fax: 01635-53329
E-mail: sales@hiway.co.uk
Web: www.hiway.co.uk
Contact: Michael Tweedie

Wadworth Breweries	*www.wadworth.co.uk*
Digital First	*www.digitalfirst.com*
PersonnelStore	*www.personnelstore.com*
Used Online	*www.used-on-line.com*

Dumfries & Galloway

Thornhill

Alphawaves
Tel: 01848-331815
Fax: 01848-331814
E-mail: info@alphawaves.net
Web: www.alphawaves.net
Contact: Simon Meade

Sakura Corporate	*www.sakuracorporate.com*
ASCO	*www.asco.uk.com*
The Gaming Club	*www.alphawaves.net/gaming*

Durham

Darlington

Edward Robertson
Web site design, Internet consultancy, e-commerce
Tel: 01325-489 300
Fax: 01325-288 219
Web: www.edwardrobertson.co.uk
Contact: Graham Miller

Flowers Direct	*www.flowersdirect.co.uk*
Chipsworld	*www.chipsworld.co.uk*
Durham School	*www.durhamschool.co.uk*
RSR Fasteners	*www.rsrfasteners.co.uk*

East Sussex
Brighton

The Wendy House
Tel: 01273-748903
Fax: 01273-774140
E-mail: info@thewendyhouse.com
Web: www.thewendyhouse.com
Contact: Michael Mason
www.great-grooms.co.uk
www.englishconcert.co.uk
www.davincifinefoods.co.uk

Dreamteam Design
E-commerce, online multimedia, Intranet development, dynamic content
Tel: 01273-204206
Fax: 01273-204201
E-mail: info@dreamteam.co.uk
Web: www.dreamteam.co.uk
Contact: Malcolm Duffitt - Commercial Director
Suntext Holidays *www.suntext.com*
Brighton Fringe Festival
www.dreamteam.co.uk/adrenalin99
Games Terminal *www.gamesterminal.com*

Eastbourne

PixelWeb Multimedia
Web design, e-commerce and custom database applications, IT consultancy.
Tel: 01323-735666
Fax: 01323-734666
E-mail: sales@pixelWeb.co.uk
Web: www.pixelWeb.co.uk
Contact: Ross Eldridge
Icc records *www.iccrecoreds.com*
PIPuk *www.pipuk.co.uk*
Jazzemporium *www.jazzemporium.com*
Harlow Lubricants *www.harlube.co.uk*

East Yorkshire
Hull

Web Images Limited
Web design company specialising in e-commerce and training.
Tel: 01482-587256
Fax: 01482-620399
E-mail: tony@Webimages.co.uk
Web: www.Webimages.co.uk
Contact: Tony Hales
Meadowhall Shopping Centre
www.meadowhall.co.uk
Tilcon UK *www.tilcon-contracting.co.uk*
Magna, Hull City *www.magna-online.co.uk*

Essex
Barking

Intuitive.net
Search engines, user interface design, graphic design, database integrationt
Tel: 0208-507 1110
E-mail: info@intuitive.net
Web: intuitive.net
Contact: Shawn Richard
Air Menzies *www.airmenzies.co.uk*
Ukdirectory *www.ukdirectory.co.uk*
Sonitus *www.timmol.co.uk*
Andersen Products *www.anpro.com*

Hampshire
Basingstoke

Adline Web Design
Tel: 01256-840498
Fax: 01256-40498
E-mail: sales@adline.co.uk
Web: www.adline.co.uk
Contact: Darren Hall
Bayer *www.health-village.org*
EurostarNetwork *www.euro-star.com*
Chase Research *www.chaser.co.uk*

Hertfordshire
Berkhamsted

Omniplex New Media
Web site design, electronic commerce, Web hosting and database integration
Tel: 01442-71002
Fax: 01442-71005
E-mail: da@omniplex.co.uk
Web: www.omniplex.co.uk
Contact: David Acton

LinguaTel	*www.linguaTel:.co.uk*
21 Store	*www.21store.com*
40 Savile Row	*40savilerow.co.uk*

Kent
New Ash Green

Eye Design
Web site design specialist
Tel: 01474-73 817
Fax: 0870-88 9724
E-mail: info@oneeye.co.uk
Web: www.oneeye.co.uk
Contact: G. Catchpole

County Ambulance	*www.ambulance.co.uk*
BSB Electrical	*www.bsbelectrical.co.uk*
The Abba Magic Tribute Band	*www.abbamagic.com*
New Ash Green Online	*www.newashgreen.co.uk*

London

AKQA
Tel: 020-7494 9200
Fax: 020-7494 9300
E-mail: incof@akqa.com
Web: www.akqa.com

Mini	*www.mini.co.uk*
Tetley's Bitter	*www.smoothlydoesit.co.uk*
Orange Media Centre	*www.media.orange.net*

Art on the Web
Web site design for SMEs, searchable databases, e-commerce .
Tel: 0207-604 4116
Fax: 0207-681 4775
E-mail: gb@art-on-the-Web.com
Web: www.art-on-the-Web.com
Contact: Gary Bortz
www.eliko-carpets.com
www.thelinenmerchant.com
www.cedar-antiques.com
www.european-paintings.net

Brand New Media
Web design, research, consultancy and media buying services
Tel: 0800-0186 444
Fax: 0800-0189 913
E-mail: info@bnm.co.uk
Web: www.bnm.co.uk
Contact: Simon Wadsworth

Heinz	*www.heinz.co.uk*
Hula Hoops	*www.hulahoops.co.uk*
Tizer (AG Barr)	*www.tizer.co.uk*
NTL	*www.ntl.com/athome*

Clarity
Tel: 020-7397 2900
Fax: 020-7397 2939
E-mail: martin@marketing.co.uk
Web: www.marketing.co.uk
Contact: Martin Chilcott

The Carphone Warehouse	*www.carphonewarehouse.com*
Railtrack	*www.railtrack.co.uk*
Royal & Sunalliance	*www.royalsunalliance.com*

CreateX Design
Tel: 020-8203 9500
E-mail: info@createx.com
Web: www.createx.com
Jongleurs Comedy

Clubs *www.jongleurs.com*
Night-Out
Entertainment Guide *www.night-out.co.uk*
Key Account *www.keyaccount.com*
Workstations UK *www.workstationsuk.com*

Global Beach
Tel: 020-7384 1188
Fax: 020-7384 8599
E-mail: gill@globalbeach.com
Web: www.globalbeach.com
Contact: Gill Freshwater
Jaguar Cars *www.jaguar.com*
Hewlett Packard *www/hp.com/go/fish*
www.hp.com/go/racing
Stewart Grand
Prix *www.stewart-ford.com*

Hyperlink
Tel: 020-7240 8121
Fax: 020-7240 8098
E-mail: postbox@hyperlink.com
Web: www.hyperlink.com
Contact: David Long
Liberty *www.liberty-of-london.com*
Allders *www.allders.co.uk*
Somerfield Recruitment microsite
jobs.somerfield.co.uk

Morgan Internet Design
Tel: 0208-785 4291
E-mail: netprofit@mid.co.uk
Web: www.mid.co.uk
Contact: Zack Morgan
Cheshire Constabulary
www.cheshire.police.uk
Leyland Exports *www.leylandexports.com*
JoJo Maman Bébe *www.jojomamanbebe.co.uk*

Nethead Web Productions
Creative design, background in advertising and media
Tel: 0870-730 6466
Fax: 0870-730 5959
E-mail: richard@nethead.ltd.uk
Web: www.nethead.ltd.uk
Contact: Richard Parkes
X-stream *www.x-stream.com*
Robot Wars BBC2 *www.robotwars.co.uk*
Motability Finance *www.mfl.co.uk*

Nettec
Strategy, design and implementation
Tel: 020-7514 9500
E-mail: info@nettec.net
Misco *www.misco.co.uk*
The Jockey Club *www.thejockeyclub.co.uk*
Oddbins *www.oddbins.co.uk*

Razorfish
Tel: 020-7549 4200
Fax: 020-7236 2605
E-mail: info@razorfish.co.uk
Web: www.razorfish.co.uk
Contact: Rassami Hok Ljungberg
RAC *www.rac.co.uk*
NMEC *www.dome2000.co.uk*
Johnson Fry *www.johnsonfry.co.uk*
British Aerospace *www.bae.co.uk*

RVC
Tel: 020-7490 3320
Fax: 020-7490 3327
E-mail: info@rvc.co.uk
Web: www.rvc.co.uk
www.atomik-xt.com
Contact: Nick Reed
Net Profit Publications
www.netprofit.co.uk (Web watch database)
Smallfish Records *www.smallfish.co.uk*
Central Saint Martins School of Art &
Design *195.195.65.205/shortcourse/*

Sebastian Kennedy Associates
Web design and online marketing, e-commerce for SME market
Tel: 0208-673 7797
Fax: 0208-673 5722
E-mail: john@skaltd.com
Web: www.skaltd.com
Contact: John Rahim
Cafe Coton *www.cafecoton.co.uk*
Tim Little *www.timlittle.com*
Kelsey Tailors *www.kelseytailors.co.uk*
Babette Wasserman *www.babette-wasserman.com*

Wirestation
Tel: 0207-336 6510
Fax: 0207-336 6511
E-mail: ian@wirestation.co.uk
Web: www.wirestation.co.uk
Contact: Ian Capon
Contracts365 *www.contracts365.com*
NSPCC *www.nspcc.org.uk*
Dudley Stationery *www.dudley.co.uk*
Alex Lawrie *www.alexlawrie.co.uk*

WWWsolutions
Tel: 0800-783 5255
Fax: 020-7355 5056
E-mail: info@wwwsolutions.co.uk
Web: www.wwwsolutions.co.uk
Contact: Nigel Rodrigues
Littlestar *www.littlestar.co.uk*
Sound Tactics *www.sound-tactics.co.uk*
BYC *www.wwwsolutions.co.uk/company/byc/*

Oxfordshire
Kingston Bagpuize

Domino Systems
Tel: 01865-821821
Fax: 01865-821881
E-mail: Web@domino.com
Web: www.domino.com
Contact: Tracey Iles
Dell Computers *www.euro.dell.com*
Condomania *www.flash.condoms4u.com*
Jaguar *www.collection.co.uk*

Oxford

Big Oxford Computer Co
Tel: 01865-784490
Fax: 01865-773456
E-mail: info@bocc.co.uk
Web: www.bocc.co.uk/
Contact: Mark Hall
Oxford Instruments *www.oxford-instruments.com*
UKOOA *www.oilandgas.org.uk/*
English Nature *www.english-nature.org.uk/*
Trading Standards Central *www.tradingstandards.gov.uk/*

Shropshire
Oswestry

Milk Design
Tel: 01691-680086/680380
Fax: 01691-680335
E-mail: si@milkdesign.co.uk
Web: www.milkdesign.co.uk
Contact: Simon Russell
BT Wireplay *www.wireplay.co.uk (client software interface)*
Gosh! Films *www.gosh-films.com*
Greenpeace International *www.greenpeace.org/climate/arctic99*
Virgin *www.virginballoons.co.uk*

Surrey
Kingston-upon-Thames

deMont designs
Tel: 020-8549 9553
Fax: 020-8541 4715
E-mail: charlie@demont.co.uk
Web: www.demont.co.uk
Contact: Charles de Montagnac
Net Profit *www.netprofit.co.uk*
Semaphore *www.semaphore-systems.co.uk*
Colourmation Media q *www.colourmation.com*

Red Fuse
Tel: 020-8977 3830
Fax: 020-8977 9987
E-mail: talk@redsquare.com
Web: www.redsquare.com
Contact: Ed Butcher
QBS Software *www.qbss.com*
The Leisure Industry Week *www.liw.co.uk*
Everywoman *www.everywoman.co.uk*

Soft Options UK
Tel: 0208-395 3100
Fax: 0208-395 3101
E-mail: info@softopt.co.uk
Web: www.softopt.co.uk
Contact: James Neill
Environment Agency of England and Wales *www.environment-agency.gov.uk*
Apple Computer Europe *europe.apple.com*
Systems Capital *www.syscap.com*
Cutty Sark Whisky *www.cutty-sark.com*

West Midlands
Coventry

Internet Solutions for Business
Tel: 0247-663 3177
Fax: 0247-663 3040
E-mail: sales@is4b.net
Web: www.is4b.net
Contact: Rik Pipe
London Taxis Int *www.london-taxis.com*
Museum of British Road Transport *www.mbrt.co.uk*
Zunsport *www.zunsport.co.uk*
Aussie Homes *www.aussie-home.com*

West Yorkshire
Leeds

ATG Design
Tel: 0113-279 6767
E-mail: richard@atg-design.co.uk
Web: www.atg-design.co.uk
Contact: Richard Armitage
www.recommended-cottages.co.uk
www.ledsigns.co.uk
www.virginholidays.co.uk
www.eurocamp.co.uk

Worcestershire
Norton

Kevin Tea
Web site design and maintenance, e-commerce, marketing for SME market
Tel: 0702-110 2409
Fax: 0870-0888711
E-mail: kevin@ktc.co.uk
Web: www.ktc.co.uk
Contact: Kevin Tea
www.gon.org
www.etw.org
www.tweuro.com
www.acorns.org.uk

Appendix D: Cyber cafés

ENGLAND

Avon

Internet Café
140 Whiteladies Road
Clifton
Bristol
Tel: 0117-973 6323
E-mail: info@l-ot.demon.co.uk

Internet Exchange
The Mall
Cribbs Causeway
Bristol
Tel: 0117-959-2628
E-mail: admin@internet-exchange.co.uk

NetGates Café
51 Broad Street
Bristol
Tel: 0117-907 4000
E-mail: cafe@netgates.co.uk

Weston Netgates
Knightstone Road
Weston-super-Mare
Tel: 01934-411579
E-mail: netgates@weston.ac.uk

Bedfordshire

Hard Drive Cafe
16 King Street
Luton LU1 2DP
Tel: 01582-485621
E-mail: hdc@hardcafe.co.uk

Berkshire

3W Cafe
4 Market Place
Bracknell
Tel: 01344-862445
E-mail: dave@3w.co.uk

WEBcentre
The Centre
Farnham Road
Slough
Tel: 01753-787555
E-mail: admin@sloughcentre.co.uk

Buckinghamshire

Crusoe's Internet Café
Cherry Tree House
7 Dean Street
Marlow
Tel: 01628-488376
E-mail: info@crusoes.co.uk

Cambridgeshire

CB1 - for Coffee, Books and the Internet
32 Mill Road
Cambridge
Tel: 01223-576306
E-mail: dan@cb1.com

International Telecom Centre
2 Wheeler Street
Cambridge
Tel: 01223-357358
Fax: 01223-357358
E-mail: itccam@hotmail.com

The Internet Experience
11 Fishers Yard Market Square
St Neots, Huntingdon
Tel: 01480-386836
E-mail: experience@intecc.co.uk

Cheshire

Cyber Cafe @ Macclesfield Leisure Centre
Priory Lane
Macclesfield
Tel: 01625-421114
E-mail: leisureconnect@hotmail.com

Cornwall

The Inner Space
26 Commercial Street
Camborne
Tel: 01209-610091
E-mail: service@inner-space.co.uk

The Internet Place
5 Frances Street
Truro
E-mail: tip@cornwall.net

Global Lounge
Unit 13, Lemon Street Market
Truro TR1 3JT
E-mail: info@globallounge.co.uk

Net 1
10 The Moor
Tel: 01326-277870
E-mail: falmouth@net1fal.co.uk

Seaview Inn
The Seaview Inn
Wodehouse Terrace, Falmouth
Tel: 01326-311 359
E-mail: seaview@dircon.co.uk

Derbyshire

Javas Internet Coffee House
8 Stephenson Place
Chesterfield
Tel: 01246-274455
E-mail: Javascoffeehouse@hotmail.com

Peak Art CyberCafe
30 Market Street
New Mills, High Peak
Tel: 01663-747770
E-mail: info@peakcafe.demon.co.uk

Devon

Cyberpoint
238 Union Street, Torre
Torquay
Tel: 01803-297675
E-mail: cyberpoint@torquay.com

Hyperactive
1B Queen Street
Central Station, Exeter
Tel: 01392-201544
E-mail: enquiries@hyperactive-cafe.co.uk

Internet Express
Central Station
Tel: 01392-201 544
E-mail: cafe@mail.InXpress.co.uk

Net-Zone Internet Cafe
6 Newton Road
Torquay
Tel: 01803-291215
E-mail: cafe@net-zone.co.uk

Project COSMIC
The Station
Exeter Road
Ottery St. Mary
Tel: 01404-813226
E-mail: WebMaster@cosmic.org.uk

Dorset

CouchNet Internet Cafe
117 Charminster Rd
Bournemouth
Tel: 01202-297222
E-mail: info@couchnet.com

The Cyber Place
132 Charminster Road
Bournemouth
Tel: 0403-451865
E-mail: surf@cyberplace.co.uk

Global Surf And Shoot
30a Princes Street
Yeovil
E-mail: enquiries@global-sas.co.uk

Durham

Beiderbeckes
30-32 Bondgate
Darlington
Tel: 01325-282 675
E-mail: wired@beiderbeckes.co.uk

East Sussex

Cybercave
9-12 Middle St
Brighton
Tel: 01273-707 900
E-mail: info@cybar.co.uk

Cybercafe
75 Middle Street
Tel: 01273-777717
E-mail: cybercave@brightonbackpack-ers.com

Global Info Centre
22 Pevensey Rd
Eastbourne
Tel: 01323-431 770
E-mail: mail@gic.co.uk

PCcorner Cybercafe
218 Portland Road,
Hove
Tel: 01273-383848
E-mail: barry@bullnet.co.uk

Surfers@Paradise
18a Bond Street
Brighton
Tel: 01273-684184
E-mail: info@surfers-paradise.co.uk

East Yorkshire

Net 21
15 Savile St
Hull
Tel: 01482-322 488
E-mail: kevin@net21.co.uk

Essex

BHi Net Centre
701 High Road
Seven Kings, Ilford
E-mail: info@bhi-netcentre.co.uk

Cyberdine
Market Square
Harlow

Tel: 01279-423 910
E-mail: newstem@btlip23.bt.co.uk

Webs NetCafe
2a Queens Street
Colchester
Tel: 01206-560400
E-mail: mus@aspects.net

Gloucestershire

Intercafe
124 -126 Barton Street
Gloucester
Tel: 01452-305303
E-mail: info@iconcafe.co.uk

Netscafe
9 Bennington St
Cheltenham
Tel: 01242-232 121
E-mail: info@netscafe.co.uk

Hampshire

Carlos Cybergate
Sanderson Centre
Lees Lane
Gosport
Tel: 01705-602900
E-mail: cybergate@termlow.co.uk

Internet Exchange
The Bargate Centre
Southampton
Tel: 01703-233548
E-mail: admin@internet-exchange.co.uk

Herefordshire

The Office
Unit E Homend Mews
The Homend
Ledbury
Tel: 01531-635888
E-mail: hcomuk@globalnet.co.uk

Isle of Man

Cyberia Internet Cafe
31 North Quay
Douglas
E-mail: cyberia@manxisle.com

Cyberia Internet Cafe
1st floor, Crescent Leisure Centre
Central Promenade
Douglas
Tel: 01624-617510
E-mail: cyberia.mcb.net

Dot-UK
2 St James Street
Newport
Tel: 01983-526044
E-mail: izzy@dot-uk.co.uk

Feegan's Lounge
22 Duke Street
Douglas
Tel: 01624-679280
Fax: 01624-679280
E-mail: feegan@feegan.co.uk

Kent

Chaucer Cyberspace
Chaucer Technology School
Spring Lane
Canterbury
Tel: 01227-763636
Fax: 01227-762352
E-mail: isocts@mail.chaucer.ac.uk

CommsPort
The Water Circus
South Village
Greenhithe
Tel: 01322-381098

Costa Coffee / Sony Store
Bluewater Shopping Center
Tel: 01322-381098
Fax: 01322-381098
E-mail: bwadmin@commsport.com

Electr@net
316 High Street
Orpington
Tel: 01689-877878
E-mail: info@electranet.com

Seadrive Internet Cafe
62 Harbour Parade
Ramsgate
Tel: 01843-570140
E-mail: martin@seadrive.co.uk

Lancashire

Cybernet
South Promenade
St. Annes, Blackpool
Tel: 01253-724 000
E-mail: cybernet@cyberscape.co.uk

Leicestershire

Environ
The Ark
2-4 St Martins Square
Leicester
Tel: 0116-233 9660
E-mail: ravi@ark.org

London

A1 Internet Cafe
19 Leinster Terrace W2 3ET
Tel: 020-7402 1177
E-mail: a1ic@aol.com

battersea.net
40 St. Johns Hill SW11 1RZ
Tel: 020-7738 0015
E-mail: post@battersea.net

bushbang cyber cafe
49 The Broadway
Stratford E15 4BQ
Tel: 020-8227 1008
E-mail: info@bushbang.com

Café Cyberia
39 Whitfield Street W1P 5RE
Tel: 020-7681 4200
E-mail: cyberia@cyberiacafe.net

Café Internet
22/24 Buckingham Palace Rd SW1
Tel: 020-7233 5786
E-mail: cafe@cafeinternet.co.uk

C@fe.Net
40 Sheen Lane SW14
Tel: 020-8255 4022
E-mail: cafemail@cafenet.uk.com

Costa Coffee
153 Earls Court Road SW5 9RQ
Tel: 020-7370 3304
E-mail: ecadmin@commsport.com

Costa Coffee
11-13 Golders Green Rd NW11 9PU
Tel: 020-8731 9247
E-mail: ggadmin@commsport.com

Costa Coffee
32 Maddox Street W1R 9PF
Tel: 020-7408 0345
E-mail: msadmin@commsport.com

Cyber café
229 Great Portland Street W1N 5HD
Tel: 020-7631 8359
E-mail: Info@cybercafe.org.uk

Cyberia Ealing
73, New Broadway
Ealing W5 5AL
Tel: 020-8840 3131
E-mail: ealing@cyberiacafe.net

The Cyber Centre BiblioTech
Biblio@Tech
631 Fulham Road
Tel: 020-7460 4343
E-mail:
thecybercentre@postmaster.co.uk

CyberNet InterNet & Game Centre
287 Putney Bridge Road SW15 2PT
Tel: 020-8789 7196
E-mail: info@cybernet-filmstudio.com

Cyber Park
1 Hogarth Place SW5 0QT
Tel: 020-7259 2680
E-mail:info@cyberpark.demon.co.uk

Cyber Space
31c Market Place NW11 6JY
Tel: 020-8731 8047
E-mail: cyberspace64@hotmail.com

Cyberspace@doddington.co.uk
263-265 Battersea Pk Rd SW11 4NE
Tel: 020-7498 1952
E-mail: Cyberspace@doddington.co.uk

Cyberzone Cybercafe
1 Dingwall Rd, Croydon
Tel: 020-8681 6500
E-mail: zone1@cyberzone.co.uk

declare computer studios
58 Kenway Road
Earls Court SW5 0RA
Tel: 020-7835 0203
E-mail: doit@declare.com

declare computer studios
14 Neals Yard
Covent Garden WC2H 9DP
Tel: 020-7379 5113
E-mail: doit@declare.com

declare computer studios
206 Camden Lock Market
Camden Town NW1 8AF
Tel: 020-7482 0102
E-mail: doit@declare.com

easyEverything
12 Wilton Road SW1 1LV
Tel: 020-7482 9502
E-mail: tony.a@easyeverything.com

Hephzibah Cybercafe
40 The Broadway N9 0TJ
Tel: 020-8884 0686
E-mail: Hackemp10@AOL.Com

IDM CyberCafe
8 Stanley Rd
Wimbledon SW19 8RF
Tel: 020-8542 0011
E-mail: training@idm.co.uk

Intercafe
25 Great Portland Street W1
Tel: 020-7631 0063
E-mail: postmaster@intercafe.co.uk

Input Output Centres
Marylebone Library
nr Baker St NW1
Tel: 020-7486 3161
E-mail: iocentre@iocentre.co.uk

Interactive Traveller
4 Grand Parade
Forty Avenue
Wembley Park HA98 9GS
Tel: 020-8908 2266
E-mail:
traveller@interactivetraveller.co.uk

Interactive Traveller
12a High Road
Willesden Green HA9 9QG
Tel: 020-8451 8975
E-mail: traveller@interactivetraveller.co.uk

Internet.Com Ltd.
The Plaza
120 Oxford Street W1N 9DP
Tel: 020-7580 5558
E-mail: info@askinternet.com

Internet Exchange
117 Putney High Street SW15 1SS
Tel: 020-8785 1485
E-mail: admin@internet-exchange.co.uk

Internet Exchange
47/49 Queensway W2 4QH U
Tel: 020-7792 5790
E-mail: admin@internet-exchange.co.uk

Internet Exchange
2nd Floor, Whiteleys Shopping Centre
Queensway W2 4YN
Tel: 020-7792 0619
E-mail: admin@internet-exchange.co.uk

Internet Exchange
The Trocadero Centre
Piccadilly W1V 8DH
Tel: 020-7437 3704
E-mail: admin@internet-exchange.co.uk

Internet Lounge
24A Earl's Court Gardens SW5 0SZ
Tel: 020-7370 1734
E-mail: info@internetlounge.co.uk

Internet Journey
1421 London Road SW16 4AH
Tel: 020-8679 1200
E-mail: admin@internet-journey.co.uk

Internet Centre
Heathrow Airport
Tel: 020-8759 2434

Kinko's, Inc.
326 High Holborn WC1V 7DD
Tel: 020-7539 2900

Microplay Internet Centre
165 Ballards Lane N3 1LP
Tel: 020-8371 0422
E-mail: sales@mvg.co.uk

Microplay Games
165 Ballards Lane
Tel: 020-8371 0422
E-mail: netsurf@microply.demon.co.uk

Netdome Internet Café
193 Holloway Road N7 8DJ

Tel: 020-7607 0589
E-mail: info@netdome.co.uk

Network City
Marylebone High St
Tel: 020-7224 4400
E-mail: nc@networkcity.co.uk

Off key
101 High Street NW10 4TS
Tel: 020-8961 2568
E-mail: offkey@offkey.org.uk

The Portobello Gold
95-97 Portobello Rd
Tel: 020-7460 4906
E-mail: mike@portobellogold.com

Rainbow Cybercafé
5 Kings Place
Chiswick High Road W4 4HT
Tel: 020-8994 0053
E-mail: d-bell@dircon.co.uk

Shoot N Surf
13 New Oxford St
Tel: 020-7419 1183
E-mail: info@shootnsurf.co.uk

Surf.net Café
13 Deptford Church Street SE8 4RX
Tel: 020-8488 1200
E-mail: richard@surfnet.co.uk

tnab.com
49 The Broadway E15 4BQ
Tel: 020-8227 1008
E-mail: info@tnab.com

The Vibe Bar
91 Brick Lane
Tel: 020-7247 2406
E-mail: info@hyena.co.uk

Webshack
15 Dean Street W1V 6AS
Tel: 020-7439 8000
E-mail: rupal@webshack-cafe.com

Websurfer Cafe
79 Goldhawk Road W12 8EG
Tel: 020-8932 0117

Manchester

Cyberia Manchester
12 Oxford St
Tel: 0161-236 6300
E-mail: barbie@cyberiacafe.net

Kaleida
448 Wilmslow Rd
Tel: 0161-291 1525
E-mail: office@kscope.u-net.com

Wet, Dry Bar
28 Oldham St
Tel: 0161-236 5920
E-mail: dry@wet.u-net.com

Middlesex

Chaplin Video & Internet Cafe
142 Marsh Road
Pinner
Tel: 020-8357 0057
E-mail: cafe@chaplin-multimedia.com

The Harrow Internet Cafe
4-6 Peterborough Rd, Harrow
Tel: 020-8426 4446
E-mail: bindu@getsurfed.co.uk

Norfolk

The Internet Café
145A King St
Great Yarmouth
Tel: 01493-856 523
E-mail: tom@comdoc.demon.co.uk

RJT Internet Services
North Quay
Great Yarmouth
E-mail: rjt@rjt.co.uk

The Workshop
Jolly Butchers Yard, Ber St
Norwich
Tel: 01603-630223
E-mail: anne@nbd-recordings.demon.co.uk

North Yorkshire

The Gateway Internet Cafe
Gateway House
26 Swinegate
York
Tel: 01904-646446
E-mail: gateway@ymn.net

Northumberland

Oasis
The Coffee House
4 Myrtel St
Ashington
Tel: 01670-521 702
Web: oasis.netexpress.co.uk

Oxfordshire

The Internet Centres
193 Cowley Rd, Oxford
Tel: 01865-295 066
E-mail: angie@mail.cts-group.co.uk

Internet Exchange
6-12 George Street
Oxford
Tel: 01865-241601
E-mail: admin@internet-exchange.co.uk

Somerset

Internet Cafe
KCS, Mart Road
Minehead
Tel: 01643-709970
E-mail: kevin_kcs@hotmail.com

South Yorkshire

Elektra Cafe
9 Westfield Terrace
Sheffield
Tel: 0114-270 1171
E-mail: webmaster@elektra-cafe.co.uk

Havana
32/34 Division Street
Sheffield
Tel: 0114-249 5452
E-mail: info@havana.co.uk

Punters CyberCafe
111 Arundel St
Sheffield
Tel: 0114-276 2668
E-mail: webmaster@mail.punters.co.uk

Spiders Web
39-41 Cleveland Street
Doncaster
Tel: 01302-814777
Fax: 01302-814777

Staffordshire

Netcafe
15-19 Marsh Parade
Newcastle-under-Lyme
Tel: 0870-787 1821
E-mail: manager@netcafe-uk.co.uk

Suffolk

Garland Café
4 Garland St
Bury St. Edmonds
Tel: 01284-753 373
E-mail: garland_cafe@post.dungeon.com

Surrey

Café Net
2-3 Phoenix Court
Guildford
Tel: 01483-451 945
E-mail: cafenet@cafenet.co.uk

Quarks
7 Jeffries Passage
Guildford
Tel: 01483-451 166
E-mail: nick@quarks.co.uk

The Network Club
163 Victoria Road
Horley
Tel: 01293-432111
E-mail: bfewtrell@networkclub.co.uk

Tolworth Digital Access Centre
37/39 Tolworth Broadway
Kingston-upon-Thames
Tel: 020-8339 6950
E-mail: Tolworth.Library
@rbk.kingston.gov.uk

Tyne & Wear

Design Works
William St, Felling
Gateshead
Tel: 0191-495 0066
E-mail: nickoliver@aol.com

McNulty's Internet Cafe
26-30 Market St
Newcastle-upon-Tyne
Tel: 0191-2320922
E-mail: craig.johnson@mcnultynet.co.uk

Terminal 1
11 Derwent Street, Sunderland
E-mail: alan@terminal1.co.uk

West Midlands

Internet Exchange
The Pallasades Shopping Centre
Birmingham
Tel: 0121-633 9803
E-mail: admin@internet-exchange.co.uk

NetPlay Cafe
8 Fletchers Walk
Paradise Forum
Birmingham
Tel: 0121-248 2228
E-mail: hdc@hardcafe.co.uk

West Yorkshire

The Café
55 Kirkstall Lane, Leeds
Tel: 0113-294 4271
E-mail: info@thecafe.co.uk

Spiderz Web
60 Carlisle Road Business Centre
Bradford
Tel: 01274-223300
E-mail: info@spiderzweb.co.uk

Window on the World Cyber Cafe
Kirklees Media Centre
7 Northumberland Street
Huddersfield
Tel: 01484-454401
E-mail: WoW_Cafe@architechs.com

Netbytes at the Cafe
6-8 Chapel Place
Headingley, Leeds
Tel: 0113-294 4270
E-mail: info@thecafe.co.uk

Wiltshire

The Cyber Den
21a Market Place
Devizes
Tel: 01380-726320
E-mail: cyberden@netcomuk.co.uk

Megabites Cafe
69 Victoria Road
Swindon
Tel: 01793-539600
E-mail: info@megabites.co.uk

Worcestershire

Cyber Centre
27 College Road
Worcester
Tel: 01905-617666
E-mail: info@the-cyber-centre.co.uk

SCOTLAND

Ayrshire

Viviante Cyber Diner
3 South Beach, Troon
Tel: 01292-316181
E-mail: viviante@btinternet.com

Central

Networx
68 Murray Place
Stirling
Tel: 01786-471122
E-mail: mail@networxcafe.com

Edinburgh

Cafe Cyberia
88 Hanover Street
Tel: 0131-220 4403
E-mail: angela@cybersurf.co.uk

CommsPort Limited
35 Shandwick Place
Tel: 0131-228 6322

Costa Coffee
Shandwick Place

Entertainment World
138 Lothian Rd
Tel: 0131-229 5333
E-mail: eworld@btinternet.com

Hog's Head
62 South Clerk St
Tel: 0131-667 5274
E-mail: tv-eye@easynet.co.uk

International Telecom Centre
52 High Street, Royal Mile
Tel: 0131-558 7114
E-mail: itcedinburgh@hotmail.com

The Tinsley Lockhart Group Internet Centre
66/68 Thistle Street
Tel: 0131-225 5000
E-mail: info@inform.org.uk

web13
13 Bread Street
Tel: 0131-229 8883
E-mail: ian@web13.co.uk

Highland

Invernet
Bridge Street
Inverness
Tel: 01463-729154
E-mail: info@invernet.co.uk

Strathclyde

Cafe Internet
2nd Floor, Waterstones
153-157 Sauchiehall St
Glasgow
Tel: 0141-353 2484
E-mail: glasgow@cafeinternet.co.uk

Café Roslin
Dalrymple St
Greenock
Tel: 01475-730 576
E-mail: roslin@easynet.co.uk

The Link Cafe Limited
569 Sauchiehall Street
Glasgow
Tel: 0141-564 1052
E-mail: info@linkcafe.co.uk

Lochgilphead Cyber Cafe
1 Argyll St
Lochgilphead
Tel: 01546-602547
E-mail: donald@lochgilphead-cafe.co.uk

WALES

Dyfed

Caffi'r WEB Café
13 Terrace Road
Aberystwyth
Tel: 01970-623340
E-mail: cafe@gweb-cafe.co.uk

Gwynedd

Dimension 4
4 Bangor Street
Caernarfon
Tel: 01286-678777
E-mail: information@dimensiwn4.co.uk

South Glamorgan

Cardiff Cybercafé
9 Duke St
Cardiff
Tel: 01222-235 757
E-mail: pauls@cardiffcybercafe.co.uk

Grassroots Cybercafé
58 Charles St
Tel: 01222-231 700
E-mail: cafe@ccyp.celtic.co.uk

West Glamorgan

Cyberstop Internet Services
Portland Street
Swansea
E-mail: edgar@cyberstop.net

NORTHERN IRELAND

Bytes
Morglen Gardens, Turf Lodge
Belfast
Tel: 01232-749 955
E-mail: bytes@worknet.thegap.com

Cybernet C@fe
21 Hamilton Rd.
Bangor
Tel: 01247-479703
E-mail: cybernet@dial.pipex.com

Hotwired Internet Cafe
Jail Square, Enniskillen
E-mail: hotwired@enterprise.net

Jack's Other-worlds Internet Cafe
110 High Street
Holywood
E-mail: jacks@other-worlds.com

Revelations Internet Cafe
27 Shaftesbury Square
Belfast
Tel: 01232-320337

IRELAND, REPUBLIC OF

Clare

MacCools Internet Cafe
Brewery Lane
Ennis
Tel: 353-65 21988
E-mail: maccools@clarenet.ie

Kilrush Internet Bureau
The 'Monastery'
Kilrush
Tel: 353-65 51061
E-mail: cwglynn@tinet.ie

Dublin

Cyberia Cafe
Arthouse, Curved St
Temple Bar, Dublin 2
Tel: 353-1 679 7607
E-mail: alexa@cyberia.ie

Cyberspace @ Cafe Bleu
88b Lower Georges Street
Dun Laoghaire

Global Cafe
The Basement
8 Lower O'Connell Street, Dublin 1
Tel: 353-1 878 0295
E-mail: info@globalcafe.ie

The Pembroke
31 Lower Pembroke Street, Dublin 2
Tel: 353-1 676 2780
E-mail: info@pembroke.ie

Planet Cafe
23 South Great George's Street Dublin 2

Tel: 353-1 679 0583

The Underground Club
55 Dame Street, Dublin 2
Tel: 353-1 679 3010
E-mail: patnpat@underground.ie

Galway

Net@ccess
Olde Malte Mall
E-mail: info@netaccess.ie

Jamie Starlights
Dominick Street
E-mail: j_starlights@hotmail.com

Kerry

DingleWeb
Main St, Dingle
Tel: 353-166 52477
E-mail: info@dingleweb.com

Kildare

CyberX
Glenroyal Centre Maynooth Co
E-mail: Aidan@CyberX.ie

Leitrim

Gartlan's Cyber Cafe
Bridge St
Carrick-On-Shannon
Tel: 353-78 21735
E-mail: gartlan@iol.ie

Limerick

Websters Internet Cafe
The Newtown Pery
Thomas Street
Tel: 353-61 317799
E-mail: info@websters.ie

Meath

Megabyte Cyber Cafe
Unit 1, Abbey Rd
Navan
Tel: 046 74322 **??**
Fax: 046 79438 **??**
E-mail: megabyte@tinet.ie

Sligo

Galaxy Cyber Cafe
Millbrook
Riverside
E-mail: webmaster@cisl.ie

Waterford

Voyager Internet Café
Parnell Court
Parnell St
Tel: 353-51 843 843
E-mail: stan@voyager.ie

Westmeath

Sherwood Systems
Austin Friar St
Mullingar
Tel: 353-44 49838
E-mail: sales@sherwood-systems.com

Appendix E: Glossary

See Chapter One for definitions of the Internet and its main parts - e-mail, Web, newsgroups.

Address: A Web address is the domain name or URL (qv). An e-mail address is in the form jo@myhouse.co.uk

Bandwidth: The capacity of the telecom link – the speed data can be transferred over the Net is partly a function of bandwidth.

Banner: A strip advertisement on a Web page.

Browser: The software that allows you to view a Web page. Netscape and Microsoft Explorer are the most popular.

Clickthrough: Clicking on a banner (qv) advertisement, to see the advertiser's site.

Digital: A way of breaking data up into a string of noughts and ones that can be transmitted by computer. Digital means finger-like - the data consist of distinct units, rather than a continuous stream (which is analogue).

Digital certificate (or digital ID): an electronic guarantee that the sender of a message is who he says he is. Provided by Certification Authorities (CAs).

Domain: Technical name for the sites' main address (eg www.companyname.co.uk). Also known as a URL (Uniform Resource Locator). The last part (.uk, .com etc) is the "top level domain".

Download: Import a computer file, often via the Internet.

Encryption: The coding of information, for example to stop people reading credit card numbers sent over the Net.

Extranet: An intranet (qv) that allows limited access by outsider, usually customers or suppliers.

Hit: A visit to an element of a Web page, often used to measure its popularity (but see page impressions). There can be anything from one to dozens of hits per page.

HTML: Hypertext Mark-up Protocol: the programming language of the Web.

Hypertext: A way of jumping from one Web page to another, by clicking on a highlighted word.

Internet Service Provider (ISP): a company that connects you to the Internet..

Intranet: A private network using Internet technology and Web browsers, which may or may not be connected to the public Internet.

ISDN: Integrated Services Digital Network. A high bandwidth phone line, which gives fast access to the Web.

Java: A programming language that adds intelligence to the browser (qv).

Leased line: A permanently open, high bandwidth line that can be used to give a company's computer network access to the Internet.

Modem: A device to connect a computer to an ordinary phone line.

Multimedia: The mixing of different media on a computer – these could include text, sound, photographs and video.

Page: Referring to the Internet, the sub-division of a Web site (qv) that is loaded onto the computer at any one time. .

Page impression: the downloading (qv) of a single page (qv) – the auditable unit that has replaced the hit (qv).

Plug-in: Software that can be downloaded to increase the functionality of the browser (qv).

Server: The computer on which a Web site lives. Also called a host.

Smart card: a plastic card with a computer chip embedded in it.

TCP/IP: The "language" of the Internet, allowing computers to communicate.

Upload: send a file from computer (eg to update a Web site).

URL: See domain (qv)

Virus: A program that can damage or destroy programs anf files. Can be spread via the Internet.